Born and raised in Hawaii, **Robert T. Kiyosaki** co-founded an international education company that operated in seven countries, teaching business to tens of thousands of graduates. Now retired, Robert does what he enjoys most . . . he invests. Concerned about the growing gap between the haves and have nots, Robert created the board game Cashflow, which teaches the game of money, before only known by the rich.

**Sharon L. Lechter** is a wife, the mother of three, a consultant to the toy and publishing industries, and a business owner. As co-author of many of the *Rich Dad, Poor Dad* books, she now focuses her efforts in helping to create educational tools for anyone interested in bettering their own financial education.

# Rich Dad's

# GUIDE TO INVESTING

## What the Rich Invest In That the Poor and Middle Class Do Not!

BY ROBERT T. KIYOSAKI
WITH SHARON L. LECHTER C.P.A.

timewarner
paperbacks

A *Time Warner* Paperback

First published in the United States in 2000 by Warner Books,
Inc., in association with CASHFLOW Technologies, Inc.
CASHFLOW is the trademark of CASHFLOW Technologies, Inc.

E B  E B  E B  ◇  ▲  are trademarks of
S I  S I  S I        CASHFLOW Technologies, Inc.

First published in Great Britain in 2003 by
Time Warner Paperbacks
Reprinted 2003, 2004, 2005

A CIP catalogue record for this book
is available from the British Library.

ISBN 0 7515 3316 5

Typeset by Palimpsest Book Production Limited,
Polmont, Stirlingshire
Printed and bound in Great Britain by
Clays Ltd, St Ives plc

Time Warner Paperbacks
An imprint of
Time Warner Book Group UK
Brettenham House
Lancaster Place
London WC2E 7EN

www.twbg.co.uk

# *Acknowledgments*

On April 8, 1997, *Rich Dad Poor Dad* was formally launched. We printed a thousand copies, thinking that quantity would last us for at least a year. Over a million copies later, and not a dollar spent on formal advertising, the success of *Rich Dad Poor Dad* and the *CASHFLOW Quadrant* continues to amaze us. Sales have been driven primarily by word of mouth, the best kind of marketing.

*Rich Dad's Guide to Investing* is a thank you to you for helping make *Rich Dad Poor Dad* and the *CASHFLOW Quadrant* so successful.

We have made many new friends through this success and some of them have contributed to the development of this book. The following are friends, new and old, whom we would like to personally thank for their contribution to this book. If you are not on this list, and you have helped in any way, please pardon our oversight and know that we also thank you.

For both technical and moral support we thank: Diane Kennedy, CPA; Rolf Parta, CPA; Dr Ann Nevin, Educational Psychologist; Kim Butler, CFP; Frank Crerie, Investment Banker; Rudy Miller, Venture Capitalist; Michael Lechter, Intellectual Property Attorney; Chris Johnson, Securities Attorney; Dr Van Tharp, Investor Psychologist; Craig Coppola, Commercial Real Estate; Dr Dolf DeRoos, Investment Real Estate; Bill and Cindy Shopoff, Investment Real Estate; Keith Cunningham, Corporate Restructuring; Wayne and Lynn Morgan, Real Estate Education; Hayden Holland, Trusts; Larry Clark, Real Estate

Entrepreneur; Marty Weber, Social Entrepreneur; Tom Weisenborn, Stockbroker; Mike Wolf, Entrepreneur; John Burley, Real Estate Investor; Dr Paul Johnson, Professor of Business at Thunderbird University; The American School of International Management; Carolita Oliveros, Professor, University of Arizona and Thunderbird; Larry Gutsch, Investor Advisor; Liz Berkenkamp, Investment Advisor; John Milton Fogg, Publishing; Dexter Yager and the Internet Services family; John Addison, Trish Adams, Mortgage Banker; Bruce Whiting, CPA, Australia; Michael Talarico, Real Estate Investor, Australia; Harry Rosenberg CPA, Australia; Dr Ed Koken, Financial Advisor, Australia; John Hallas, Business Owner, Australia; Dan Osborn, Foreign Exchange Advisor, Australia; Nigel Brunel, Securities Trader, Australia; David Reid, Securities Attorney, Canada; Thomas Allen, Securities Attorney, Canada; Kelvin Dushnisky, General Counsel, Canada; Alan Jacques, Business, Canada; Raymond Aaron, Business, Canada; Dan Sullivan, Business, Canada; Brian Cameron, Securities, Canada; Jannie Tay, Business Investments, Singapore; Patrick Lim, Real Estate Investments, Singapore; Dennis Wee, Real Estate Investments, Singapore; Richard and Veronica Tan, Business, Singapore; Bellum and Doreen Tan, Business, Singapore; C.K. Teo, Business, Singapore; Nazim Kahn, Attorney, Singapore; K.C. See, Business, Malaysia; Siew Ka Wei, Business, Malaysia; Kevin Stock, Sara Woolard, Joe Sposi, Ron Barry, Loral Langemeier, Mary Painter and Kim Arries.

With great appreciation and in loving memory we acknowledge Cynthia Oti. Cynthia was a Financial Commentator for radio station KSFO-San Francisco, California, a stockbroker, a fellow teacher, and most importantly, a friend. She is truly missed.

Our list would not be complete without thanking the incredible team members we have at CASHFLOW Technologies.

*Thank you,*

*Robert and Kim Kiyosaki*        *Sharon Lechter*

# Contents

## Phase Three   How Do You Build a Strong Business?

## Phase Four   Who Is a Sophisticated Investor?

## Phase Five   Giving It Back

## In Conclusion

# A Father's Advice on Investing

Years ago, I asked my rich dad,
*'What advice would you give
to the average investor?'*

His reply was,
*'Don't be average.'*

## The 90/10 Rule of Money

Most of us have heard of the 80/20 rule. In other words, 80% of our success comes from 20% of our efforts. Originated by the Italian economist Vilfredo Pareto in 1897 it is also known as the Principle of Least Effort.

Rich dad agreed with the 80/20 rule for overall success in all areas but money. When it came to money, he believed in the 90/10 rule. Rich dad noticed that 10% of the people had 90% of the money. He pointed out that in the world of movies, 10% of the actors made 90% of the money. He also noticed that 10% of the athletes made 90% of the money as did 10% of the musicians. The same 90/10 rule applies to the world of investing, which is why his advice to investors was 'Don't be average.' An article in *The Wall Street Journal* recently validated his opinion. It stated that 90% of all corporate shares of stock in America are owned by just 10% of the people.

This book explains how some of the investors in the 10% have gained 90% of the wealth and how you might be able to do the same.

## Rich Dad's Guide to Investing

# The Introduction

### What You Will Learn from Reading this Book

The Securities and Exchange Commission (SEC) of the United States defines an individual as an Accredited Investor if the individual has:

1. $200,000 or more in annual income or
2. $300,000 or more in annual income as a couple, or
3. $1 million or more in net worth.

The SEC established these requirements to protect the average investor from some of the worst and most risky investments in the world. The problem is, these investor requirements also shield the average investor from some of the best investments in the world, which is one reason why rich dad's advice to the average investor was, 'Don't be average.'

### Starting with Nothing

This book begins with me returning from Vietnam in 1973. I had less than a year to go before I was going to be discharged from the Marine Corps. That meant that in less than a year, I was going to have no job, no money, and no assets. So this book begins at a point that many of you may recognize and that is a point of starting with nothing.

Writing this book has been a challenge. I have written and rewritten it four times. The first draft began at the SEC's Accredited Investor Level, the level that begins with a $200,000 minimum annual income. After the book was completed the first time, it was Sharon Lechter, my co-author, who reminded me of rich dad's 90/10 rule of money. She said, 'While this book is about the investments that the rich invest in, the reality is less than 10% of the population in America earn more than $200,000 a year. In fact, I believe it is less than 3% that earns enough to qualify as an Accredited Investor.' So the challenge of this book was to write about the investments the rich invest in, investments that begin at the minimum requirement of $200,000 in earnings and still include all readers regardless of whether they have money to invest or not. That was quite a challenge and why it required writing and rewriting the book four times.

It now begins at the most basic of investor levels and goes to the most sophisticated investor level. Instead of beginning at the Accredited Investor level, the book now begins in 1973 because that is when I had no job, no money, and no assets. A point in life many of us have shared. All I had in 1973 was the dream of someday being very rich and becoming an investor who qualified to invest in the investments of the rich. Investments that few people ever hear about, or that are written about in the financial newspapers, or sold over the counter by investments brokers. This book begins when I had nothing but a dream and my rich dad's guidance to become an investor who could invest in the investments of the rich.

So regardless of whether you have very little money to invest or have a lot to invest today, and regardless of whether you know very little about investing or you know a lot about investing, this book should be of interest to you. It is written as simply as possible about a very complex subject. It is written to include anyone interested in becoming a better informed investor regardless of how much money they have.

If this is your first book on investing, and you are concerned that it might be too complicated, please do not be concerned. All Sharon and I ask is that you have a willingness to learn and read this book from the beginning to the end with an open mind. If there are parts of the book that you do not understand, then just read the words but continue on to the end. Even if you do not understand everything, just by reading all the way through to the conclusion of this book, you will know more about the subject of investing than many people who are currently investing in the market. In fact, by reading the entire book, you will know a lot more about investing than many people who are giving investment advice and being paid to give their investment advice. This book begins with the simple and goes into the sophisticated without getting too bogged down in detail and complexity. In many ways, this book starts simple and remains simple although covering some very sophisticated investor strategies. This is a story of a rich man guiding a young man, with pictures and diagrams to help explain the often confusing subject of investing.

## *The 90/10 Rule of Money*

My rich dad appreciated Italian economist Vilfredo Pareto's discovery of the 80/20 rule, also known as the Principle of Least Effort. Yet when it came to money, rich dad was more aware of the 90/10 rule which meant that 10% of the people always made 90% of the money.

The September 13, 1999, issue of *The Wall Street Journal* ran an article supporting my rich dad's point of view on the 90/10 rule of money. A section of the article read:

> For all the talk of mutual funds for the masses, of barbers and shoe shine boys giving investment tips, the stock market has remained the privilege of a relatively elite group. Only 43.3% of all households owned any stock in 1997, the most recent year for which data is available, according to New York University economist

Edward Wolf. Of those, many portfolios were relatively small. Nearly 90% of all shares were held by the wealthiest 10% of households. The bottom line: That top 10% held 73% of the country's net worth in 1997, up from 68% in 1983.

In other words, even though more people are investing today, the rich continue to get richer. When it comes to stocks, the 90/10 rule of money holds true.

Personally I am concerned because more and more families are counting on their investments to support them in the future. The problem is that while more people are investing very few of them are well educated investors. If or when the market crashes, what will happen to all these new investors? The federal government of the United States insures our savings from catastrophic loss but it does not insure our investments. That is why when I asked my rich dad, 'What advice would you give the average investor?' his reply was, 'Don't be average.'

## *How Not to Be Average*

I became very aware of the subject of investing when I was just 12 years old. Up until that age, the concept of investing was not really in my head. Baseball and football were on my mind but not investing. I had heard the word, but I had not really paid much attention to the word until I saw what the power of investing could do. I remember walking along a small beach with the man I call my rich dad and his son Mike, my best friend. Rich dad was showing his son and me this piece of real estate he had just purchased. Although only 12 years old, I did realize that my rich dad had just purchased one of the most valuable pieces of property in our town. Even though I was young I knew that oceanfront property with a sandy beach in front of it was more valuable than property without a beach on it. My first thought was, 'How can Mike's dad afford such an expensive piece of property?'

I stood there with the waves washing over my bare feet looking at a man the same age as my real dad, who was making one of the biggest financial investments in his life. I was in awe of how he could afford such a piece of land. I knew that my dad made much more money because he was a highly paid government official with a bigger salary. But I also knew that my real dad could never afford to buy land right on the ocean. So how could Mike's dad afford this land when my dad couldn't? Little did I know that my career as a professional investor had begun the moment I realized the power built into the word 'investing.'

Some 40 years after that walk on the beach with my rich dad and his son Mike, I now have people asking me many of the same questions I began asking that day. In the investment classes I teach, people are now asking me similar questions. I began asking my rich dad questions such as:

1. 'How can I invest when I don't have any money?'
2. 'I have $10,000 to invest. What would you recommend I invest in?'
3. 'Do you recommend investing in real estate, mutual funds, or stocks?'
4. 'Can I buy real estate or stocks without any money?'
5. 'Doesn't it take money to make money?'
6. 'Isn't investing risky?'
7. 'How do you get such high returns with low risk?'
8. 'Can I invest with you?'

Today more and more people are beginning to realize the power hidden in the word investing. Many want to find out how to acquire that power for themselves. After reading this book, it is my intention that many of these questions will be answered for you and if not answered, it should inspire you to dig further to find the answers that work for you. Over 40 years ago, the most important thing my rich dad did for me was spark my curiosity on this subject of investing. My curiosity was aroused when I realized that my best friend's dad, a man who made less money than my real dad, at least when comparing paycheck to paycheck, could afford to acquire investments that only rich people could afford. I realized that my rich dad had a power my real dad did not have and I wanted to have that power also.

Many people are afraid of this power, stay away from it and many even fall victim to it. Instead of running from the power or condemning it by saying such things as, 'The rich exploit the poor,' or 'Investing is risky,' or 'I'm not interested in becoming rich,' I became curious. It is my curiosity and my desire to acquire this power, also known as knowledge and abilities, that set me off on a lifelong path of inquiry and learning.

## Investing Like a Rich Person

While this book may not give you all the technical answers you may want, the intention is to offer you an insight into how many of the richest self-made individuals made their money and went on to acquire great wealth. Standing on the beach at the age of 12, looking at my rich dad's newly acquired piece of real estate, my mind was opened to a world of possibilities that did not exist in my home. I realized that it was not money that made my rich dad a rich investor. I realized that my rich dad had a thinking pattern that was almost exactly opposite and often contradicted the thinking of my real dad. I realized that I needed to understand the thinking pattern of my rich dad if I wanted to have the same financial power he had. I knew that if I thought like him I would be rich forever. I knew that if I did not think like him, I would never really be rich, regardless of how much money I had. Rich dad had just invested in one of the most expensive pieces of land in our town, and he had no money. I realized that wealth was a way of thinking and not a dollar amount in the bank. It is this thinking pattern of rich investors that Sharon and I want to deliver to you in this book, and why we rewrote the book four times.

## Rich Dad's Answer

Standing on the beach 40 years ago, I finally worked up the courage to ask my rich dad, 'How can you afford to buy these 10 acres of very expensive oceanfront land, when my dad can't afford it?' Rich dad then put his hand on my shoulder and gave me an answer I have never forgotten. With his arm draped over my shoulder, we turned and began walking down the beach at the water line and he began to warmly explain to me the fundamentals of the way he thought about money and investing. His answer began with, 'I can't afford this land either. But my business can.' We walked on the beach for an hour that day, rich dad with his son on one side and me on his other side. My investor lessons had begun.

A few years ago, I was teaching a three-day investment course in Sydney, Australia. The first day and a half I spent discussing the ins and outs of building a business. Finally, in frustration, a participant raised his hand and said, 'I came to learn about investing. Why are you spending so much time on business?'

My reply was, 'There are two reasons. Reason number one is because what we ultimately invest in is a business. If you invest in stocks, you are investing in a business. If you buy a piece of real estate, such as an apartment building, that building is also a business. If you buy a bond, you are also investing in a business. In order to be a good investor, you first need to be good at business. Reason number two is the best way to invest is to have your business buy your investments for you. The worst way to invest is to invest as an individual. The average investor knows very little about business and often invests as an individual. That is why I spend so much time on the subject of business in an investment course.' And that is why this book will spend some time on how to build a business as well as how to analyze a business. I will also spend time on investing through a business because that is how rich dad taught me to invest. As he said to me 40 years ago, 'I can't afford to buy this land either. But my business can.' In other words my rich dad's rule was 'My business buys my investments. Most people are not rich because they invest as individuals and not as owners of businesses.' In this book, you will see why most of the 10% who own 90% of the stocks are owners of businesses and invest through their businesses and how you can do the same.

Later in the course the individual understood why I spent so much time on business. As the course progressed, that individual and the class began to realize that the richest investors in the world do not buy investments, most of the 90/10 investors created their own investments. The reason we have billionaires who are still in their twenties is not because they bought investments. They created investments, called businesses, that millions of people want to buy.

Nearly every day I hear people say, 'I have an idea for a new product that will make millions.' Unfortunately most of those creative ideas will never be turned into fortunes. The second half of this book will focus on how the 10% turn their ideas into multi-million, even multi-billion dollar businesses that other investors invest in. That is why rich dad spent so much time teaching me to build businesses as well as to analyze businesses to invest in. So if you have an idea that you think could make you rich, maybe even help you join the 90/10 club, the second half of this book is for you.

## *Buy, Hold and Pray*

Over the years rich dad pointed out that investing means different things to different people. Today I often hear people saying such things as:

1. 'I just bought 500 shares of XYZ company for $5.00 a share, the price went up to $15.00 and I sold it. I made $5,000 in less than a week.'
2. 'My husband and I buy old houses, we fix them up and sell them for a profit.'
3. 'I trade commodity futures.'
4. 'I have over a million dollars in my retirement account.'
5. 'Safe as money in the bank.'
6. 'I have a diversified portfolio.'
7. 'I'm investing for the long term.'

As rich dad said, 'Investing means different things to different people.' While the above statements reflect different types of investment products and procedures, rich dad did not invest in the same way. He said instead, 'Most people are not investors. Most people are speculators or gamblers. Most people have the "buy, hold, and pray the price goes up mentality." Most investors live in hopes that the market stays up and live in fear of the market crashing. A true investor makes money regardless if the market is going up or crashing down; they make money regardless if they are winning or losing, and they go both long and short. The average investor does not know how to do that and that is why most investors are average investors who fall into the 90% that make only 10% of the money.'

## More than Buying, Holding and Praying

Investing meant more to rich dad than buying, holding, and praying. This book will cover such subjects as:

1. The 10 Investor Controls: Many people say that investing is risky. Rich dad said, 'Investing is not risky. Being out of control is risky.' This book will go into rich dad's 10 investor controls that can reduce risk and increase profits.

2.  The 5 phases of rich dad's plan to guide me from having no money to investing with a lot of money. Phase One of rich dad's plan was preparing my mind to become a rich investor. This is a simple yet very important phase for anyone who wants to invest with confidence.

3.  The different tax laws for different investors. In book number two, *CASHFLOW Quadrant*, I cover the four different people found in the world of business.

    They are:

The E stands for employee. The S stands for self-employed or small business. The B stands for business owner. The I stands for investor.

The reason rich dad encouraged me to invest from the B quadrant is because the tax laws are better for investing from the B quadrant. Rich dad always said, 'The tax laws are not fair; they are written for the rich and by the rich. If you want to be rich, you need to use the same tax laws the rich use.' One of the reasons why 10% of the people control most of the wealth is because only 10% know which tax laws to use.

In 1943, the federal government plugged most tax loopholes

for all employees. In 1986, the federal government took away the tax loopholes enjoyed by the B quadrant from individuals in the S quadrant, individuals such as doctors, lawyers, accountants, engineers, and architects.

In other words, another reason 10% of the investors make 90% of the money is because only 10% of all investors know how to invest from the four different quadrants in order to gain different tax advantages. The average investor often only invests from one quadrant.

4. Why and how a true investor will make money regardless of whether the market goes up or crashes down.

5. The difference between Fundamental Investors and Technical Investors.

6. In *CASHFLOW Quadrant*, I went into the six levels of investors. This book starts at the last two levels of investors and further classifies them into the following types of investors:

> The Accredited Investor
> The Qualified Investor
> The Sophisticated Investor
> The Inside Investor
> The Ultimate Investor

By the end of this book, you will know the different skill and education requirements between each different investor.

7. Many people say, 'When I make a lot of money, my money problems will be over.' What they fail to realize is that having too much money is as big a problem as having not enough money. In this book you will learn the difference between the two kinds of money problems. One problem is the problem

of not enough money. The other problem is the problem of too much money. Few people realize how big a problem having too much money can be.

One of the reasons so many people go broke after making a lot of money is because they do not know how to handle the problem of too much money.

In this book you will learn how to start with the problem of having not enough money, how to make a lot of money and then how to handle the problem of too much money. In other words, this book will not only teach you how to make a lot of money but more importantly it will teach you how to keep it. As rich dad said, 'What good is making a lot of money if you wind up losing it all?'

A stockbroker friend of mine once said to me, 'The average investor does not make money in the market. They do not necessarily lose money, they just fail to make money. I have seen so many investors make money one year and give it all back the next year.'

8. How to make much more than just $200,000, the minimum income level to begin investing in the investments of the rich. Rich dad said to me, 'Money is just a point of view. How can you be rich if you think $200,000 is a lot of money? If you want to be a rich investor, you need to see that $200,000, the minimum dollar amount to qualify as an accredited investor, is just a drop in the bucket.' And that is why Phase One of this book is so important.

9. Phase One of this book, which is preparing yourself mentally to be a rich investor, has a short mental quiz for you at the end of each chapter.

Although the quiz questions are simple, they are designed to have you think and maybe discuss your answers with the people you love. It was the soul searching questions my rich dad asked me that helped me find the answers I was looking for. In other words, many of the answers I was looking for, regarding the subject of investing, were really inside of me all along.

## What Makes the 90/10 Investor Different?

One of the most important aspects of this book is the mental differences between the average investor and the 90/10 investor. Rich dad often said, 'If you want to be rich, just find out what everyone else is doing and do exactly the opposite.' As you read this book you will find out that most of the differences between the 10% of investors who make 90% of the money and the 90% that make only 10% of the money is not what they invest in, but that their thinking is different. For example:

1. Most investors say 'Don't take risks.' The rich investor takes risks.
2. Most investors say 'diversify.' The rich investor focuses.
3. The average investor tries to minimize debt. The rich investor increases debt in their favor.
4. The average investor tries to decrease expenses. The rich investor knows how to increase expenses to make themselves richer.
5. The average investor has a job. The rich investor creates jobs.
6. The average investor works hard. The rich investor works less and less to make more and more.

## The Other Side of the Coin

So an important aspect of reading this book is to notice when your thoughts are often 180 degrees out from the guiding thoughts of my rich dad. Rich dad said, 'One of the reasons so few people become rich is because they become set in one way of thinking. They think there is only one way to think or do something. While the average investor thinks "Play it safe and don't take risks," the rich investor must also think about how to improve skills so he or she can take more risks.' Rich dad called this kind of thinking, 'Thinking on both sides of the coin.' He went on to say, 'The rich investor must have more flexible thinking than the average investor. For example, while both the average investor and rich investor must think about safety, the rich investor must also think about how to take more risks. While the average investor thinks about cutting down debt, the rich investor is thinking about how to increase debt. While the average investor lives in fear of market crashes, the rich investor looks forward to market crashes. While this may sound like a contradiction to the average investor, it is this contradiction that makes the rich investor rich.'

As you read through this book, be aware of the contradictions in thinking between average investors and rich investors. As rich dad said, 'The rich investor is very aware that there are two sides to every coin. The average investor sees only one side. And it is the side the average investor does not see that keeps the average investor average and the rich investor rich.' The second part of this book is about the other side of the coin.

## *Do You Want to Be More than an Average Investor?*

This book is much more than just a book about investing, hot tips, and magic formulas. One of the main purposes for writing it is to offer you the opportunity to gain a different point of view on the subject of investing. It begins with me returning from Vietnam in 1973 and preparing myself to begin investing as a rich investor. In 1973, rich dad began teaching me how to acquire the same financial power he possessed, a power I first became aware of at the age of 12. While standing on the sandy beach in front of my rich dad's latest investment 40 years ago, I realized that when it came to the subject of investing, the difference between my rich dad and my poor dad went far deeper than merely how much money each man had to invest. The difference is first found in a person's deep desire to be much more than just an average investor. If you have such a desire, then read on.

**FREE!**

### A Special Audio Report from Robert Kiyosaki
### For Readers of *Rich Dad's Guide to Investing* Only

As our way of saying thank you for taking an active role in your financial education, Robert has prepared a special audio report. 'My rich dad said that one of the most important investor skills an investor can learn is how to get rich when a market is crashing. When everyone else is panicking and selling, how do you stay calm, stay in the market and make a lot of money?'

### Please listen to
### 'My Rich Dad Said, "Profit Don't Panic"'

All you have to do to get this audio report is visit our special website at www.richdadbook3.com, and the report is yours free.

Thank you and good luck.

# *Are You Mentally Prepared to Be an Investor?*

*Chapter One*

# What Should I Invest In?

In 1973, I returned home from my tour of Vietnam. I felt fortunate to have been assigned to a base in Hawaii near home rather than to a base on the East Coast. After settling in at the Marine Corps Air Station, I called my friend Mike and we set up a time to have lunch together with his dad, the man I call my rich dad. Mike was anxious to show me his new baby and his new home so we agreed to have lunch at his house the following Saturday. When Mike's limousine came to pick me up at the drab gray base BOQ, the Bachelor Officers' Quarters, I began to realize how much had changed since we had graduated together from high school in 1965.

'Welcome home,' Mike said as I walked into the foyer of his beautiful home with marble floors. Mike was beaming from ear to ear as he held his seven-month-old son. 'Glad you made it back in one piece.'

'So am I,' I replied as I looked past Mike at the shimmering blue Pacific Ocean, which touched the white sand in front of his home. The home was spectacular. It was a tropical one-level mansion with all the grace and charm of old and new Hawaiian living. There were beautiful Persian carpets, tall dark green potted plants, and a large pool that was surrounded on three sides by his home, with the ocean on the fourth side. It was very open, breezy, and the model of gracious island living with the finest of detail. The home fit my fantasies of living the luxurious life in Hawaii.

'Meet my son James,' said Mike.

'Oh,' I said in a startled voice. My jaw must have been hanging open as I had slipped into a trance taking in the stunning beauty of this home. 'What a cute kid,' I replied as any person should reply when looking at a new baby. But as I stood there waving and making faces at a baby blankly staring back at me, my mind was still in shock at how much had changed in eight years. I was living on a military base in old barracks, sharing a room with three other messy beer-drinking young pilots, while Mike was living in a multi-million-dollar estate with his gorgeous wife and newborn baby.

'Come on in,' Mike continued. 'Dad and Connie are waiting for us on the patio.'

The lunch was spectacular and served by their full-time maid. I sat there enjoying the meal, the scenery, and the company when I thought about my three roommates who were probably dining at the officer's mess hall at that very moment. Since it was Saturday, lunch on the base was probably a sub sandwich and a bowl of soup.

After the pleasantries and catching up on old times was over, rich dad said, 'As you can see, Mike has done an excellent job investing the profits from the business. We have made more money in the last two years than I made in the first twenty. There is a lot of truth to the statement that the first million is the hardest.'

'So business has been good?' I asked, encouraging further disclosure on how their fortunes had jumped so radically.

'Business is excellent,' said rich dad. 'These new 747s bring so many tourists from all over the world to Hawaii that business cannot help but keep growing. But our real success is from our investments more than our business. And Mike is in charge of the investments.'

'Congratulations,' I said to Mike. 'Well done.'

'Thank you,' said Mike. 'But I can't take all the credit. It's dad's investment formula that is really working. I'm just doing exactly what he has been teaching us about business and investing for all these years.'

'It must be paying off,' I said. 'I can't believe you live here in the richest neighborhood in the city. Do you remember when we were poor kids, running with our surfboards between houses trying to get to the beach?'

Mike laughed. 'Yes I do. And I remember being chased by all those mean old rich guys. Now I'm the mean old rich guy who is chasing those kids away. Who would have ever thought that you and I would be living . . .?'

Mike suddenly stopped talking once he realized what he was saying. He realized that while he was living here, I was living on the other side of the island in drab military barracks.

'I'm sorry,' he said. 'I . . . didn't mean to . . .'

'No apologies necessary,' I said with a grin. 'I'm happy for you. I'm glad you're so wealthy and successful. You deserve it because you took the time to learn to run the business. I'll be out of the barracks in a couple of years as soon as my contract with the Marine Corps is done.'

Rich dad, sensing the tension between Mike and me, broke in and said, 'And he's done a better job than I have. I'm very proud of him. I'm proud of both my son and his wife. They are a great team and have earned everything they have. Now that you're back from the war, it's your turn Robert.'

## May I Invest With You?

'I'd love to invest with you,' I eagerly replied. 'I saved nearly $3,000 while I was in Vietnam and I'd like to invest it before I spend it. Can I invest with you?'

'Well, I'll give you the name of a good stockbroker,' rich dad said. 'I'm sure he'll give you some good advice, maybe even a hot tip or two.'

'No, no, no,' I said. 'I want to invest in what you are investing in. Come on. You know how long I've known you two. I know you've always got something that you're working on or investing in. I don't want to go to a stockbroker. I want to be in a deal with you guys.'

The room went silent as I waited for rich dad or Mike to respond. The silence grew into tension.

'Did I say something wrong?' I asked finally.

'No,' said Mike. 'Dad and I are investing in a couple of new projects that are exciting but I think it is best you call one of our stockbrokers first and begin investing with him.'

Again there was silence, punctuated only by the clinking of the dishes and glasses as the maid cleared the table. Mike's wife Connie excused herself and took the baby to another room.

'I don't understand,' I said. Turning to rich dad more than Mike, I continued, 'All these years I've worked right alongside the two of you building your business. I've worked for close to nothing. I went to college as you advised and I fought for my country as you said a young man should. Now that I'm old enough and I finally have a few dollars to invest, you seem to hesitate when I say I want to invest in what you invest in. I don't understand. Why the cold shoulder – are you trying to snub me or push me away? Don't you want me to get rich like you?'

'It's not a cold shoulder,' Mike replied. 'And we would never snub you or not wish you to attain great wealth. It's that things are different now.'

Rich dad nodded his head in slow and silent agreement.

'We'd love to have you invest in what we invest in,' rich dad finally said. 'But it would be against the law.'

'Against the law?' I echoed in loud disbelief. 'Are you two doing something illegal?'

'No, no,' said rich dad with a chuckle. 'We would never do anything illegal. It's too easy to get rich legally to ever risk going to jail for something illegal.'

'And it is because we want to always remain on the right side of the law that we say it would be illegal for you to invest with us,' said Mike.

'It's not illegal for Mike and me to invest in what we invest in. But it would be illegal for you,' rich dad tried to summarize.

'Why?' I asked.

'Because you're not rich,' said Mike softly and gently. 'What we invest in is for rich people only.'

Mike's words went straight through me. Since he was my best friend, I knew they were difficult words for him to say to me. And although he said them as gently as possible, they still hurt and cut like a knife through my heart. I was beginning to sense how wide the financial gap between us was. While his dad and my dad both started out with nothing, he and his dad had achieved great wealth. My dad and I were still from the other side of the tracks, as they say. I could sense that this big house with the lovely white-sand beach was still far away for me, and the distance was measured in more than miles. Leaning back in my chair and crossing my arms in introspective thought, I sat there nodding quietly as I summarized that moment in our lives. We were both 25 years old but in many ways, Mike was 25 years ahead of me financially. My own dad had just been more or less fired from his government job and he was starting over with nothing at age 52. I had not even begun.

'Are you OK?' asked rich dad gently.

'Yeah, I'm OK,' I replied, doing my best to hide the hurt that came from feeling sorry for myself and for my family. 'I'm just doing some deep thinking and some soul searching,' I said, mustering a brave grin.

The room was silent as we listened to the waves and as the cool breeze blew through the beautiful home. Mike, rich dad, and I sat there while I came to terms with the message and its reality.

'So I can't invest with you because I'm not rich,' I finally said as I came out of my trance. 'And if I did invest in what you invest in, it would be against the law?'

Rich dad and Mike nodded. 'In some instances,' Mike added.

'And who made this law?' I asked.

'The federal government,' Mike replied.

'The SEC,' rich dad added.

'The SEC?' I asked. 'What is the SEC?'

'The Securities and Exchange Commission,' rich dad responded. 'It was created in the 1930s under the direction of Joseph Kennedy, father of our late President John Kennedy.'

'Why was it created?' I asked.

Rich dad laughed. 'It was created to protect the public from wild unscrupulous dealmakers, businessmen, brokers, and investors.'

'Why do you laugh?' I asked. 'It seems like that would be a good thing to do.'

'Yes, it is a very good thing,' rich dad replied, still chuckling a little. 'Prior to the stock market crash of 1929, many shady, slippery, and shoddy investments were being sold to the public. A lot of lying and misinformation was being put forth. So the SEC was formed to be the watchdog. It is the agency that helps make – as well as enforce – the rules. It serves a very important role. Without the SEC, there would be chaos.'

'So why do you laugh?' I persisted.

'Because while it protects the public from the bad investments, it also keeps the public out of the best investments,' replied rich dad in a more serious tone.

'So if the SEC protects the public from the worst investments and from the best investments, what does the public invest in?' I asked.

'The sanitized investments,' rich dad replied. 'The investments that follow the guidelines of the SEC.'

'Well, what is wrong with that?' I asked.

'Nothing,' said rich dad. 'I think it's a good idea. We must have rules and enforce the rules. The SEC does that.'

'But why the chuckle?' I asked. 'I've known you too many years and I know you are holding back something that is causing you to laugh.'

'I've already told you,' said rich dad. 'I chuckle because in protecting the public from the bad investments, the SEC also protects the public from the best investments.'

'Which is one of the reasons the rich get richer?' I asked tenuously.

'You got it,' said rich dad. 'I chuckle because I see the irony in the big picture. People invest because they want to get rich. But because they're not rich, they're not allowed to invest in the investments that could make them rich. Only if you're rich can you invest in a rich person's investments. And so the rich get richer. To me, that is ironic.'

'But why is it done this way?' I asked. 'Is it to protect the poor and middle class from the rich?'

'No, not necessarily,' Mike responded. 'I think it is really to protect the poor and the middle class from themselves.'

'Why do you say that?' I asked.

'Because there are many more bad deals than good deals. If a person is not aware, all deals – good and bad – look the same. It takes a great deal of education and experience to sort the more sophisticated investments into good and bad investments. To be sophisticated means you have the ability to know what makes one investment good and the others dangerous. And most people simply do not have that education and experience,' said rich dad. 'Mike, why don't you bring out the latest deal we are considering?'

Mike left the table for his office and returned with a three-ring binder that was about two inches thick filled with pages, pictures, figures, and maps.

'This is an example of something we would consider investing in,' said Mike as he sat down. 'It is known as a non-registered security. This particular investment is sometimes called a private placement memorandum.'

My mind went numb as Mike flipped though the pages and showed me the graphs, charts, maps, and pages of written text that described the risks and rewards of the investment. I felt drowsy as Mike explained what he was looking at and why he thought it was such a great investment opportunity.

Rich dad, seeing me begin to fade away with the overload of unfamiliar information, stopped Mike and said, 'This is what I wanted Robert to see.'

Rich dad then pointed to a small paragraph at the front of the book that read 'Exemptions from the Securities Act of 1933.'

'This is what I want you to understand,' he said.

I leaned forward to be better able to read the fine print his finger was pointing to. The fine print said,

'This investment is for accredited investors only. An accredited investor is generally accepted to be someone who:

- has a net worth of $1 million or more; or
- has had an annual income of $200,000 or more in each of the most recent years (or $300,000 jointly with a spouse) and who has a reasonable expectation of reaching the same income level in the current year.'

Leaning back in my chair, I said, 'This is why you say I cannot invest in what you invest in. This investment is for rich people only.'

'Or people with high incomes,' said Mike.

'Not only are these guidelines tough, but the minimum amount you can invest in this investment is $35,000. That is how much each investment "unit," as it is called, costs.'

'$35,000!' I said with a gasp. 'That is a lot of money and a lot of risk. You mean that is the least someone can invest in this deal?'

Rich dad nodded. 'How much does the government pay you as a Marine Corps pilot?'

'I was earning about $12,000 a year with flight pay and combat pay in Vietnam. I really don't know what my pay will be here now that I am stationed in Hawaii. I might get some COLA, cost of living allowance, but it sure isn't going to be much, and it certainly will not cover the cost of living in Hawaii.'

'So for you to have saved $3,000 was quite an accomplishment,' said rich dad, doing his best to cheer me up. 'You saved nearly 25% of your gross income.'

I nodded yet silently I realized how very, very far behind I was from becoming a so-called accredited investor. I realized that even if I became a General in the Marine Corps, I would probably not earn enough money to be considered an accredited investor. Not even the president of the United States, unless he or she were already rich, could qualify on salary alone.

'So what should I do?' I finally asked. 'Why can't I just give you my $3,000 and you combine it with your money and we split the profits when the deal pays off?'

'We could do that,' said rich dad. 'But I wouldn't recommend it. Not for you anyway.'

'Why?' I asked. 'Why not for me?'

'You already have a pretty good financial education foundation. So you can go way beyond just being an accredited investor. If you want, you could become a sophisticated investor. Then you will find wealth far beyond your wildest dreams.'

'Accredited investor? Sophisticated investor? What's the difference?' I asked, actually feeling a spark of renewed hope.

'Good question,' Mike said with a smile, sensing that his friend was coming out of a slump.

'An accredited investor is by definition someone who qualifies because he or she has money. That is why an accredited investor is often called a qualified investor,' rich dad explained. 'But money alone does not qualify you to be a sophisticated investor.'

'What is the difference?' I asked.

'Well, did you see the headlines in yesterday's newspaper about the Hollywood movie star who lost millions in an investment scam?' asked rich dad.

I nodded my head saying, 'Yes I did. Not only did he lose millions, he had to pay the tax department for untaxed income that went into that deal.'

'Well, that is an example of an accredited or qualified investor,' rich dad continued. 'But just because you have money does not mean you're a sophisticated investor. This is why we often hear of so many high-income people such as doctors, lawyers, rock stars, and professional athletes losing money in less-than-sound investments. They have the money but they lack the sophistication. They have money but don't know how to invest it safely and for high returns. All the deals look the same to them. They can't tell a good investment from a bad one. People like them should stay only in sanitized investments or hire a professional money manager they trust to invest for them.'

'So what is your definition of a sophisticated investor?' I asked.

'A sophisticated investor knows the three Es,' said rich dad.

'The three Es,' I repeated. 'What are the three Es?'

Rich dad then turned over the private placement memorandum

we were looking at and wrote the following on the back of one of
the pages.

1.  Education
2.  Experience
3.  Excessive cash

'Those are the three Es,' he said, looking up from the page. 'Achieve
those three items and you will be a sophisticated investor.'

Looking at the three items, I said, 'So the movie star had excessive cash, but he lacked the first two items.'

Rich dad nodded. 'And there are many people with the right education but they lack the experience, and without real life experience,
they often lack the excessive cash.'

'People like that often say, "I know" when you explain things to
them, but they do not do what they know,' added Mike. 'Our banker
always says, "I know" to what dad and I do, but for some reason, he
does not do what he claims he knows.'

'And that is why your banker lacks the excessive cash,' I said.

Rich dad and Mike nodded.

Again, the room went silent as the conversation ended. All three
of us were deep in our own private thoughts. Rich dad signaled the
maid for more coffee and Mike began putting the three-ring binder
away. I sat with my arms crossed, gazing out upon the deep blue
Pacific Ocean at Mike's beautiful home and contemplating my next
direction in life. I had finished college as my parents had wished, my
military obligation would soon be over, and then I would be free to
choose the path that was best for me.

'What are you thinking about?' asked rich dad, sipping from his
fresh cup of coffee.

'I'm thinking about what I want to become now that I have grown
up,' I replied.

'And what is that?' asked Mike.

'I'm thinking that maybe I should become a sophisticated investor,' I replied quietly. 'Whatever that is.'

'That would be a wise choice,' said rich dad. 'You've got a pretty good start, a financial education foundation. Now it's time to get some experience.'

'And how will I know when I have enough of both?' I asked.

'When you have excessive cash,' smiled rich dad.

With that, the three of us laughed and raised our water glasses, toasting, 'To excessive cash.'

Rich dad then toasted, 'And to being a sophisticated investor.'

'To being a sophisticated investor and to excessive cash,' I repeated again silently to myself. I liked the ring of those words in my head.

Mike's limousine driver was summoned and I returned to my dingy bachelor officers' quarters to think about what I was going to do with the rest of my life. I was an adult and I had fulfilled my parents' expectations . . . expectations such as getting a college education and serving my country during a time of war. It was now time for me to decide what I wanted to do for myself. The thought of studying to become a sophisticated investor appealed to me. I could continue my education with rich dad as I gained the experience I needed. This time, my rich dad would be guiding me as an adult.

## 20 Years Later

By 1993, rich dad's wealth was split between his children, grandchildren, and their future children. For the next hundred years or so, his heirs would not have to worry about money. Mike received the primary assets of the business and has done a magnificent job of growing the balance of rich dad's financial empire, a financial empire that rich dad had built from nothing. I had seen it start and grow during my lifetime.

It took me 20 years to achieve what I thought I should have been able to do in 10 years. There is some truth to that saying, 'It's the first million that is the hardest.'

In retrospect, making $1 million was not that difficult. It's keeping the million and having it work hard for you that I found to be difficult. Nevertheless, I was able to retire in 1994 at the age of 47, financially free with ample money with which to enjoy life.

Yet, it was not retirement that I found exciting. It was finally being able to invest as a sophisticated investor that was exciting. To be able to invest alongside Mike and rich dad was a goal worth achieving. That day back in 1973, when Mike and rich dad said I was not rich enough to invest with them, was a turning point in my life and the day I set the goal to become a sophisticated investor.

The following is a list of some of the investments in which so-called 'Accredited Investors and Sophisticated Investors' invest:

1. Private placements
2. Real estate syndication and limited partnerships
3. Pre-initial public offerings (IPOs). While available to all investors, IPOs are not usually easily accessible.
4. Sub-prime financing
5. Mergers and acquisitions
6. Loans for startups
7. Hedge funds

For the average investor, these investments are too risky, not because the investment itself is necessarily risky, but because all too often, the average investor lacks the education, experience, and excessive capital to know what he or she is getting into. I now tend to side with the SEC that it is better to protect unqualified investors by restricting their access to these types of investments because I made some errors and false steps along the way.

As a sophisticated investor today, I now invest in such ventures. If you know what you're doing, the risk is very low while the potential reward can be huge. Investments such as these are where the rich routinely invest their money.

Although I have taken some losses, the returns on the investments that do well have been spectacular, far exceeding the few losses. A 35% return on capital is normal, but returns of 1,000% and more are occasionally achieved. I would rather invest in these investments because I find them more exciting and more challenging. It's not simply a matter of 'Buy me 100 shares of this or sell 100 shares of that.' Nor is it 'Is the p/e high or is the p/e low?' That is not what being a sophisticated investor is about. Investing in these investments is about getting very close to the engine of capitalism. In fact, some of the investments listed are venture capital investments, which for the average investor are far too risky. In reality, the investments are not risky, it's the lack of education, experience, and excessive cash that makes the average investor risky.

This Book is not about investments.<br>This Book is about the investor.

## The Path

This book is not necessarily about investments. This book is about the investor specifically, and the path to becoming a sophisticated investor. It is about you finding your path to acquiring the three Es: education, experience, and excessive cash.

*Rich Dad Poor Dad* is a book about my educational path as a child. *CASHFLOW Quadrant* is *Rich Dad Poor Dad* part II and is my educational path as a young adult between the years 1973 and 1994. This book, *Rich Dad's Guide to Investing*, builds on the lessons from all previous years with my real-life experiences and converts the lessons into the three Es in order to qualify as a sophisticated investor.

In 1973, I barely had $3,000 to invest and I did not have much education and real-life experience. By 1994, I had become a sophisticated investor.

Over 20 years ago, rich dad said, 'Just as there are houses for the rich, the poor, and the middle class, there are investments for each of them. If you want to invest in investments that the rich invest in, you have to be more than rich. You need to become a sophisticated investor, not just a rich person who invests.'

## *The Five Phases of Becoming a Sophisticated Investor*

Rich dad broke my development program into five distinct phases, which I have organized into phases, lessons, and chapters. The phases are:

1. Are You Mentally Prepared to Be an Investor?
2. What Type of Investor Do You Want to Become?
3. How Do You Build a Strong Business?
4. Who Is the Sophisticated Investor?
5. Giving It Back.

This book is written as a guide. It will not give you specific answers. The purpose of this book is to help you understand what questions to ask. And if this book does that, it has done its job. Rich dad said, 'You cannot teach someone to be a sophisticated investor. But a person can learn to become a sophisticated investor. It's like learning to ride a bicycle. I cannot teach you to ride a bicycle, but you can learn to ride a bicycle. Learning to ride a bicycle requires risk, trial and error, and proper guidance. The same is true with investing. If you do not want to take risks, then you're saying you do not want to learn. And if you do not want to learn, then I cannot teach you.'

If you're looking for a book on hot investment tips, or how to get rich quick, or the secret investment formula of the rich, this book is not for you. This book is really about learning more than investing. It is written for people who are students of investing, students who seek their own path to wealth rather than look for the easy road to wealth.

This book is about rich dad's five phases of development, the five phases that he went through and that I am currently going through. If you are a student of great wealth, you may notice while reading this book that rich dad's five phases are the same five phases that the richest businesspeople and investors in the world went through in order to become very, very rich. Bill Gates, founder of Microsoft; Warren Buffet, America's richest investor; and Thomas Edison, founder of General Electric, all went through these five phases. They are the same five phases that the young new millionaires and billionaires of the Internet or the 'dot com' generation are currently going through while still in their twenties and thirties. The only difference is that because of the Information Age, these young people went through the same phases faster . . . and maybe so can you.

## *Are You Part of the Revolution?*

Great wealth, vast fortunes, and mega-rich families were created during the Industrial Revolution. The same is going on today during the Information Revolution.

I find it interesting that today we have self-made multi-millionaires and billionaires who are twenty, thirty, and forty years of age; yet we still have people forty and over having a tough time hanging on to $50,000-a-year jobs. One reason causing this great disparity is the shift from the Industrial Age to the Information Age. When we shifted into the Industrial Age, people like Henry Ford and Thomas Edison became billionaires. Today, shifting into the Information Age, we have Bill Gates, Michael Dell, and the founders of the Internet companies becoming young millionaires and billionaires. These twenty-some-things will soon be passing Bill Gates – who is old at 39 – in wealth. That is the power of a shift in ages, the shift from the Industrial Age to the Information Age. It has been said that there is nothing so powerful as an idea whose time has come . . . and there is nothing so detrimental as someone who is still thinking old ideas.

For you, this book may be about looking at old ideas and possibly finding new ideas for wealth. It may also be about a paradigm shift in your life. It may be about a transition as radical as the shift from the Industrial Age to the Information Age. It may be about you defining a new financial path for your life. It may be about thinking more like a businessperson and investor rather than an employee or a self-employed person.

It took me years to go through the phases, and in fact, I am still going through them. After reading this book, you may consider going through the same five phases or you may decide that this developmental path is not for you. If you decide to embark upon the same path, how fast you choose to go through these five phases of development is up to you. Remember that this book is not about getting rich quickly. The choice to undergo such a personal development and education program begins in Phase One . . . the phase of mental preparation.

## Are You Mentally Prepared to Be an Investor?

Rich dad often said, 'Money will be anything you want it to be.'

What he meant was that money comes from our minds, our thoughts. If a person says, 'Money is hard to get,' it will probably be hard to get. If a person says, 'Oh I'll never be rich,' or 'It's really hard to get rich,' it will probably be true for that person. If a person says, 'The only way to get rich is to work hard,' then that person will probably work hard. If the person says, 'If I had a lot of money, I would put it in the bank because I wouldn't know what to do with it,' then it will probably happen just that way. You'd be surprised how many people think and do just that. And if a person says, 'Investing is risky,' then it is. As rich dad said, 'Money will be anything you want it to be.'

Rich dad warned me that the mental preparation needed to become a sophisticated investor was probably similar to the mental preparation it would take to climb Mt Everest, or to prepare for the priesthood. He was kidding, yet he was putting me on notice that such an undertaking was not to be taken lightly. He said to me, 'You start as I did. You start without any money. All you have is hope and a dream of attaining great wealth. While many people dream of it, only a few achieve it. Think hard and prepare mentally because you are about to learn to invest in a way that very few people are allowed to invest. You will see the investment world from the inside rather than from the outside. There are far easier paths in life and easier ways to invest. So think it over and be prepared if you decide this is the path for your life.'

# Chapter 2

# *Pouring a Foundation of Wealth*

Returning to the dingy gray officers' quarters on base that night was very difficult. They had been fine when I left earlier that day, but after spending the afternoon in Mike's new home, the officers' quarters seemed cheap, old, and tired.

As expected, my three roommates were drinking beer and watching a baseball game on television. There were pizza boxes and beer cans everywhere. They did not say much as I passed through the shared living area. They just stared at the TV set. As I retired to my room and closed the door, I felt grateful that we all had private rooms. I had much to think about.

At 25 years of age, I finally realized things that I could not understand as a kid of 9, the age at which I first began working with rich dad. I realized that my rich dad had been working hard for years pouring a solid foundation of wealth. They had started on the poor side of town, living frugally, building businesses, buying real estate, and working on their plan. I now understood that rich dad's plan was to become very wealthy. While Mike and I were in high school, rich dad had made his move by expanding to different islands of the

Hawaiian chain, buying businesses and real estate. While Mike and I were in college, he made his big move and became one of the major private investors in businesses in Honolulu and parts of Waikiki. While I was flying for the Marine Corps in Vietnam, his foundation of wealth was set in place. It was a strong and firm foundation. Now he and his family were enjoying the fruits of their labor. Instead of living in the poorest of neighborhoods on an outer island, they lived in one of the wealthiest neighborhoods in Honolulu. They did not just look rich on the surface as many of the people in that neighborhood did. I knew that Mike and his dad were rich because they allowed me to review their audited financial statements. Not many people were given that privilege.

My real dad, on the other hand, had just lost his job. He had been climbing the ladder in the state government when he fell from grace from the political machine that ran the State of Hawaii. My dad lost everything he had worked to achieve when he ran against his boss for governor and lost. He had been blacklisted from state government and was trying to start over. He had no foundation of wealth. Although he was 52 and I was 25, we were in exactly the same financial position. We had no money. We both had a college education and we could both get another job, but when it came to real assets, we had nothing. That night, lying quietly on my bunk, I knew I had a rare opportunity to choose a direction for my life. I say rare because very few people have the luxury of comparing the life paths of two fathers and then choosing the path that was right for them. It was a choice I did not take lightly.

### *Investments of the Rich*

Although many things ran through my mind that night, I was most intrigued by the idea that there were investments only for the rich, and then there were investments for everyone else. I remembered that when I was a kid working for rich dad, all he talked about was building his businesses. But now that he was rich, all he talked about was his investments . . . investments for the rich. That day over lunch, he had explained, 'The only reason I built business was so I could invest in the investments of the rich. The only reason you build a business is so that your business can buy your assets. Without my business, I could not afford to invest in the investments of the rich.'

Rich dad went on to stress the difference between an employee buying an investment and a business buying an investment. He said, 'Most investments are too expensive when you purchase them as an employee. But they are much more affordable if my business buys them for me.' I did not know what he meant by that statement, but I knew this distinction was important. I was now curious and anxious to find out what the difference was. Rich dad had studied corporate and tax law and had found ways to make a lot of money using the laws to his advantage. I drifted off that night excited about calling rich dad in the morning and saying softly to myself, 'investments of the rich.'

### *The Lessons Resume*

I had spent many hours as a child sitting at a table in one of rich dad's restaurants as rich dad discussed the affairs of his business. At these discussions, I would sit and sip my soda, while rich dad talked with his bankers, accountants, attorneys, stockbrokers, real estate brokers, financial planners, and insurance agents. It was the beginning of my business education. Between the ages of 9 and 18, I spent hours listening to these men and women solve intricate business problems. But those lessons around the table ended when I left for four years of college in New York, followed by five years of service with the Marine Corps. Now that my college education was complete and my military duty nearly over, I was ready to continue the lessons with rich dad.

When I called him the next day, he was ready to begin my lessons again. He had turned the business over to Mike and was now semi-retired. He was looking for something to do rather than play golf all day.

When I was young, I did not know which dad to listen to when it came to the subject of money. Both were good, hard-working men. Both were strong and charismatic. Both said I should go to college and serve my country in the military. But they did not say the same things about money or give the same advice about what to become when I grew up. Now I could compare the results of the career paths chosen by my rich dad and my poor dad.

In *CASHFLOW Quadrant*, the book that follows *Rich Dad Poor Dad*, my poor dad advised me to 'Go to school, get good grades, and then find a safe, secure job with benefits.' He was recommending a career path in this direction:

On the other hand, my rich dad said, 'Learn to build businesses and invest through your businesses.' He was recommending a career path that looked like this:

The *CASHFLOW Quadrant* is about the core emotional differences and the technical differences among the people found in each of the quadrants. These core emotional and technical differences are important because they ultimately determine which quadrant a person tends to favor and operate from. For example, a person who needs job security will most likely seek the E quadrant. In the E quadrant are people from janitors to presidents of companies. A person who needs to do things on his or her own is often found in the S quadrant, the quadrant of the self-employed or small business. I also say that 'S' stands for solo and smart, because this is where many of the professionals such as doctors, attorneys, accountants, and other technical consultants are found.

The *CASHFLOW Quadrant* explains a lot about the difference between the S quadrant – which is where most small-business owners operate – and the B quadrant – which is the quadrant where big businesses are found. In this book, we will go into much more detail about the technical differences, because it is here that the differences between the rich and everyone else are found.

## *The Tax Laws Are Different*

The differences between the quadrants play a very important role in this book. The tax laws are different for the different quadrants. What may be legal in one quadrant is illegal in another. These subtle differences make big differences when it comes to the subject of investing. When discussing the subject of investing, my rich dad was very careful to ask me from which quadrant I was planning to earn my money.

## *The Lessons Begin*

While Mike was busy running their empire, rich dad and I were having lunch at a hotel on Waikiki Beach. The sun was warm, the ocean beautiful, the breeze light, and the setting as close to paradise as you can get. Rich dad was shocked to see me walk in wearing my uniform. He had never seen me in uniform before. He had only seen me as a kid, dressed in casual clothes such as shorts, jeans, and T-shirts. I guess he finally realized that I had grown up since leaving high school, and by now had seen a lot of the world and fought in a war. I had worn my uniform to the meeting because I was between flights and had to get back to the base to fly that evening.

'So that is what you have been doing since leaving high school,' said rich dad.

I nodded my head and said, 'Four years at the military academy in New York, and four years in the Marine Corps. One more year to go.'

'I am very proud of you,' said rich dad.

'Thanks,' I replied. 'But it will be nice to get out of a military uniform. It's really tough being spit on or stared at, or called "baby-killers" by all these hippies and people who are against the war. I just hope it ends soon for all of us.'

'I'm just glad Mike did not have to go,' said rich dad. 'He wanted to enlist but his poor health kept him out.'

'He was fortunate,' I replied. 'I lost enough friends to that war. I would have hated to have lost Mike too.'

Rich dad nodded his head and asked, 'So what are your plans once your military contract is up next year?'

'Well, three of my friends have been offered jobs with the airlines as pilots. It's tough getting hired right now but they say they can get me in through some contacts they have.'

'So you're thinking of flying with the airlines?' asked rich dad.

I nodded slowly. 'Well, that's all I've been doing . . . thinking about it. The pay is OK, and benefits are good. And besides, my flight training has been pretty intense,' I said. 'I've become a pretty good pilot after flying in combat. If I fly for a year with a small airline and get some multi-engine time, I will be ready for the major carriers.'

'So is that what you think you are going to do?' asked rich dad.

'No,' I replied. 'Not after what has happened to my dad and after having lunch at Mike's new home. I lay awake for hours that night and I thought about what you said about investing. I realized that if I took a job with the airlines I might someday become an accredited investor. But I realized that I might never go beyond that level.'

Rich dad sat in silence, nodding ever so slightly. 'So what I said hit home,' rich dad said in a low voice.

'Very much so,' I replied. 'I reflected on all the lessons you gave me as a kid. Now I am an adult and the lessons have a new meaning to me.'

'And what did you remember?' asked rich dad.

'I remember you taking away my 10 cents per hour and making me work for free,' I replied. 'I remembered that lesson of not becoming addicted to a paycheck.'

Rich dad laughed at himself and said, 'That was a pretty tough lesson.'

'Yes it was,' I replied. 'But a great lesson. My dad was really angry with you. But now he is the one trying to live without a paycheck. The difference is he's 52 and I was 9 when I got that lesson. After lunch at Mike's, I vowed that I would not spend my life clinging to job security just because I needed a paycheck. That is why I doubt that I will seek a job with the airlines. And that is why I'm here having lunch with you. I want to review your lessons on how to have money work for me, so I don't have to spend my life working for money. But this time, I want your lessons as an adult. Make the lessons harder and give me more detail.'

'And what was my first lesson?' asked rich dad.

'The rich don't work for money,' I said promptly. 'They know how to have money work for them.'

A broad smile came over rich dad's face. He knew that I had been listening to him all those years as a kid. 'Very good,' he said. 'And that is the basis of becoming an investor. All investors do is learn how to have their money work hard for them.'

'And that is what I want to learn,' I said quietly. 'I want to learn and maybe teach my dad what you know. He is in a very bad way right now, trying to start over again at the age of 52.'

'I know,' said rich dad. 'I know.'

So on a sunny day, with surfers riding the beautiful waves of the deep blue ocean, my lessons on investing began. The lessons came in five phases, each phase taking me to a higher level of understanding . . . understanding the thought process of rich dad and his invest-ment plan. The lessons began with preparing mentally and taking control of myself . . . because that is the only place that investing really takes place anyway. Investing ultimately begins and ends with taking control of yourself.

The lessons on investment in Phase One of rich dad's investment plan are all about the mental preparation it takes before actually begin-ning to invest. Lying in my bunk that night in 1973, in a dingy room on base, my mental preparation had begun. Mike was fortunate enough to have a father who had accumulated great wealth. I was not that fortunate. In many ways, he had a 50-year head start on me. I had yet to start. That night, I began my mental preparation by making a decision between job security, as chosen by my poor dad, or pouring a foundation of real wealth as chosen by my rich dad. That is where the process of investing truly begins and where rich dad's lessons on investing start. It starts with a very personal decision . . . a mental choice to be rich, poor, or middle class. It is an important decision, because whichever financial position in life you choose — be it rich, poor, or middle class — everything in your life then changes.

# Chapter 3
## Investor Lesson #1:

# The Choice

Rich dad's lessons on investing began. 'When it comes to money and investing, people have three fundamental reasons or choices for investing. They are:

1. To be secure,
2. To be comfortable, or
3. To be rich.'

Rich dad went on to say, 'All three choices are important. The difference in one's life occurs when the choices are prioritized.' He continued by saying that most people make their money and investment choices in that exact order. In other words, their first choice when it comes to money decisions is security, second is comfort, and third is to be rich. That is why most people make job security their highest priority. After they have a secure job or profession, then they focus on comfort. The last choice for most people is to be rich.

That day in 1973, rich dad said, 'Most people dream of becoming rich, but it is not their first choice.' He went on to say, 'Only three out of a hundred people in America are rich because of this priority of choices. For most people, if becoming rich disturbs their comfort or makes them feel insecure, they will forsake becoming rich. That is why so many people want that one hot investment tip. People who make security and comfort their first and second choices look for ways to get rich quick that are easy, risk free, and comfortable. A few people do get rich on one lucky investment, but all too often they lose it all again.'

### Rich or Happy

I often hear people say, 'I'd rather be happy than be rich.' That comment has always sounded very strange to me since I have been both rich and poor. And in both financial positions, I have been both happy and unhappy. I wonder why people think they have to choose between happiness and being rich.

When I reflect upon this lesson, it occurs to me that what people are really saying is that 'I'd rather feel secure and comfortable than be rich.' That is because if they felt insecure or uncomfortable, they were not happy. For me, I was willing to feel insecure and uncomfortable in order to be rich. I have been rich and poor as well as happy and unhappy. But I assure you that when I was poor and unhappy, I was much unhappier than when I was rich and unhappy.

I have also never understood the statement 'Money does not make you happy.' While there is some truth in it, I have always noticed that when I have money, I feel pretty good. The other day, I found a $10 bill in my jeans pocket. Even though it was only $10, it felt great finding it. Receiving money has always felt better than receiving a bill for money I owe. At least that is my experience with money. I feel happy when it comes in and sad when it leaves me.

Back in 1973, I put my priorities in this order:

1. To be rich
2. To be comfortable
3. To be secure

As stated earlier, when it comes to money and investing, all three priorities are important. Which order you put them in is a very personal decision that should be made before beginning to invest. My poor dad put 'to be secure' as priority one, and rich dad put 'to be rich' as priority one. Before beginning to invest, it is important to decide what your priorities are.

## Mental Attitude Quiz

To be rich, comfortable, and secure are really personal core values. One is not better than the other. I do know, however, that making the choice of which core values are most important to you often has a significant long-term impact upon the kind of life you choose. That is why it is important to know which core values are most important to you, especially when it comes to the subject of money and financial planning.

**So the mental attitude quiz is:**

List in order of importance which core values are most important to you:

1. _____

2. _____

3. _____

Some of you may need to work through your true feelings. Talk seriously with your spouse or mentor. Make 'pro' and 'con' lists. Knowing what your personal priorities are will save you many agonizing decisions and sleepless nights later.

One of the reasons the 90/10 rule of money applies may be because 90% of the people choose comfort and security over being rich.

## Chapter 4
## Investor Lesson #2:

# What Kind of World Do You See?

One of the most startling differences between my rich dad and poor dad was what kind of world they saw. My poor dad always saw a world of financial scarcity. That view was reflected when he said, 'Do you think money grows on trees?' or 'Do you think I'm made of money?' or 'I can't afford it.'

When I spent time with my rich dad, I began to realize that he saw a completely different world. He could see a world of too much money. That view was reflected when he said, 'Don't worry about money. If we do the right thigns, there will always be plenty of money,' or 'Don't let not having money be an excuse for not getting what you want.'

In 1973, during one of rich dad's lessons, he said, 'There are only two kinds of money problems. One problem is not enough money. The other problem is too much money. Which type of money problem do you want?'

In my classes on investing, I spend a lot of time on this subject. Most people come from families where the money problem was not enough money. Since money is only an idea, if your idea is that there is not enough money, then that is what your reality will be. One of the advantages I had, coming from two families, was that I could see both types of problems . . . and rest assured, both are problems. My poor dad always had problems of not enough money and my rich dad always had problems of too much money.

Rich dad had a comment on that strange phenomenon. He said, 'People who suddenly become rich – by things such as inheritance, a big jackpot from Las Vegas, or the lottery – suddenly become poor again because psychologically, all they know is a world of not enough money. So they lose all their suddenly found wealth and go back to repeating the only world of money they know: a world of not enough money.'

One of my personal struggles was shaking the idea that the world was a world of not enough money. From 1973 on, rich dad had me become very aware of my thoughts when it came to the subjects of money, working, and becoming rich. Rich dad truly believed that poor people remained poor simply because that was the only world they knew. Rich dad would say, 'Whatever your reality is about money inside of you is the reality of money outside of you. You cannot change your outside reality until you first change your inside reality about money.'

Rich dad once outlined what he saw as some of the causes of scarcity as differences in peoples' attitudes:

1. The more security you need, the more scarcity there is in your life.

2. The more competitive you are, the more scarcity in your life. Which is why people compete for jobs and promotions at work and compete for grades in school.

3. To gain more abundance a person needs more skills and needs to be more creative and cooperative. People who are creative have good financial and business skills, and people who are cooperative often have lives of increasing financial abundance.

I could see these differences in attitudes between my two dads. My real dad always encouraged me to play it safe and seek security. My rich dad encouraged me to develop skills and be creative. The second half of this book is about how to take your creative ideas and create a world of abundance rather than a world of scarcity.

During our discussions about scarcity rich dad would break out a coin and say, 'When a person says "I can't afford it," that person sees only one side of the coin. The moment you say "How can I afford it?" you begin to see the other side. The problem is, even when people see the other side, they see it with only their eyes. That is why poor people see rich people doing what rich people do on the surface but they fail to see what rich people are doing inside their minds. If you want to see the other side of the coin, you have to see what is going on inside a very rich person's mind.' The second half of this book is about what goes on in a rich person's mind.

Years later, when lottery winners began going broke I asked rich dad why this was happening. His reply was, 'A person who suddenly comes into a lot of money and goes broke, goes broke because they still see only one side of the coin. In other words they handle the money in the same way they always did, which was the reason they were poor or struggled in the first place. They see only a world of not enough money. The safest thing that person can do is just put the money in the bank and live off the interest only. People who can see the other side of the coin would take that money and multiply it rapidly and safely. They can do that because they see the other side of the coin, the side of the coin where there is a world of too much money and they use their money to get to the other side faster while everyone else uses money to become poorer faster.'

In the late 1980s after rich dad retired and turned his empire over to Mike, he called me in for a brief meeting. Before the meeting began he showed me a bank statement with 39 million dollars in cash in it. I gasped as he said, 'And this is only in one bank. I am retired now because it is a full-time job to keep taking this cash out of my banks and moving it into more productive investments. I repeat, it is a full-time job that becomes more challenging every year.'

As the meeting ended rich dad said, 'I spent years training Mike to build the engine that produces this much money. Now that I am retired he is running the engine that I built. The reason I can retire with confidence is because Mike knows not only how to run the engine, he can fix it if it breaks. Most rich kids lose their parents' money because although they grew up in extreme wealth, they never really learned how to build an engine or fix it after it is broken. In fact, too many rich kids are the very people who break the engine. They grew up on the rich side of the coin, but they never learned what it takes to get to that side. You have a chance, with my guidance, to make the transition and stay on the other side.'

A big part of taking control of myself was taking control of my internal reality about money. I have had to constantly remind myself that there is a world of too much money, because in my heart and soul, I have often felt like a poor person.

One of the exercises rich dad had me do whenever I felt the surge of panic in my heart and stomach, the panic that comes from the fear of not having enough money, was to simply say, 'There are two kinds of money problems. One problem is not enough money and the other is too much money. Which one do I want?' I would ask this question mentally even though my core being was in a state of financial panic.

I am not one of these wishful-thinking people or a person who believes solely in the power of affirmation. I asked myself that question to combat my inherited point of view on money. Once my gut was calmed down, I would then ask my mind to begin finding solutions to whatever was financially challenging me at the time. Solutions could mean seeking new answers, finding new advisors, or attending a class on a subject I was weak on. The main purpose for combating my core panic was to allow me to calm down so I could move forward again.

I have noticed that most people let their panic about money defeat them and dictate the terms and conditions of their lives. Hence, they remain terrified about risk and money. As I wrote in *CASHFLOW Quadrant*, people's emotions often run their lives. Emotions such as fear and doubt lead to low self-esteem and a lack of self-confidence.

In the early 1990s, Donald Trump was nearly $1 billion in debt personally and $9 billion in debt corporately. An interviewer asked Trump if he was worried. Trump replied, 'Worrying is a waste of time. Worrying gets in my way of working to solve these problems.' I have noticed that one of the main reasons people are not rich is that they worry too much about things that might never happen.

Rich dad's investment lesson #2 was to mentally choose to see both worlds . . . a world of not enough money and a world of too much money. Later, rich dad went into the importance of a financial plan. Rich dad strongly believed in having a financial plan for when you did not have enough money as well as a financial plan for when you did have too much money. He said, 'If you do not have a plan for having too much money, then you will lose all your money and go back to the only plan you know, which is what 90% of the population knows: a world of not enough money.'

## *Security and Scarcity*

Rich dad said, 'The more a person seeks security the more scarcity they will have in their life. Security and scarcity go hand in hand. That is why people who seek job security or guarantees are often the people with less abundance in their life. One of the reasons the 90/10 rule of money holds true is because most people spend their lives seeking more security instead of seeking more financial skills. The more financial skills you have the more abundance you will have in your life.'

It was these financial skills that gave rich dad the power to begin acquiring some of the most valuable real estate in Hawaii even though he had very little money. These same financial skills give people the power to take an opportunity and turn it into millions of dollars. Most people can see opportunities, they just cannot turn that opportunity into money and that is why they often seek even more security. Rich dad also said, 'The more a person seeks security, the less they can see of the opportunities that abound. They see only one side of the coin and never see the other side. That is why the more they seek security the less opportunity they see on the flip side of the coin. As the great baseball player Yogi Bera once said, "Strike out just 7 out of 10 times and you're in the Hall of Fame."' In other words, if he came to bat one thousand times in his baseball career, and if he could strike out only 700 times, he would be in the Hall of Fame. After reading Yogi Bera's quote, rich dad said, 'Most people are so security conscious that they live their entire lives avoiding striking out just once.'

## Mental Attitude Quiz

I came from a family that saw the world as a world of not enough money. My personal challenge was to repeatedly remind myself that another kind of world existed and that I needed to keep an open mind to see a world of both possibilities for me.

**So the mental attitude questions are:**

1.  Can you see that two different worlds of money can exist? A world of not enough money and a world of too much money.

    Yes _____ No _____

2.  If you currently live in a world of not enough money, are you willing to see the possibility of you living in a world of too much money?

    Yes _____ No _____

# Chapter 5
## Investor Lesson #3:

# Why Investing Is Confusing

One day, I was waiting in rich dad's office and he was speaking on the phone. He was saying things such as, 'So you're long today?' and 'If the prime drops, what will that do to the spread?' and 'OK, OK, OK, now I understand why you're buying an option straddle to cover that position' and 'You're going to short that stock? Why not use a put option instead of a short?'

After rich dad put his phone down, I said, 'I have no idea what you were talking about. Investing seems so confusing.'

Rich dad smiled and said, 'What I was talking about was not really investing.'

'It wasn't investing? Then what was it? It sounded like what investors on TV and in the movies sound like.'

Rich dad smiled and laughed, saying, 'First of all, investing means different things to different people. That is why it seems so confusing. What most people call investing is not really investing. People are all talking about different things yet they often think they are talking about the same thing.'

'What?' I said, screwing up my face. 'People are talking about different things yet thinking they are talking about the same thing?'

Again rich dad laughed. The lesson had begun.

## Investing Means Different Things to Different People

As rich dad began the lesson that day, he repeatedly stressed that main point. Investing means different things to different people. The following are some of the highlights of this important lesson:

## Different People Invest in Different Things

1.  Rich dad explained some of the differences in value.
    a.  Some people invest in large families. A large extended family is a way to ensure care for the parents in their old age.
    b.  People invest in a good education, job security, and benefits. The individual and his or her marketable skills become the assets.
    c.  Some people invest in external assets. In America, about 45% of the population owns shares in companies. This number is growing as people realize that job security and lifetime employment are less and less guaranteed.

## There Are Many Different Investment Products

2.  Here is a sample of some of the different types of investments:
    a.  Stocks, bonds, mutual funds, real estate, insurance, commodities, savings, collectibles, precious metals, hedge funds, etc.
    b.  Each one of these groups can then be broken down into different subgroups. Let's take stocks, for example.

### Stocks can be subdivided into:
1. Common stock
2. Preferred stock

3. Stocks with warrants
4. Small cap stock
5. Blue chip stock
6. Convertible stock
7. Technical stock
8. Industrial stock
9. And on and on and on

**Real estate can be subdivided into:**

1. Single family
2. Commercial office
3. Commercial retail
4. Multi-family
5. Warehouse
6. Industrial
7. Raw land
8. Raw land to the curb
9. And on and on and on

**Mutual funds can be subdivided into:**

1. Index fund
2. Aggressive growth fund
3. Sector fund
4. Income fund
5. Closed end fund
6. Balanced fund
7. Municipal bond fund
8. Country fund
9. And on and on and on

**Insurance can be subdivided into:**

1. Whole, Term, Variable Life
2. Universal, Variable Universal
3. Blended (whole and term in one policy)

    4. First, second, or last to die

    5. Used for Funding Buy-Sell Agreement

    6. Used for Executive Bonus and Defferred Compensation

    7. Used for Funding Estate taxes

    8. Used for Non Qualified retirement benefits

    9. And on and on and on

  c. There are many different investment products, each designed to do something different. That is another reason why the subject of investing is so confusing.

## There Are Different Investment Procedures

3. Rich dad used the word 'procedure' to describe the technique, method, or formula for buying, selling, trading, or holding these investment products. The following are some of the different types of investment procedures:

    1. Buy, hold, and pray (long)

    2. Buy and sell (trade)

    3. Sell then buy (short)

    4. Option buying and selling (trade)

    5. Dollar cost averaging (long)

    6. Brokering (trade no position)

    7. Saving (collecting)

4. Many investors are classified by their procedures and their products. For example:

    1. I am a stock trader

    2. I speculate in real estate.

    3. I collect rare coins.

    4. I trade commodity future options.

    5. I am a day trader.

    6. I believe in money in the bank.

These are all examples of different types of investors, their product specialties, and their investing procedure. All of this adds to the confusion on the subject of investing because under the banner of investing there are people who are really:

a. Gamblers
b. Speculators
c. Traders
d. Savers
e. Dreamers
f. Losers

Many of these individuals call themselves investors, and technically they are, which is why the subject of investing is even more confusing.

### No One Is an Expert at Everything

'Investing means different things to different people.' Rich dad also said, 'There is no one person who can possibly be an expert at the entire subject. There are many different investment products and many different investment procedures.'

### Everyone Has a Bias

A person who is good at stocks will say, 'Stocks are your best investment.' A person who loves real estate will say, 'Real estate is the basis of all wealth.' Someone who hates gold will say, 'Gold is an obsolete commodity.'

Then you add procedure bias and you really become confused. Some people say, 'Diversify. Don't put all your eggs in one basket,' and still others such as Warren Buffet, America's greatest investor, say, 'Don't diversify. Put all your eggs in one basket and watch that basket closely.'

All of this personal bias from so-called experts adds to the confusion that shrouds the subject of investing.

## Same Market, Different Directions

Adding to the confusion is that everyone has a different opinion on the direction of the market and the future of the world. If you watch the financial news stations, they will have one so-called expert who says, 'The market is over-heated. It will crash in the next six weeks.' Ten minutes later, another expert will come on and say, 'The market is set to go up even further. There will be no crash.'

## Late to the Party

A friend of mine recently asked, 'Every time I hear of a hot stock, by the time I buy it, the stock is heading down. So I buy at the top because it's the hot popular stock and then a day later it starts heading down. Why am I always late to the party?'

Another complaint I often hear is: 'The stock drops in price so I sell it, and the next day it goes up. Why does that happen?'

I call this the 'late to the party' phenomenon or the 'you sold too early' phenomenon. The problem with investing in something because it's popular or rated as the #1 fund for the past two years is that real investors have already made their money in that investment. They were in it early and got out at the top. For me, nothing is more frustrating than to hear someone say, 'I bought it at $2 a share and it's now at $35 a share.' Such stories or hot tips do me no good and only frustrate me. That is why today, when I hear such tales of instant wealth and fast money in the market, I just walk away and choose not to listen . . . because such stories are not really stories about investing.

## This Is Why Investing Is Confusing

Rich dad often said, 'Investing is confusing because it is a very large subject. If you look around you, you'll see that people have invested in many different things. Look at your appliances. Those are all products from companies that people invested in. You receive your electricity from a utility company that people invest in. Once you understand that, then look at your car, the gas, the tires, seat belts, windshield wipers, spark plugs, the roads, the stripes on the road, your soft drinks, the furniture in your house, the shopping center your favorite store is in, the office buildings, the bank, the hotels, the airplane overhead, the carpet in the airport, etc. All of these things are there because someone invested in the business or building that delivers you the things that make life civilized. That is what investing really is all about.'

Rich dad often ended his lessons on investing with this statement: 'Investing is such a confusing subject for most people because what most people call investing is not really investing.'

In the next chapter, rich dad guides me into reducing the confusion and into what investing really is.

### *Mental Attitude Quiz*

Investing is a vast subject with many different people having as many different opinions:

1. Do you realize that investing means different things to different people?

    Yes_____ No_____

2. Do you realize that no one person can know all there is to know about the subject of investing?

    Yes_____ No_____

3. Do you realize that one person may say an investment is good and another person may say the same investment is bad, and realize both could have valid points?

    Yes_____ No_____

4. Are you willing to keep an open mind to the subject of investing and listen to different points of view on the subject?

        Yes _____    No _____

5. Are you now aware that focusing on specific products and procedures may not necessarily be investing?

        Yes _____    No _____

6. Do you realize that an investment product that is good for one person may not be good for you?

        Yes _____    No _____

## Chapter 6
### Investor Lesson #4:

# Investing Is a Plan, Not a Product or Procedure

I am often asked questions like, 'I have $10,000 to invest. What do you recommend I invest in?'

And my standard reply is, 'Do you have a plan?'

A few months ago, I was on a radio station in San Francisco. The program was on investing and was hosted by a very popular local stockbroker. A call came in from a listener wanting some investment advice. 'I am 42 years old, I have a good job, but I have no money. My mother has a house with a lot of equity in it. Her home is worth about $800,000 and she owes only $100,000 on it. She said she would let me borrow some of the equity out so I could begin investing. What do you think I should invest in? Should it be stocks or real estate?'

Again my reply was, 'Do you have a plan?'

'I don't need a plan,' was the reply. 'I just want you to tell me what to invest in. I want to know if you think the real estate market is better or the stock market.'

'I know that is what you want to know . . . but do you have a plan?' I again asked as politely as possible.

'I told you I don't need a plan,' said the caller. 'I told you my mother will give me the money. So I have money. That's why I don't need a plan. I'm ready to invest. I just want to know which market you think is better, the stock market or the real estate market. I also want to know how much of my mom's money I should spend on my own home. Prices are going up so fast here in the Bay Area that I don't want to wait any longer.'

Deciding to take another tack, I asked, 'If you're 42 years old and have a good job, why is that you have no money? And if you lose your mother's equity money from her home, can she continue to afford the home with the added debt? And if you lose your job or the market crashes, can you continue to afford a new house if you can't sell it for what you paid for it?'

To an estimated 400,000 listeners came his answer. 'That is none of your business. I thought you were an investor. You don't need to dig into my private life to give me tips on investing. And leave my mother out of this. All I want is investment advice, not personal advice.'

### *Investment Advice Is Personal Advice*

One of the most important lessons I learned from my rich dad was that 'Investing is a plan, not a product or procedure.' He went on to say, 'Investing is a very personal plan.'

During one of my lessons on investing, he asked, 'Do you know why there are so many different types of cars and trucks?'

I thought about the question for a while, finally replying, 'I guess because there are so many different types of people and people have different needs. A single person may not need a large nine-passenger station wagon but a family with five kids would need one. And a farmer would rather have a pickup truck than a two-seater sports car.'

'That's correct,' said rich dad. 'And that is why investment products are often called "investment vehicles."'

'They're called "vehicles"?' I repeated. 'Why investment vehicles?'

'Because that is all they are,' said rich dad. 'There are many different investment products, or vehicles, because there are many different people with many different needs, just as a family with five children has different needs from a single person or a farmer.'

'But why the word "vehicles"?' I again asked.

'Because all a vehicle does is get you from point A to point B,' said rich dad. 'An investment product or vehicle simply takes you from where you are financially to where you want to be, sometime in the future, financially.'

'And that is why investing is a plan,' I said nodding my head quietly. I was beginning to understand.

'Investing is like planning a trip, let's say from Hawaii to New York. Obviously, you know that for the first leg of your trip, a bicycle or car will not do. That means you will need a boat or a plane to get across the ocean,' said rich dad.

'And once I reach land, I can walk, ride a bike, travel by car, train, bus, or fly to New York,' I added. 'All are different vehicles.'

Rich dad nodded his head. 'And one is not necessarily better than the other. If you have a lot of time and really want to see the country, then walking or riding a bike would be the best. Not only that, you will be much healthier at the end of the trip. But if you need to be in New York tomorrow, then obviously flying from Hawaii to New York is your best and only choice if you want to make it on time.'

'So many people focus on a product, let's say stocks, and then a procedure, let's say trading, but they don't really have a plan. Is that what you are saying?' I asked.

Rich dad nodded. 'Most people are trying to make money by what they think is investing. But trading is not investing.'

'What is it, if it is not investing?' I asked.

'It's trading,' said rich dad. 'And trading is a procedure or technique. A person trading stocks is not much different from a person who buys a house, fixes it up, and sells it for a higher profit. One trades stocks; the other trades real estate. It's still trading. In reality, trading is centuries old. Camels carried exotic wares across the desert to consumers in Europe. So a retailer is also a trader in a sense. And trading is a profession. But it is not what I call investing.'

'And to you, investing is a plan, a plan to get you from where you are to where you want to be,' I said, doing my best to understand rich dad's distinctions.

Rich dad nodded and said, 'I know it's picky and seems a minor detail. Yet, I want to do my best to reduce the confusion around this subject of investing. Every day, I meet people who think they're investing, but financially they're going nowhere. They might as well be pushing a wheelbarrow in a circle.'

## *It Takes More Than One Vehicle*

In the previous chapter, I listed a few of the different types of investment products and procedures available. More are being created every day because so many people have so many different needs. When people are not clear on their own personal financial plans, all these different products and procedures become overwhelming and confusing.

Rich dad used the wheelbarrow as his vehicle of choice when describing many investors. 'Too many so-called investors get attached to one investment product and one investment procedure. For example, a person may invest only in stocks or a person may invest only in real estate. The person becomes attached to the vehicle and then fails to see all the other investment vehicles and procedures available. The person becomes an expert at that one wheelbarrow and pushes it in a circle forever.'

One day when he was laughing about investors and their wheelbarrows, I had to ask for further clarification. His response was, 'Some people become experts at one type of product and one procedure. That is what I mean by becoming attached to the wheelbarrow. The wheelbarrow works; it hauls a lot of cash around, but it is still a wheelbarrow. A true investor does not become attached to the vehicles or the procedures. A true investor has a plan and has multiple options as to investment vehicles and procedures. All a true investor wants to do is get from point A to point B safely and within a desired time frame. That person doesn't want to own or push the wheelbarrow.'

Still confused, I asked for greater clarification. 'Look,' he said, becoming a little frustrated, 'if I want to go from Hawaii to New York, I have a choice of many vehicles. I don't really want to own them. I just want to use them. When I climb on a 747, I don't want to fly it. I don't want to fall in love with it. I just want to get from where I am to where I am going. When I land at Kennedy Airport, I want to use the taxi to get from the airport to my hotel. Once I arrive at the hotel, the porter uses a handcart to move my bags from the curb to the room. I don't want to own or push that handcart.'

'So what is the difference?' I asked.

'Many people who think they are investors get attached to the investment vehicle. They think they have to like stocks or like real estate to use them as investment vehicles. So they look for investments they like and fail to put together a plan. These are the investors who wind up traveling in circles, never getting from financial point A to financial point B.'

'So you don't necessarily fall in love with the 747 you fly on, just as you don't necessarily fall in love with your stocks, bonds, mutual funds, or office buildings. They are all simply vehicles,' I stated, 'vehicles to take you to where you want to go.'

Rich dad nodded. 'I appreciate those vehicles, I trust that people take care of those vehicles, I just don't get attached to the vehicles . . . nor do I necessarily want to own or spend my time driving them.'

'What happens when people get attached to their investment vehicles?' I asked.

'They think that their investment vehicle is the only vehicle, or it is the best vehicle. I know people who invest only in stocks as well as people who invest only in mutual funds or real estate. That is what I mean by getting attached to the wheelbarrow. There is not anything necessarily wrong with that type of thinking. It's just that they often focus on the vehicle rather than their plan. So even though they may make a lot of money buying, holding, and selling investment products, that money may not take them to where they want to go.'

'So I need a plan,' I said. 'And my plan will then determine the different types of investment vehicles I will need.'

Rich dad nodded, saying, 'In fact, don't invest until you have a plan. Always remember that investing is a plan . . . not a product or procedure. That is a very important lesson.'

### Mental Attitude Quiz

Before a person builds a house, he or she usually calls in an architect to draw up the plans. Could you imagine what could happen if someone just called in some people and began to build a house without a plan? Well, that is what happens to many people's financial houses.

Rich dad guided me in writing out financial plans. It was not necessarily an easy process, nor did it make sense at first. But after a while, I became very clear on where I was financially, and where I wanted to go. Once I knew that, the planning process became easier. In other words, for me, the hardest part was figuring out what I wanted. So the mental attitude questions are:

1.  Are you willing to invest the time to find out where you are financially today and where you want to be financially, and are you willing to spell out how you plan to get there? In addition, always remember that a plan is not really a plan until it is in writing and you can show it to someone else.

Yes _____    No _____

2.  Are you willing to meet with at least one professional financial advisor and find out how his or her services may help you with your long term investment plans?

Yes _____    No _____

You may want to meet with two or three financial advisors just to find out the differences in their approach to financial planning.

# *Are You Planning to Be Rich or Are You Planning to Be Poor?*

'Most people are planning to be poor,' said rich dad.

'What?' I replied in disbelief. 'Why do you say that and how can you say that?'

'I just listen to what people say,' said rich dad. 'If you want to see a person's past, present, and future, just listen to his or her words.'

### *The Power of Words*

Rich dad's lesson on the power of words was very powerful. He asked, 'Have you ever heard someone say, "It takes money to make money"?'

Standing to get two soft drinks from the refrigerator, I replied, 'Yes. I hear it all the time. Why do you ask?'

'Because the idea that it takes money to make money is one of the worst ideas there is. Especially if a person wants more money,' said rich dad.

Handing rich dad his soft drink, I said, 'I don't understand. You mean it doesn't take money to make money?'

'No,' said rich dad, shaking his head. 'It does not take money to make money. It takes something available to all of us and is a lot less expensive to obtain than money. In fact, in many cases, what it takes is free.'

That statement made me very curious but he would not tell me what it was. Instead, as the lesson on investing ended, he gave me an assignment. 'Before we meet again, I want you to invite your dad out to dinner . . . a long, slow dinner. All through the dinner, I want you to pay careful attention to the specific words he uses. After you hear his words, begin to pay attention to the message his words are sending.'

By this time, I was accustomed to rich dad giving me strange assignments, assignments that seemed unrelated to the subject we were discussing or studying. Yet he was a firm believer in experience first and lesson second. So I called my dad and set up a date for dinner at his favorite restaurant.

About a week later, rich dad and I met again. 'How was dinner?' he asked.

'Interesting,' I replied. 'I listened very carefully to his choice of words and the meaning of, or thoughts behind, the words.'

'And what did you hear?'

'I heard, "I'll never be rich,"' I said. 'But I've heard that most of my life. In fact, he often said to the family, "The moment I decided to become a schoolteacher, I knew I'd never be rich."'

'So you've heard some of the same lines before?' inquired rich dad.

I nodded, saying, 'Many times. Over and over again.'

'What else have you heard repeatedly?' asked rich dad.

'"Do you think money grows on trees?" "Do you think I'm made of money?" "The rich don't care about people like I do." "Money is hard to get." "I'd rather be happy than be rich,"' I replied.

'Now do you know what I mean when I say you can see people's past, present, and future by listening to their words?' asked rich dad.

Nodding, I said, 'And I noticed something else.'

'And what was that?' asked rich dad.

'You have the vocabulary of a businessman and an investor. My dad has the vocabulary of a schoolteacher. You use words such as "capitalization rates," "financial leverage," "EBIT," "producer price index," "profits," and "cash flow." He uses words such as "test scores," "grants," "grammar," "literature," "government appropriations," and "tenure."'

Rich dad smiled as he said, 'It does not take money to make money. It takes words. The difference between a rich person and a poor person is that person's vocabulary. All a person needs to do to become richer is increase his or her financial vocabulary. And the best news is, most words are free.'

During the 1980s, I spent much time teaching entrepreneurship and investing. During that time, I became acutely aware of people's vocabulary and how their words related to their financial well-being. Upon further research, I found out that there are approximately 2 million words in the English language. The average person had command of approximately 5,000 words. If people want to begin increasing their financial success, it begins with increasing their vocabulary in a certain subject. For example, when I was investing in small real estate deals such as single-family rental properties, my vocabulary increased in that subject area. When I shifted to investing in private companies, my vocabulary had to increase before I felt comfortable investing in such companies.

In school, lawyers learn the vocabulary of law, medical doctors learn the vocabulary of medicine, and teachers learn the vocabulary of teachers. If a person leaves school without learning the vocabulary of investing, finance, money, accounting, corporate law, taxation, it is difficult to feel comfortable as an investor.

One reason I created the educational board game *CASHFLOW* was to familiarize non-investors with the vocabulary of investing. In all our games, the players quickly learn the relationships behind the words of accounting, business, and investing. By repeatedly playing the games, the players learn the true definition of such misused words as 'asset' and 'liability.'

Rich dad often said, 'More than not knowing the definitions of words, using the wrong definition to a word is what really causes long-term financial problems. Nothing is more destructive to a person's financial stability than to call a "liability" an "asset."' That is why he was a stickler for the definition of financial words. He would say, the word 'mortgage' comes from 'mort,' French for 'death.' So a mortgage is 'an engagement until death.' 'Real estate' does not mean 'real' in English. Real estate really comes from the Spanish words meaning royal estate. That is why to this day, we do not own our property. We only technically control our real estate. We do not really own it. The government owns our property and taxes us to use it.

And that is why rich dad would often say, 'It does not take money to make money. It takes a rich person's vocabulary to make money and more importantly, keep money.'

So as you read this book, please be aware of the different words that may be used. And always remember that one of the fundamental differences between a rich person and a poor person is his or her words . . . and words are free.

## Planning to Be Poor

After this lesson with rich dad, by simply listening to others' words, I began to notice why most people are unconsciously planning to be poor. Today, I often hear people say, 'When I retire, my income will go down.' And it does.

They also often say, 'My needs will go down after I retire, so that is why I will need less income.' But what they often fail to realize is that while some expenses do go down, other expenses go up. And often these expenses – such as full-time nursing home care when they are very old, if they are lucky enough to become very old – are large. An average nursing home for the elderly can cost $5,000 a month. That is more than many people's monthly incomes today.

Other people say, 'I don't need to plan. I have a retirement and medical plan from my work.' The problem with such thinking is that there is more to an investment plan than simply investments and money. A financial plan is important before someone begins to invest because it needs to take into consideration many different financial needs. These needs include college education, retirement, medical costs, and long-term health care. Many of these often large and pressing needs can be provided for by investing in products other than stocks and bonds or real estate, such as insurance products and different investment vehicles.

## *The Future*

I write about money to help educate people to provide for their long-term financial well-being. Ever since the advent of Information Age retirement plans, which are 401Ks in America and Superannuation plans in Australia and Registered Retirement Savings Plans (RRSP) in Canada, I have grown concerned about the people who are not prepared for the Information Age. At least in the Industrial Age a company and the government did provide some financial aid for a person after his or her working days were over. Today, when a person's 401K or 'cash balance retirement plan' (which isn't a traditional pension) is drained dry, it will be the individual's problem, not the company's.

It is imperative that our schools begin to teach young people to invest for their long-term health and financial well-being. If we do not, we will have a massive socioeconomic time bomb on our hands.

I often say to my classes, 'Be sure you have a plan. First, ask your-self if you are planning to be rich or if you are planning to be poor.

If you are planning to be poor, the older you get, the more difficult you will find the financial world.' Rich dad said to me many years ago, 'The trouble with being young is that you don't know what it feels like to be old. If you knew what being old felt like, you would plan your financial life differently.'

## Planning for Being Old

It is important to plan as early in life as possible. When I say this to my classes, most of my students nod in agreement. No one disagrees on the importance of planning. The problem is, very few people actually do it.

Realizing that most people agreed that they needed to write a financial plan, but few were going to take the time to do it, I decided to do something about it. About an hour before lunch in one of these classes, I found some cotton clothesline and cut it into different lengths. I asked the students to take one piece of line and tie each end around one of their ankles, much like one would hobble a horse. With their ankles tied about a foot apart, I gave them another piece of the line and had them loop it around their neck and tie it back down at their ankles. The overall result was that they were hobbled at the ankles and instead of standing erect, they stooped over at about a 45-degree angle.

One of the students asked if this was a new form of Chinese water torture. 'No,' I replied. 'I'm just taking each of you into the future, if you're lucky to live so long. The ropes now represent what old age could feel like.'

A slow moan came from the class. A few were getting the picture. The hotel staff then brought in lunch on long tables. The lunch consisted of sandwiches, salad, and beverages. The problem was, the cold cuts were simply stacked, the bread was not sliced, the salad was not made, and the beverages were the dry mix type that had to be combined with water. The students, now stooped and aged, had to prepare their own lunch. For the next two hours, they struggled to slice their bread, stack their sandwiches, make their salads, mix their drinks, sit, eat, and clean up. Naturally, many also needed to go to the rest room during these two hours.

At the end of the two hours, I asked them if they wanted to take a few moments to write out a financial plan for their life. The answer was an enthusiastic 'Yes.' It was interesting to observe them actively taking an interest in what they planned to do once the ropes came off. Their interest in planning had increased dramatically once their point of view on life had been changed.

As rich dad said, 'The problem with being young is that you don't know what it feels like to be old. If you knew what being old felt like, you would plan your financial life differently.' He also said, 'The problem with many people is that they plan only up to retirement. Planning to retirement is not enough. You need to plan far beyond retirement. In fact, if you're rich, you should plan for at least three generations beyond you. If you don't, the money could be gone soon after you're gone. Besides, if you don't have a plan for your money before you depart this earth, the government does.'

## Mental Attitude Quiz

Many times, we do not pay close attention to our silent and seemingly unimportant thoughts. Rich dad said, 'It's not what we say out loud that determines our lives. It's what we whisper to ourselves that has the most power.'

### So the mental attitude questions are:

1.  Are you planning to be rich or are you planning to be poor?

    Rich _____ Poor _____

2.  Are you willing to pay more attention to your deep, often silent, thoughts?

    Yes_____  No_____

3.  Are you willing to invest time to increase your financial vocabulary? A first goal of learning one new financial word a week is doable. Simply find a word, look it up in the dictionary, find more than one definition for the word, and make a mental note to use the word in a sentence that week.

    Yes_____  No_____

Rich dad was a stickler for words. He often said, 'Words form thoughts, thoughts form realities, and realities become life. The primary difference between a rich person and a poor person is the words he or she uses. If you want to change a person's external reality, you need to first change that person's internal reality. That is done through first changing, improving, or updating the words he or she uses. If you want to change people's lives, first change their words. And the good news is, words are free.'

## Chapter 8
### Investor Lesson #6:

# Getting Rich Is Automatic . . . If You Have a Good Plan and Stick to It

My friend Tom is an excellent stockbroker. He often says, 'The sad thing is that nine out of ten investors do not make money.' Tom goes on to explain that while these nine out of ten investors do not lose money, they just fail to make money.

Rich dad said a similar thing to me: 'Most people who consider themselves investors make money one day and then give it back a week later. So they do not lose money, they simply fail to make money. Yet they consider themselves investors.'

Years ago, rich dad explained to me that much of what people think is investing is really the Hollywood version of investing. The average person often has mental images of floor traders shouting buy/sell orders at the start of the trading day, or images of tycoons making millions of dollars in a single trade, or images of stock prices plummeting and investors diving out of tall office buildings. To rich dad, that was not investing.

I remember watching a program where Warren Buffet was being interviewed. During the course of the interview, I heard him say, 'The only reason I go to the market is to see if someone is about to do something silly.' Buffet went on to explain that he did not watch the pundits on TV or watch the ups and downs of share prices to gain his investing advice. In fact, his investing was actually done far away from all the noise and promotion of stock promoters and people who make money from so-called investment news.

### Investing Is Not What Most People Think

Years ago, rich dad explained to me that investing was not what most people thought it was. He said, 'Many people think investing is this exciting process where there is a lot of drama. Many people think investing involves a lot of risk, luck, timing, and hot tips. Some realize they know little about this mysterious subject of investing, so they entrust their faith and money to someone they hope knows more than they do. Many other so-called investors want to prove they know more than other people . . . so they invest, hoping to prove that they can outsmart the market. But while many people think this is investing, it is not what investing is to me. To me, investing is a plan, often a dull, boring, and almost mechanical process of getting rich.'

When I heard rich dad make that statement, I repeated it back to him several times. 'Investing is a plan, often a dull, boring, and almost mechanical process of getting rich?' I asked. 'What do you mean by a dull, boring, and almost mechanical process of getting rich?'

'That is exactly what I said and what I mean,' said rich dad. 'Investing is simply a plan, made up of formulas and strategies, a system for getting rich . . . almost guaranteed.'

'A plan that guarantees that you get rich?' I asked.

'I said almost guarantees,' repeated rich dad. 'There is always some risk.'

'You mean investing doesn't have to be risky, dangerous, and exciting?' I asked hesitantly.

'That's correct,' rich dad answered. 'Unless, of course, you want it to be that way or you think that is the way investing has to be. But for me, investing is as simple and boring as following a recipe to bake bread. Personally, I hate risk. I just want to be rich. So I'll simply follow the plan, the recipe, or the formula. That is all investing is to me.'

'So if investing is simply a matter of following a recipe, then how come so many people don't follow the same formula?' I asked.

'I don't know,' said rich dad. 'I've often asked myself the same question. I've also wondered why only three out of every hundred Americans is rich. How can so few people become rich in a country that was founded on the idea that each of us has the opportunity to become rich? I wanted to be rich. I had no money. So to me, it was just common sense to find a plan or recipe to be rich and follow it. Why try and make up your own plan when someone else has already shown you the way?'

'I don't know,' I said. 'I guess I did not know that it was a recipe.'

Rich dad continued. 'I now realize why it is so hard for most people to follow a simple plan.'

'And why is that?' I asked.

'Because following a simple plan to become rich is boring,' said rich dad. 'Human beings are quickly bored and want to find something more exciting and amusing. That is why only three out of a hundred people become rich. They start following a plan, and soon they are bored. So they stop following the plan and then they look for a magic way to get rich quick. They repeat the process of boredom, amusement, and boredom again for the rest of their lives. That is why they do not get rich. They cannot stand the boredom of following a simple, uncomplicated plan to get rich. Most people think there is some magic to getting rich through investing. Or they think that if it is not complicated, it cannot be a good plan. Trust me; when it comes to investing, simple is better than complex.'

'And where did you find your formula?' I asked.

'Playing *Monopoly*,' said rich dad. 'Most of us have played *Monopoly* as children. The difference is, I did not stop playing the game once I grew up. Do you remember that years ago, I would play *Monopoly* by the hours with you and Mike?'

I nodded.

'And do you remember the formula for tremendous wealth that this simple game teaches?'

Again I nodded.

'And what is that simple formula and strategy?' asked rich dad.

'Buy four green houses. Then exchange the four green houses for a red hotel,' I said quietly as my childhood memories came rushing back. 'You told us over and over again while you were poor and just starting out that playing *Monopoly* in real life was what you were doing.'

'And I did,' said rich dad. 'Do you remember me taking you to see my green houses and red hotels in real life?'

'I do,' I replied. 'I remember how impressed I was that you actually played the game in real life. I was only 12 years old, but I knew that for you, *Monopoly* was more than a game. I just didn't realize that this simple game was teaching you a strategy, a recipe, or a formula to become rich. I did not see it that way.'

'Once I learned the formula, the process of buying four green houses and then exchanging them for one red hotel, the formula became automatic. I could do it in my sleep, and many times, it seemed like I did. I did it automatically without much thinking. I just followed the plan for ten years, and one day I woke up and realized I was rich.'

'Was that the only part of your plan?' I asked.

'No, it wasn't. But that strategy was one of the simple formulas I followed. To me, if the formula is complex, it is not worth following. If you can't do it automatically after you learn it, you shouldn't follow it. That is how automatic investing and getting rich is, if you have a simple strategy and follow it.'

## A Great Book for People Who Think Investing Is Difficult

In my investment classes, there is always the cynic or doubter to the idea that investing is a simple and boring process of following a plan. This type of person always wants more facts, more data, more proof from smart people. Since I am not a technical specialist, I did not have the scholarly proof that these types of individuals demanded — that is, until I read a great book on investing.

James P. O'Shaughnessy wrote the perfect book for people who think that investing has to be risky, complex, and dangerous. It is also the perfect book for those who want to think that they can outsmart the market. This book has the academic and numerical proof that a passive or mechanical system of investing will in most cases beat a human system of investing . . . even professional investors such as fund managers. This book also explains why nine out of ten investors do not make money.

O'Shaughnessy's best-selling book is titled *What Works On Wall Street: A Guide to the Best Performing Investment Strategies of All Time*. O'Shaughnessy distinguishes between two basic types of decision-making:

1. The clinical or intuitive method. This method relies on knowledge, experience, and common sense.
2. The quantitative or actuarial method. This method relies solely on proven relationships based on large samples of data.

O'Shaughnessy found that most investors prefer the intuitive method of investment decision-making. In most instances, the investor who used the intuitive method was wrong or beaten by the nearly mechanical method. He quotes David Faust, author of *The Limits of Scientific Reasoning*, who writes, 'Human judgment is far more limited than we think.'

O'Shaughnessy also writes, 'All (speaking of money managers) of them think they have superior insights, intelligence, and ability to pick winning stocks, yet 80 percent are routinely out performed by the S&P 500 index.' In other words, a purely mechanical method of picking stocks outperforms 80 percent of the professional stock pickers. That means, even if you knew nothing about stock picking, you could beat most of the so-called well-trained and educated professionals if you followed a purely mechanical, non-intuitive method of investing. It is exactly as rich dad said: 'It's automatic.' Or, the less you think, the more money you make with less risk and with a lot less worry.

Other interesting ideas that O'Shaughnessy's book points out are:

1. Most investors prefer personal experience to simple basic facts or base rates. Again, they prefer intuition to reality.

2. Most investors prefer complex rather than simple formulas. There seems to be this idea that if the formula is not complex and difficult, it can't be a good formula.

3. Keeping it simple is the best rule for investing. He states that instead of keeping things simple, 'We make things complex, follow the crowd, fall in love with the story of a stock, let our emotions dictate decisions, buy and sell on tips and hunches, and approach each investment on a case-by-case basis, with no underlying consistency or strategy.'

4. He also states that professional institutional investors tend to make the same mistakes that average investors make. O'Shaughnessy writes, 'Institutional investors say they make decisions objectively and unemotionally, but they don't.' Here's a quotation from the book *Fortune and Folly*. 'While institu-

tional investors' desks are cluttered with in-depth analytical reports, the majority of pension executives select outside managers based on gut feelings and keep managers with consistently poor performance simply because they have good personal relationships with them.'

5. 'The path to achieving investment success is to study long-term results and find a strategy or group of strategies that make sense. Then stay on the path.' He also states, 'We must look at how well strategies, not stocks, perform.'

6. History does repeat itself. Yet people want to believe that this time, things will be different. He writes, 'People want to believe that the present is different from the past. Markets are now computerized, block traders dominate, individual investors are gone, and in their place sit money managers controlling huge mutual funds to which they have given their money. Some people think these masters of money make decisions differently, and believe that a strategy perfected in the 1950s and 1960s offers little insight into how it will perform in the future.'

But not much has changed since Sir Isaac Newton, a brilliant man indeed, lost a fortune in the South Sea Trading Company bubble of 1720. Newton lamented that he could 'calculate the motions of heavenly bodies but not the madness of men.'

7. O'Shaughnessy was not necessarily saying to invest in the S&P 500. He simply used that example as a comparison between intuitive human investors and a mechanical formula. He went on to say that investing in the S&P 500 was not necessarily the best performing formula, although it was a good one. He explained that in the last five to ten years, large cap stocks have done the best. Yet over the past 46 years of data, it was actually small cap stocks, companies of less than $25 million

in capitalization, that have made the investor the most money. The lesson was, the longer period of time for which you had data, the better your judgment. He looked for the formula that performed the best over the longest amount of time.

Rich dad had a similar view. That is why his formula was to build businesses and have his businesses buy his real estate as well as his paper assets. That formula has been a winning formula for wealth for at least 200 years. Rich dad said, 'The formula I use, and the formula I am teaching you, is the formula that has created the richest individuals over a long period of time.'

Many people think the Indians who sold Manhattan Island, a.k.a. New York City, to Peter Minuit of the Dutch West India Company for $24 in beads and trinkets got a bad deal. Yet if the Indians had invested that money for an 8 percent annual return, that $24 would be worth over $27 trillion today. They could buy Manhattan back and have plenty of money left over. The problem was not the amount of money but the lack of a plan for their money.

8.    'There is a chasm of difference between what we think might work and what really works.'

## Find a Formula That Works and Follow It

So rich dad's simple message to me years ago was: 'Find a formula that will make you rich and follow it.' I am often disturbed when people come up to me and start telling me about the stock they bought for $5 and how it went up to $30 and they sold it. I find myself disturbed because those kinds of stories distract from their plan, their success.

Such stories of hot tips and quick cash often remind me of a story rich dad told me. He said, 'Many investors are like a family taking a drive in the country. Suddenly, on the road ahead of them appear several large deer with massive horns. The driver, usually the male of the household, shouts, "Look at the big bucks." The bucks instinctively bolt from the road and onto the farmland alongside the road. The driver veers the car off the road and begins chasing the big bucks across the farm and into the trees. The ride is rough and bumpy. The family is screaming for the driver to stop. Suddenly, the car goes over a stream embankment and crashes into the water below. The moral of the story is that this is what happens when you stop following your simple plan and begin chasing the big bucks.'

## Mental Attitude Quiz

Whenever I hear someone say to me, 'It takes money to make money,' I cringe. I cringe because my rich dad said, 'You don't have to be a rocket scientist to be rich. You don't need a college education, a high-paying job, or any money at all to start. All you have to do is know what you want, have a plan, and stick to it.' In other words, all it takes is a little discipline. The problem when it comes to money, however, is a little discipline is often a rare commodity. O'Shaughnessy highlights one of my favorite quotations. It comes from the famous cartoon character Pogo, who said, 'We've met the enemy, and he is us.' That statement is very true for me. I'd be a lot better off financially if I had simply listened to rich dad and just followed my formula.

### So the mental attitude question is:

1. Are you ready to find a simple formula as part of your plan and stick to it until you reach your financial goal?

    Yes _____ No _____

## Chapter 9
### *Investor Lesson #7:*

# How Can You Find The Plan That Is Right for You?

'How do I find the plan that is right for me?' is a question I am asked often.

My standard answer is that it comes in steps:

1. Take your time. Think quietly about your life up to this point. Take days to think quietly. Take weeks if you need to.

2. Ask yourself in these moments of quiet, 'What do I want from this gift called my life?'

3. Don't talk to anyone else for a while, at least until you are certain you know what you think you want. All too often, people either innocently or aggressively want to impose what they want for you instead of what you want for yourself. The biggest killers of deep inner dreams are your friends and family members who say, 'Oh don't be silly,' or 'You can't do that,' or 'What about me?'

Remember Bill Gates was in his 20s when he started with $50,000 and became the richest man in the world with $90 billion. It's a good thing he did not ask too many people for their ideas on what they thought was possible for his life.

4. Call a financial advisor. All investment plans begin with a financial plan. If you do not like what the financial advisor says, find another one. You would ask for a second opinion for a medical problem, so why not ask for many opinions for financial challenges? Financial advisors come in many forms; a reference list is provided later in this chapter. Choose an advisor equipped to assist you in developing a written financial plan.

Many financial advisors sell different types of products. One such product is insurance. Insurance is a very important product and needs to be considered as part of your financial plan, especially when you are first starting out. For example, if you have no money but have three children, insurance is important in case you die, are injured, or for whatever reason are unable to complete your investment plan. Insurance is a safety net, or a hedge against financial liabilities and weak spots. Also, as you become rich, the role of insurance and type of insurance in your financial plan may change as your financial position and needs change. So keep that part of your plan up to date.

Two years ago, a tenant in one of my apartment buildings left his Christmas tree lights on and went out for the day. A fire broke out. Immediately, the fire crews were there to put out the fire. I was never so grateful to a bunch of men and women. The next people on the scene were my insurance agent and his assistant. They were the second most important group of people I was grateful to see that day.

Rich dad always said, 'Insurance is a very important product in anyone's life plan. The trouble with insurance is that you can never buy it when you need it. So you have to anticipate what you need and buy it hoping you'll never need it. Insurance is simply peace of mind.'

IMPORTANT NOTE: Some financial advisors specialize in helping people at different financial levels. In other words, some advisors work only with rich people. Regardless of whether or not you have money, find an advisor you like and who is willing to work with you. If your advisor has done a good job, you may find yourself outgrowing your advisor. My wife Kim and I have often changed our professional advisors, which include doctors, attorneys, accountants, etc. If the person is professional, he or she will understand. But even if you change advisors, be sure you stick to your plan.

## So How Do You Find Your Plan?

I had a goal of being a multi-millionaire before I was 30 years old. That was the end result of my plan. The problem was, I made it and then immediately lost all my money. So while I found out that there were flaws in my plan, my overall plan did not change. After losing my money after reaching my goal, I simply needed to refine my plan by what I had learned from that experience. I then had to reset my goal, which was to be financially free and a millionaire by age 45. It took me to age 47 to reach the new goal.

The point is, my plan remains the same. It just gets improved upon as I learn more and more.

So how do you find your own plan? The answer is to begin with a financial advisor. Ask the advisors to provide their qualifications to you and interview several. If you have never had a financial plan done for you, it is an eye-opening experience for most people.

Set realistic goals. I set a goal of becoming a multi-millionaire in five years because it was realistic for me. It was realistic because I had my rich dad guiding me. Yet, even though he guided me, it did not mean I was free from making mistakes . . . and I made many of them, which is why I lost my money so quickly. As I said, life would have been easier if I had just followed rich dad's plan. Being young, however, I had to do things my way.

So start with realistic goals, and then improve upon or add to the goals as your education and experience increase. Always remember that it is best to start by walking before you begin to run in a marathon.

You find your own plan first by taking action. Begin by calling an advisor, set realistic goals, knowing the goals will change as you change . . . but stick to the plan. For most people, the ultimate plan is to find a sense of financial freedom, freedom from the day-to-day drudgery of working for money.

The second step is to realize that investing is a team sport. In this book, I will go into the importance of my financial team. I have noticed that too many people think they need to do things on their own. Well, there are definitely things you need to do on your own, but sometimes you need a team. Financial intelligence helps you know when to do things on your own and when to ask for help.

When it comes to money, many people often suffer alone and in silence. Chances are, their parents did the same thing. As your plan evolves, you will begin to meet the new members of your team, which will assist you in helping make your financial dreams come true. Members of your financial team may include:

1. Financial planner
2. Banker
3. Accountant
4. Lawyer
5. Broker
6. Bookkeeper

      7. Insurance agent
      8. Successful mentor

You may want to hold meetings over lunch with all these people on a regular basis. That is what rich dad did, and it was at these meetings that I learned the most about business, investing, and the process of becoming very rich.

Remember that finding a team member is much like finding a business partner, because that is what team members are in many ways. They are partners in minding the most important business of all — the business of your life. Always remember what rich dad said: 'Regardless of if you work for someone else or for yourself, if you want to be rich, you've got to mind your own business.' And in minding your own business, the plan that works best for you will slowly appear. So take your time, yet keep taking one step a day and you will have a good chance of getting everything you want in your life.

## Mental Attitude Quiz

My plan has not really changed, yet in many ways, it has changed dramatically. What has not changed about my plan is where I started and what I ultimately want for my life. Through many of the mistakes, the learning experiences, the wins, the losses, the highs, and the lows, I have grown up and gained knowledge and wisdom along the way. Therefore, my plan is constantly under revision because I am under revision.

As someone once said, 'Life is a cruel teacher. It punishes you first, and then gives you the lesson.' Yet like it or not, that is the process of true learning. Most of us have said, 'If I knew back then what I knew today, life would be different.' Well, for me, that is exactly what has happened as I traveled along my plan. So my plan is basically the same, yet it is very different since I am different. I would not do today what I did 20 years ago. However, if I had not done what I did 20 years ago, I would not be where I am and know what I know today. For example, I would not run my business today the way I ran my business 20 years ago. Yet, it was losing my first major business and digging myself out from under the rubble and wreckage that helped me become a better businessperson. So although I did reach my goal of becoming a millionaire by age 30, it was losing the money that made me a millionaire today . . . all according to plan. It just took a little longer than I wanted.

And when it comes to investing, I learned more from my bad investments, investments where I lost money, than I learned from the investments that went smoothly. My rich dad said, if I have ten investments, three of them will go smoothly and be financial home runs. Five will probably be dogs and do nothing, and two would be disasters. Yet, I would learn more from the two financial disasters than I would from the three home runs . . . In fact, those two disasters are what make it easier to hit the home runs the next time I am up to bat. And that is all part of the plan.

## So the mental attitude question is:

1.  Are you willing to start with a simple plan, keep the plan simple, but keep learning and improving as the plan reveals to you what you need to learn along the way? In other words, the plan doesn't really change, but are you willing to allow the plan to change you?

Yes _____ No _____

## Chapter 10
## Investor Lesson #8:

# Decide Now What You Want to Be When You Grow Up

In Investor Lesson #1, which was the importance of choice, there were three financial core value choices offered. They were:

1. To be secure
2. To be comfortable
3. To be rich

These are very important personal choices and should not be taken lightly.

In 1973, when I returned from the Vietnam War, I was faced with these choices. When rich dad discussed my option of taking a job with the airlines as a pilot, he said, 'A job with the airlines may not be that secure. I suspect that they will be having a rough time in the next few years. Yet, if you keep your record clean, you might find job security in that profession . . . if that is what you really want.'

He then asked me if I wanted to get my job back with Standard Oil of California, a job I held for only five months . . . the five months before I went to flight school for the Marine Corps. 'Didn't you receive a letter saying that Standard Oil would take you back as an employee once your military duty was over?'

'They said they would be happy to have me reapply,' I replied. 'But they guaranteed nothing.'

'But wouldn't that be a good company to work for? Wasn't the pay pretty good?' asked rich dad.

'Very good,' I said. 'It was an excellent company to work for, but I don't want to go back. I want to move on.'

'And what do you want most?' asked rich dad as he pointed to the three choices. 'Do you want security, comfort, or to be rich the most?'

From deep inside me, the answer was a loud 'To be rich.' It had not changed in years, although that desire and core value was pushed down quite a bit in my family, a family where job and financial security was the highest priority and rich people were considered evil, uneducated, and greedy. I grew up in a family where money was not discussed at the table because it was an unclean subject, a subject not worthy of intellectual discussion. But now that I was 25 years old, I could let my personal truth out. I knew the priority of core values of security and comfort were not first on my list. To be rich was core value number one for me.

My rich dad then had me list my core financial priorities. My list went in this order:

1.  To be rich
2.  To be comfortable
3.  To be secure

Rich dad looked at my list and said, 'OK. Step one is to write out a financial plan to be financially secure.'

'What?' I asked. 'I just told you I wanted to be rich. Why should I bother with a plan to be secure?'

Rich dad laughed. 'Just as I thought,' he said. 'The world is filled with guys like you who only want to be rich. The problem is, most guys like you don't make it because you don't understand being secure, or being comfortable financially. While a few people like you do make it, the reality is, the road to wealth is littered with wrecked lives . . . wrecked lives of reckless people . . . people just like you.'

I sat there ready to scream. All my life, I had lived with my poor dad, a man who valued security above all. Now, I'm finally old enough to be outside of my poor dad's values and now my rich dad is saying the same thing. I was ready to scream. I was ready to get rich, not be secure.

It was three weeks before I could talk to rich dad again. I was very upset. Everything I had done my best to get away from he put back in my face. Finally I calmed down and called him for another lesson.

'Are you ready to listen?' rich dad asked when we met again.

I nodded, saying, 'I'm ready but not really willing.'

'Step one,' rich dad started. 'Call my financial advisor. Say, "I want a written financial plan for lifetime financial security."'

'OK,' I said.

'Step two,' said rich dad. 'After you have a written plan for basic financial security, call me and we'll go over it. Lesson is over. Goodbye.'

It was a month before I called him. I had my plan and I showed it to him. 'Good' was all he said. 'Are you going to follow it?'

'I don't think so,' I said. 'It's just too boring and automatic.'

'That is what it is supposed to be,' said rich dad. 'It's supposed to be mechanical, automatic, and boring. But I can't make you follow it, although I do recommend you do.'

I was calming down as I said, 'Now what?'

'Now you find your own advisor and you write a plan on how to be financially comfortable,' said rich dad.

'You mean a long-term financial plan that is little bit more aggressive?' I asked.

'That is correct,' said rich dad.

'That is more exciting,' I said. 'That one I can get into.'

'Good,' said rich dad. 'Call me when you have that one ready.'

It was four months before I could meet with rich dad again. This plan was not that easy . . . or as easy as I thought it would be. I checked in by phone with rich dad every so often, but the plan was still taking longer than I wanted. Yet the process was extremely valuable because I learned a tremendous amount talking to different financial advisors. I was gaining a better understanding of the concepts rich dad was trying to teach me. The lesson I learned was that unless I am clear, it is hard for the advisor to be clear and able to help me.

Finally, I was able to meet with rich dad and show him my plan. 'Good' was all he said for a while. He sat there looking at the plan and then asked, 'So what did you learn about yourself?'

'I learned that it is not that easy to really define what it is I want from my life because today we have so many choices . . . and so many of them look exciting.'

'Very good,' he said. 'And that is why so many people today go from job to job or from business to business . . . but never really get to where they want to go financially. So they often spend their most precious asset, their time, and wander through life without much of a plan. They might be happy doing what they are doing, but they really do not know what they are missing out on.'

'Exactly,' I agreed. 'This time, instead of just being secure, I really had to think what I wanted to do with my life . . . and surprisingly, I had to explore ideas that would never have occurred to me before.'

'Like what?' asked rich dad.

'Well, if I really wanted to be comfortable with my life, then I had to think about what I wanted to have in my life. Things like travel to faraway lands, fancy cars, expensive vacations, nice clothes, big houses, etc. I really had to expand my thoughts into the future and find out what I wanted for my life.'

'And what did you find out?' asked rich dad.

'I found out that security was so easy because I was planning on being secure only. I did not know what true comfort meant. So security was easy, defining comfort was more difficult, and I now cannot wait to define what rich means and how I plan to achieve great wealth.'

'That's good,' said rich dad. 'Very good.' He then continued on by saying, 'So many people have been conditioned to "live below their means" or "save for a rainy day" that they never know what could be possible for their lives. So people splurge, get into debt by taking the annual vacation or buying a nice car, then feel guilty. They never take the time to figure out what could be financially possible if only they had a good financial plan . . . and that is a waste.'

'That is exactly what happened,' I said. 'By meeting with advisors and discussing what was possible, I learned a lot. I learned that I was really selling myself short. In fact, I felt like I have been walking in a house with a low ceiling for years, trying to scrimp, save, be secure, and live below my means. Now that I have a plan of what is possible relative to being comfortable, I am now excited about defining what the word "rich" means.'

'Good,' said rich dad with a smile. 'The key to staying young is to decide what you want to be when you grow up, and then keep growing up. Nothing is more tragic than to see people who have sold themselves short on what is possible for their lives. They try to live frugally, scrimping and saving, and they think that is being financially smart. In reality, it is financially limiting . . . and it shows up in their faces and in their attitude in life the older they get. Most people spend their lives mentally caged in financial ignorance. They begin to look like wild lions trapped in small cages at the zoo. They just pace back and forth wondering what happened to the life they once knew. One of the most important discoveries people can make by taking the time to learn how to plan is to find out what is financially possible for their lives . . . and that is priceless.

'The continual planning process also keeps me young. I am often asked why I spend my time building more businesses, investing, and making more money. The reason is I feel good doing it. While I make a lot of money doing what I do, I do it because making money keeps me young and alive. You wouldn't ask a great painter to stop painting once he or she was successful, so why should I stop building businesses, investing, and making more money? That is what I do, just as painting is what artists do to keep their spirits young and alive, even though the body ages.'

'So the reason you asked me to take the time to plan at different levels is for me to find out what is financially possible for my life?' I asked.

'That's it,' said rich dad. 'That is why you want to plan. The more you find out what might be possible for this tremendous gift called life, the younger at heart you remain. People who plan only for security or who say, "My income will go down when I retire" are planning for a life of less, not a life of more. If our maker has created a life of unlimited abundance, why should you plan on limiting yourself to having less?'

'Maybe that is what they were taught to think,' I said.

'And that is tragic,' rich dad replied. 'Very tragic.'

As rich dad and I sat there, my mind and heart drifted to my poor dad. I knew he was hurting and struggling to start his life over again. Many times I had sat down with him and attempted to show him a few of the things I knew about money. However, we usually got into an argument. I think there is often that kind of breakdown in communication when two parties communicate from two different core values, one of security and the other of being rich. As much as I loved my dad, the subject of money, wealth, and abundance was not a subject we could communicate about. Finally, I decided to let him live his life and I would focus on living mine. If he ever wanted to know about money, I would let him ask, rather than trying to help when my help had not been requested. He never asked. Instead of trying to help him financially, I decided to just love him for his strengths and not get into what I thought were his weaknesses. After all, love and respect are far more important than money.

## Mental Attitude Quiz

In retrospect, my real dad had a plan only for financial security via job security. The problem was that his plan failed when he ran for public office against his boss. He failed to update his plan and continued to plan only for security. Luckily, he did have his financial security needs covered by a teacher's pension, Social Security, and Medicare. If not for those safety nets, he would have been in very bad financial shape. The reality was that he planned for a world of scarcity, a world of bare minimum survival, and that is what he got. My rich dad, on the other hand, planned for a world of financial abundance, and that is what he achieved.

Both lifestyles require planning. Sadly, most people plan for a world of not enough, although a parallel world of financial plenty is also possible. All it requires is a plan.

**So the mental attitude question is:**

Do you have a written financial plan to be:

| | | | |
|---|---|---|---|
| 1. | Secure? | Yes _____ | No _____ |
| 2. | Comfortable? | Yes _____ | No _____ |
| 3. | Rich? | Yes _____ | No _____ |

Please remember rich dad's lesson that all three plans are important. But security and comfort still come before being rich, even though being rich may be your first choice. The point is that if you want to be rich, you will need all three plans. To be comfortable, you need only two plans. And to be secure, you need only one plan. Remember that only three out of every hundred Americans are rich. Most fail to have more than one plan. Many don't have any kind of written financial plan at all.

## Chapter 11
### Investor Lesson #9:

# Each Plan Has a Price

'What is the difference between the plan to be rich and the other two core values?' I asked.

Rich dad turned to his yellow legal tablet and wrote down the following words:

1. To be secure
2. To be comfortable
3. To be rich

'You mean the difference between rich and secure and comfortable?'

'That's what I am asking,' I responded.

'The difference is the price,' said rich dad. 'There is a tremendous price difference between a financial plan to be rich and the other two positions.'

'You mean the investments in the rich financial plan cost more money?' I asked.

'Well, to most people, it looks like the price is measured in terms of money. But if you look closer, you'll see that the price is not measured in money; it is really measured in time. And of the assets of time and money, time is really the more precious asset.'

A scowl came over my face as I tried to comprehend what rich dad was saying. 'What do you mean the price is measured in time? Give me an example.'

'Sure,' said rich dad. 'If I wanted to go from LA to New York, how much would a bus ticket cost?'

'I don't know. I'd guess under $100,' I replied. 'I've never purchased a bus ticket from LA to New York.'

'Neither have I,' said rich dad. 'Now tell me how much a ticket by a 747 jetliner from LA to New York would cost.'

'Again, I don't really know. But I guess it would be around $500,' I replied.

'That's close enough,' said rich dad. 'Now let me ask you. Why the difference in price? You're traveling from LA to New York in both instances. Why would you pay so much more for a ticket on a jet airliner?'

'Oh, I got it,' I said as I began to understand what rich dad was getting at. 'I pay more for the jet airliner ticket because I am saving time.'

'Think of it more like buying time than saving time. The moment you begin to think of time as precious and that it has a price, the richer you will become.'

I sat thinking silently. I really was not getting what rich dad was talking about . . . yet I knew that it was important to him. I wanted to say something but I did not know what to say. I did understand the idea that time was precious but I never really thought of it as having a price. And the idea of buying time rather than saving time was important to rich dad, but it was not important to me yet.

Finally, sensing my mental struggle, rich dad broke the silence by saying, 'I'll bet in your family you use the words "save" or "saving" a lot. I'll bet your mom often says she goes shopping and tries to save money. And your dad thinks that how much money he has in savings is important.'

'Yes they do,' I replied. 'So what does that mean to you?'

'Well they may work hard at trying to save but they waste a lot of time. I've seen shoppers in grocery stores spend hours trying to save a few dollars,' said rich dad. 'They may save money but they waste a lot of time.'

'But isn't saving important?' I asked. 'Can't you get rich by saving?'

'I'm not saying that saving is not important,' rich dad continued. 'And yes you can become rich by saving. All I am saying is that the price is really measured in time.'

Again I scrunched up my face, struggling with what he was saying.

'Look,' said rich dad. 'You can get rich by saving and you can become rich by being cheap, but it takes a heck of a long time, just as you can go from LA to New York by bus so you can save some money. However, your real price will be measured in time. In other words, it takes five hours by jet for $500 or it can take up to five days by bus for $100. Poor people measure in money and rich people measure in time. That may be why there are more poor people who ride buses.'

'Because they have more time than money?' I asked. 'That is why they ride the bus?'

'That is part of it,' said rich dad, shaking his head, indicating that he was not happy with the way our conversation was going.

'Because they value money more than time?' I asked, guessing in the dark.

'Closer,' said rich dad. 'I have noticed that the less money a person has the harder that person clings to it. I have met a lot of poor people with a lot of money.'

'Poor people with a lot of money?' I asked.

'Yes,' said rich dad. 'They have a lot of money because they cling to money like it has some magical value. So they have a lot of money but are just as poor as if they had no money.'

'So poor people often cling to money more than rich people?' I asked.

'I think of money as only a medium of exchange. In reality, money by itself has very little value. So as soon as I have money, I want to exchange it for something of value. The irony is that for many people who cling desperately to money, the money they spend for things of very little value . . . is why they are poor. They say things like "safe as money in the bank," and when they do spend their hard-earned money, they turn their cash into trash.'

'So they value money more than you do,' I said.

'Yes,' said rich dad. 'In many cases, the poor and middle class struggle because they place far too much importance on money itself. So they cling to it, work hard for it, work hard at living frugally, shop at sales, and do their best to save as much of it as they can. Many of these people try to get rich by being cheap. But at the end of the day, you may have a lot of money, but you're still cheap.'

'I don't understand,' I replied. 'You're talking about the values my mom and dad tried to instill in us. You're talking about the way I currently think. I'm in the Marine Corps, and they don't pay much money so I find myself naturally thinking that way.'

'I understand,' rich dad replied. 'Thrift and frugality have their place. But today we are talking about the difference between the plan to be rich and the other two plans.'

'And the difference is the price,' I restated.

'Yes,' said rich dad. 'And most people think the price is measured in money.'

'And what you're saying is that the price is measured in time,' I added, beginning to understand what rich dad was getting at. 'Because time is more important than money.'

Nodding, rich dad said, 'Many people want to get rich, or invest in the investments the rich invest in, but most are not willing to invest the time. That is why only three out of a hundred Americans are rich — and one of those three inherited that money.'

Rich dad again wrote on his yellow legal tablet the three core values we had been discussing:

1. To be secure
2. To be comfortable
3. To be rich

'You can invest to be secure and comfortable using an automatic system or plan. In fact, I recommend that for most people. Simply work and turn your money over to professional managers or institutions and invest for the long term. People who invest in this manner will probably do better than the individual who thinks he or she is the Tarzan of Wall Street. A steady program of putting money away following a plan is the best way to invest for most people.'

'But if I want to be rich, I have to invest in something more valuable than money, and that is time. Is this what you've been getting at with this lesson?'

'I wanted to make sure you understood the lesson,' said rich dad. 'You see, most people want to be rich but they are not willing to first invest the time. They operate on hot tips or wild get-rich-quick schemes. Or they want to start a business so they rush out and start a business without the basic skills of business. And then we wonder why 95% of all small businesses fail in the first five to ten years.'

'They are in such a hurry to make money, they eventually lose both time and money,' I added. 'They want to do things on their own rather than invest in a little study.'

'Or follow a simple long-term plan,' rich dad repeated. 'You see, almost anyone in the Western world can easily become a millionaire if he or she simply follows a long-term plan. But again, most people aren't willing to invest the time; they want to get rich now.'

'Instead they say things like "investing is risky" or "it takes money to make money" or "I don't have the time to learn to invest. I'm too busy working and I have bills to pay,"' I added as I began to understand rich dad's point.

Rich dad nodded. 'And those very common ideas or excuses are why so few people achieve great wealth in a world that is filled with money.

Those ideas or words are why 90% of the population has the problem of having not enough money rather than the problem of too much money. Their ideas about money and investing cause their money problems. All they have to do is change a few words, a few ideas, and their financial world will change like magic. But most people are too busy working and they do not have the time. Many often say, "I'm not interested in learning to invest. It is a subject that does not interest me." Yet they fail to see that by saying that, they become slaves to money, working for money, having money dictate the financial boundaries of their lives, living frugally and within their means, instead of investing a little time, following a plan, and having money work for them.'

'So time is more important than money,' I said.

'That is true for me,' said rich dad. 'So if you want to move on to the rich level of investing, you are going to have to invest much more time than you do at the other two levels. Most people do not go beyond secure and comfortable because they are not willing to invest the time. That is a personal decision we all need to make. At least the person has a financial plan to be secure and/or comfortable. There is nothing more high risk than a person who does not have those two basic plans, who is focused only on becoming rich. While a few make it, most don't. You see them in the later years of their lives, broke, spent, and talking about the deal they almost made or the money they once had. At the end of their lives, they have neither time nor money.'

'So I think it is time I began to invest more time, especially since I want to invest at the rich level,' I said, shuddering at the thought of being a broke and broken old man, muttering in my beer about the deals that almost happened. I had already seen and met such investors. It is not pretty to see a person who is out of both time and money.

## *Mental Attitude Quiz*

Investing at the secure level and the comfortable level should be as mechanical or as formulated as possible. They should be 'no-brainers.' All you do is turn your money over to professional – and hopefully reputable – managers, and all they do is follow your plan. If you start early and if the stars shine on you, at the end of the rainbow should be the pot of gold. Investing can – and should – be that simple, at these two fundamental levels.

There is a word of caution, however. There is no such thing in life as risk free. There are lower-risk things, and that is so for investing. So, if you feel uncertain about the fate of the financial world and don't trust the people or the industry, then you have much more research to do.

It is important to be true to your emotions and instinct but don't let them run your entire life. So if you cannot shake this nervousness, then invest with greater caution . . . but always remember the price; the more secure an investment, the more time it takes to make money . . . if it makes money. So there is always a tradeoff, or as they say, 'There is no such thing as a free lunch.' Everything has a price, and in the investment world, that price is measured in both time and money.

Once your investment plans of being financially secure and/or comfortable are in place and on track, then you are better able to speculate on that hot stock tip you heard from a friend. Speculating in the world of financial products is fun, yet it should be done responsibly. There are many so-called investors in the markets who are really addicts with a gambling problem.

When people ask me questions such as 'What stocks are you investing in?' I have to say, 'I don't pick stocks. Professional money managers do that for me.'

They then often say, 'I thought you were a professional investor.'

And I reply, 'I am. But I do not invest in the ways that most people invest. I invest how my rich dad taught me to invest.'

I personally and actively invest in the rich level of investing. Very few people invest or play the game of investing at this level. The remainder of this book is dedicated to that level of investing, which my rich dad taught me. It is not a method for everyone . . . especially if you do not already have the security and comfort levels already in place.

## So the mental attitude questions are:

1.  Are you willing to set in place an investment plan to cover your financial needs to be secure and/or comfortable?

    Yes _____ No _____

2.  Are you willing to invest the time to learn to invest at the rich level, the level of my rich dad?

    Yes _____ No _____

    If you are not sure of your answer and want to find out what level of commitment rich dad's investment in study requires, the rest of the book will give you some insights as to what it takes to invest at the rich level.

*Chapter 12*
*Investor Lesson #10*

# Why Investing Isn't Risky

People say, 'investing is risky' for three main reasons:

1. They have not been trained to be investors. If you read *CASH-FLOW Quadrant*, the sequel to *Rich Dad Poor Dad*, you will recall that most people go to school to be trained for the left side of the Quadrant rather than the right side of the Quadrant.

2. Secondly, most investors lack control or are out of control. My rich dad used this example: He would say, 'There is risk driving

a car. But driving the car with your hands off the steering wheel is really risky.' He then said, 'When it comes to investing, most people are driving with their hands off the steering wheel.' Phase One of this book is taking control of yourself before investing. If you didn't have a plan, a little discipline, and some determination, the other investor controls would not mean much. The rest of this book will go into the remainder of rich dad's ten investor controls.

3.  Thirdly, people say investing is risky because most people invest from the outside rather than from the inside. Most of us know intuitively that if you want a real deal, you have to be on the inside. You often hear someone say, 'I have a friend in the business.' It does not matter what the business is. It could be to buy a car, tickets to a play, or a new dress. We all know that on the inside is where the deals are made. The investment world is no different. As Gordon Gekko, the villainous character played by Michael Douglas in the movie *Wall Street*, said, 'If you're not on the inside, you're outside.'

We will review this relationship between being on the outside or inside later. What is interesting to note at this time is that people on the left side of the Quadrant usually invest from the outside. In contrast, Bs and Is are able to invest from the inside as well as the outside.

### *An Important Note*

As this book progresses, many sacred money cows may be slaughtered. Inside investing is one of them. In the real world, there is legal inside investing and there is illegal inside investing. That is an important distinction. What makes the news is the illegal insider investing. Yet, there is more legal insider investing in the real world that does not make the news, and that is the type of inside investing I am talking about.

A hot tip from a taxi driver is in many ways an insider tip. The real question in insider investing is really: 'How close to the inside are you?'

## Rich Dad's Plan

When rich dad listed the three core financial values, which are:

1. To be secure,
2. To be comfortable and
3. To be rich,

he said, 'It makes perfect sense to invest from the outside when you invest at the secure and the comfortable level of investing. That is why you turn your money over to a professional you hope is closer to the inside than you. But if you want to be rich, you have to be closer to the inside than the professional to whom most people entrust their money.'

And that was the focus of rich dad's plan to be rich. That is what he did and that was why he was so rich. To follow his plan, I needed the education and experiences found on the right side of the Quadrant, not the left. To do that, I needed to invest a lot more time than the average investor . . . and that is what the rest of this book is really about. This book is about what it takes to move from the outside to the inside.

## Before You Decide

I realize that many people do not want to invest that much time into the subject of investing just to get to the inside. But before you decide, and before getting into a little more detail about rich dad's plan, I thought I would give you a very simplified overview of the subject of investing. Hopefully, after reading the next few chapters, you may learn a few new ways to reduce your investment risk to become more successful as an investor, even if you do not want to be an inside investor. As I said earlier, investing is a very personal subject, and I completely respect that reality. I know that many people do not want to commit the time to the subject of investing the way rich dad and I did.

Before going into rich dad's educational plan to teach me to be an investor at the rich level, the next few chapters are dedicated to offering the reader a simple overview of rich dad's investment plan.

## Mental Attitude Quiz

The business of investing has many parallels to the business of professional sports. For example, let's use the game of professional football. At Super Bowl time, the entire world watches. On the field are the players, the fans, the blimp overhead, the cheerleaders, the vendors, the sports commentators, and the fans at home watching the event on television.

Today, for many investors, the world of investing looks like a professional football game. You have the same cast of characters. You have the TV commentators describing the play-by-play battle of the blue chip giants on the field. There are the adoring fans purchasing shares instead of tickets, cheering for their favorite team. You also have the cheerleaders, telling you why the stock price is going up; or, if the market goes down, they want to keep cheering you up with new hope that the price will soon rise. There are the bookmakers, called stockbrokers, who give you stock quotes over the phone and record your bets. Instead of reading the sports page, you read the financial pages. There are even the equivalent of ticket scalpers, but in the financial world they don't sell over-priced tickets to latecomers; they sell over-priced financial tip sheets to people who want to get closer to the inside game. Then there are the hot dog vendors, who also dispense antacid pills, as well as the people who sweep up the mess after the trading day is over. And of course we have the viewers at home.

What most people do not see in both arenas of the sports world and the investment world is what is going on behind the scenes. And that is the business behind both games. Oh, you may see the owner of the team occasionally, just as you may see a CEO or the president of the company, but the figurehead is not really the business. So as rich dad said, 'The business behind the business is the real game. It's the business behind the business that makes money regardless of who wins the game or which way the market goes – up or down. It's the business that sells the tickets to the game; it does not buy the tickets.' That is the investment game rich dad taught me, and what the rest of this book is about. It is the investment game that creates the richest people in the world.

## So the mental attitude questions are:

1. Are you willing to start taking control over yourself?

Yes _____ No _____

2. Based on what you know so far, are you willing to invest the time to gain the education and experience to become a successful investor as an insider?

Yes _____ No _____

## Chapter Thirteen
### Investor Lesson #11:

# On Which Side of the Table Do You Want to Sit?

### Why Investing Isn't Risky

My poor dad always said, 'Work hard and save money.'

My rich dad said, 'Working hard and saving money are important if you want to be secure and comfortable. But if you want to be rich, working hard and saving money will probably not get you there. On top of that, people who work hard and save money are often the same people that say, "Investing is risky."'

There were many reasons rich dad reminded Mike and me that working hard and saving money was not the way he got rich. He knew that working hard and saving money was good for the masses but not for anyone wanting to become rich.

There were three reasons why he recommended finding a different plan to becoming rich. These are the reasons.

1.  He would say, 'People who work hard and save money have a hard time getting rich because they pay more than their fair share of taxes. The government taxes people like this when they earn, when they save, when they spend, and when they die. If you want to be rich you will need greater financial sophistication than merely working hard and saving money.'

Rich dad explained further by saying, 'To put $1,000 in savings, the government has already taken its fair share out in taxes. So it might take $1,300 or more in earnings just to save $1,000. Then that $1,000 is immediately being eaten away by inflation, so each year your $1,000 is worth less. The meager sum of interest you are paid is also eaten by inflation as well as taxes. So let's say your bank pays you 5% interest, and inflation runs at 4% and taxes run at 30% of the interest, your net result is a loss of money.' That is why rich dad thought that working hard and saving money was a hard way to try and get rich.

2.  The second reason was, 'People who work hard and save often think investing is risky. People who think things are risky often also avoid learning something new.'
3.  The third reason was, 'People who believe in hard work, saving, and that investing is risky, rarely ever see the other side of the coin.'

This chapter covers some of the reasons why or how investing does not have to be risky.

Rich dad had a way of taking very complex subjects and simplifying them so almost everyone could understand at least the basics of what he was talking about. In *Rich Dad Poor Dad*, I shared the diagrams of the income statement and the balance sheet that he used to teach me the basics of accounting and financial literacy. In *CASH-FLOW Quadrant*, I shared his diagram that explains the core emotional and educational differences between the people found in the four quadrants. In order for me to understand investing, I first needed to fully understand the lessons taught in those two books.

When I was between the ages of 12 and 15, rich dad would occasionally have me sit at his side while he interviewed people who were looking for a job. At 4:30 p.m., which was the time he did all his interviews, I would sit behind a large brown wooden table in a chair next to rich dad. Across the table was a single wooden chair for the person being interviewed. One by one, his secretary would let the prospective employees into the large room and instruct each person to sit in the lone open chair.

I saw grown adults asking for jobs that paid $1.00 an hour, with minimal benefits. Even though I was a young teenager, I knew that it was difficult to raise a family, much less get rich, on $8.00 a day. I also saw people with college degrees, even several with Ph.D.s, asking rich dad for managerial or technical jobs that paid less than $500 a month.

After a while, the novelty of sitting behind the table on rich dad's side wore off. Rich dad never said anything to me before, during, or after these interviewing days. Finally, when I was 15 and bored of sitting behind the table, I asked him, 'Why do you want me to sit here and watch people ask for jobs? I'm not learning anything and it's getting boring. Besides, it is painful to see grownups so needy for a job and money. Some of those people are really desperate. They can't afford to quit their present job unless you give them another job. I doubt some of them could last three months without a paycheck. And some of them are older than you and obviously have no money. What's happened to them? Why do you want me to see this? It hurts me every time I do this with you. I have no problem with them asking for a job, but it's the desperation for money I can see in their eyes that really bothers me.'

Rich dad sat still at the table for a moment, collecting his thoughts. 'I've been waiting for you to ask this question,' he said. 'It hurts me too and that is why I wanted you to see this before you got much older.' Rich dad took his legal pad and drew the *CASHFLOW Quadrant*.

'You are just starting high school. You are soon going to be making some very important decisions about what you will be when you grow up, if you haven't already made them. I know your dad is encouraging you to go to college so you can get a high-paying job. If you listen to his advice, you will be going in this direction.' Rich dad then drew an arrow to the E and S side of the Quadrant.

'If you listen to me, you will be studying to become a person on this side of the Quadrant.' He then drew an arrow to the B and I side of the Quadrant.

'You've shown me this and told me this many times,' I replied quietly. 'Why do you continue to go over it?'

'Because if you listen to your dad, you will soon find yourself sitting in that solitary wooden chair on the other side of the table. If you listen to me, you will be sitting in the wooden chair on my side of the table. That is the decision you are making, consciously or unconsciously, as you enter high school. I've had you sit on my side of the table because I wanted you to know that there is a difference in points of view. I'm not saying one side of the table is better than the other side. Each side has its pluses and minuses. I just want you to start choosing now which side you want to sit on because what you study from this day forward will determine which side of the table you wind up on. Will you wind up on the E and S side or the B and I side of the table?'

## *A Gentle Reminder 10 Years Later*

In 1973, rich dad reminded me of that discussion we had when I was 15 years old. 'Do you remember me asking you which side of the table you want to sit on?' he asked.

I nodded and said, 'Who could have predicted back then that my dad, the proponent for job security and lifelong employment, would be sitting on the other side of the table again, at the age of 50? He had everything going for him at 40, and it was all over just 10 years later.'

'Well, your dad is a very courageous man. Unfortunately, he did not plan for this happening to him and now he's getting into professional as well as financial trouble. It could get worse if he does not make some rapid changes. If he keeps going with his old beliefs about jobs and job security, I am afraid he will waste the last years of his life. I cannot help him right now but I can help guide you,' said rich dad.

'So you're saying choose which side of the table to sit on?' I replied.

'You mean choose a job as a pilot with the airlines or make my own path?'

'Not necessarily,' said rich dad. 'All I want to do in this lesson is point something out to you.'

'And what is that?' I asked.

Rich dad again drew the *CASHFLOW Quadrant*:

He then said, 'Too many young people focus on only one side of the Quadrant. Most people are asked as children, 'What do you want to be when you grow up?' If you notice, most children will reply such things as "a fireman," or "a ballerina," or "a doctor," or "a teacher."'

'So most kids choose the E and S side of the Quadrant,' I added.

'Yes,' said rich dad. 'And the I quadrant, the investor quadrant, is an afterthought, if any thought is given to it at all. In many families, the only thought given to the "I" quadrant is when parents say, "Make sure the job you have has excellent benefits and a strong retirement plan." In other words, the idea is to let the company be responsible for your long-term investment needs. That is changing rapidly as we speak.'

'Why do you say that?' I asked. 'Why do you say it's changing?'

'We are entering a period of a global economy,' said rich dad. 'For companies to compete in the world, they need to get their costs down. And one of their major costs is employee compensation and employee retirement plan funding. You mark my words, in the next few years businesses will begin shifting the responsibility of investing for retirement to the employee.'

'You mean people will have to provide for their own pension instead of relying on their employer or the government?' I asked.

'Yes. The problem will be the worst for poor people, and they are who I worry about,' said rich dad. 'That is why I reminded you about sitting across the table from people whose only financial support was a job. By the time you are my age, what to do with people without financial and medical support when they are older will be a massive problem. And your generation, the Baby Boomer generation, will probably be tasked with solving that problem. The severity of this problem will be very prominent sometime around 2010.'

'So what should I do?' I asked.

'Make the "I" quadrant the most important quadrant, not the others. Choose to be an investor when you're grown up. You'll want to have your money working for you so you don't have to work if you don't want to, or cannot, work. You don't want to be like your dad at 50 — starting all over again, trying to figure out which quadrant he can earn the most money from, and realizing he is trapped in the E quadrant,' said rich dad.

'You want to learn how to operate from all quadrants. Being able to sit on both sides of the table allows you to see both sides of the coin,' rich dad said in summary, referring to his two-sided coin story.

## The Most Important Quadrant

Rich dad explained to me that one of the differences between rich people and poor people comes from what the parents teach their kids at home. He said, 'Mike already had a personal investment portfolio of over $200,000 by the time he was 15. You had nothing. All you had was the idea of going to school so you could get a job with benefits. That is what your dad thought was important.'

Rich dad reminded me that his son Mike knew how to be an investor before he left high school. 'I never tried to influence him in his choice of careers,' said rich dad. 'I wanted him to follow his interests, even if it meant he did not take over my business. But whether he chose to be a policeman, politician, or a poet, I wanted him to first be an investor. You'll become far richer if you learn to be an investor, regardless of what you do to earn the money along the way.'

Years later, as I met more and more people who came from well-to-do families, many of them said the same thing. Many of my wealthy friends said that their families started an investment portfolio for them when they were very young and then guided them in learning to be investors – before deciding what type of profession they wanted to enter.

## *Mental Attitude Quiz*

In the Industrial Age, the rules of employment were that your company would employ you for life and take care of your investing needs once your working days were over. In 1980, the average length of retirement before death was only one year for men and two years for women. In other words, all you had to do was focus on the E quadrant and your employer would take care of the I quadrant. That message was very comforting, especially to my parents' generation, since they lived through a horrible world war, and the Great Depression. Those events had a tremendous impact upon their mental attitude and financial priorities. Many still live with that financial attitude and they often taught that same attitude to their children. Many people also continue to believe that their home is an asset and their most important investment. That idea is an Industrial Age way of thinking. In the Industrial Age, that was all a person needed to know about money management because the company or labor union and the government took care of the rest.

The rules have changed. In the Information Age of today, most of us need greater financial sophistication. We need to know the difference between an asset and a liability. We are living much longer and therefore need more financial stability for our retirement years. If your home is your biggest investment, then you're probably in financial trouble. Your financial portfolio needs to be a much bigger investment than your home.

The good news is that the I quadrant is a great quadrant to place first — to learn to be responsible for — because freedom comes from this quadrant.

**So the mental attitude questions are:**
1. Which quadrant will you place first (is the most important to you)?

       E ___ S ___ B ___ I ___

2. What side of the table do you eventually plan to sit on?

I have asked question two and left it without an answer because of this phenomenon: You may have noticed that when a major company announces a lay-off of thousands of employees, the company's share price often goes up. That is an example of the two sides of the table. When a person shifts to the other side, his or her point of view of the world also changes. And when a person shifts quadrants, if only mentally and emotionally, then loyalties often change. And I believe that this shift is brought on by the change of ages, the change from Industrial Age thinking to Information Age thinking, and it will cause businesses and business leaders some of the biggest challenges in the future. As they say, 'The rules have just begun to change.'

# Chapter 14
## Investor Lesson #12:

# The Basic Rules of Investing

One day, I was feeling frustrated about my financial progress in life. I had about four months before I was to leave the military and enter the civilian world. I had stopped all efforts to get a job with the airlines. I had decided that I was going to enter the business world in June of 1974 and see if I could make it in the B quadrant. It was not a hard decision since rich dad was willing to guide me, but the pressure to become financially successful was building. I felt that I was so far behind financially, especially when I compared myself to Mike.

During one of our meetings, I shared my thoughts and frustrations with rich dad. I said, 'I've got my two plans in place. One plan is to ensure that I have basic financial security, and the other, more aggressive, investment plan is so I will be comfortable financially. But at the rates those plans will be successful, if they are successful, I'll never be rich like you and Mike.'

Rich dad grinned when he heard that. Smiling and laughing quietly to himself, he said, 'Investing is not a race. You are not in competition with anyone else. People who compete usually have huge ups and downs in their financial life. You are not here to try to finish first. All you need to do to make more money is simply focus on becoming a better investor. If you focus on improving your experience and education as an investor, you will gain tremendous wealth. If all you want to do is to get rich quickly, or have more money than Mike, then the chances are you will be the big loser. It's OK to compare and compete a little, but the real objective of this process is for you to become a better and more educated investor. Anything other than that is foolish and risky.'

I sat there nodding and feeling a little bit better. I knew then that rather than try to make more money and take bigger risks, I would focus on studying harder. That made more sense to me, it seemed less risky, and it certainly took less money . . . and money was not something I had much of then.

Rich dad went on to explain his reasons for starting Mike out in the I quadrant, rather than the B or E quadrant. He said, 'Since the objective of the rich is to have your money work for you so you don't have to work, why not start where you want to wind up?' He went on to explain why he encouraged Mike and me to play golf when we were 10 years old. He said, 'Golf is a game you can play all your life. Football is a game you can play for only a few years. So why not start with the game you will end with?'

Of course I had not listened to him. Mike continued playing golf and I went on to baseball, football, and rugby. I was not very good at any of them, but I loved the games and I am glad I played them.

Fifteen years after starting to play golf and beginning to invest, Mike was now a great golfer, had a substantial investment portfolio, and had years more investment experience than I did. At 25, I was just beginning to learn the basics of the game of golf and the game of investing.

I make this point because regardless of how young or old you are, learning the basics of anything, especially a game, is important. Most people take some kind of golf lessons to learn the basics before playing golf, but unfortunately, most people never learn the simple basics of investing before investing their hard-earned money.

## *The Basics of Investing*

'Now that your two plans are in place – the plan for security and the plan for comfort – I will explain the basics of investing,' said rich dad. He went on to explain that too many people begin investing without having the first two plans in place, and that was risky in his mind. He said, 'After you have those two plans firmly in place, then you can experiment and learn more exotic techniques utilizing different investment vehicles. That is why I waited for you to take the time to put those two automatic or mechanical investment plans in place before I continued on with your lessons.'

## *Basic Rule Number One*

'Investment basic rule number one,' said rich dad, 'is to always know what kind of income you are working for.'

For years, rich dad had always said to Mike and me that there were three different kinds of income:

1. **Earned Income:** income generally derived from a job or some form of labor. In its most common form, it is income from a paycheck. It is also the highest-taxed income, so it is the hardest income with which to build wealth. When you say to a child, 'Get a good job,' you are advising the child to work for earned income.

2. **Portfolio Income:** income generally derived from paper assets such as stocks, bonds, mutual funds, etc. Portfolio income is by far the most popular form of investment income, simply because paper assets are so much easier to manage and maintain than any others.

3. **Passive Income:** income generally derived from real estate. It can also be income derived from royalties from patents or license agreements. Yet approximately 80% of the time, passive income is from real estate. There are many tax advantages available for real estate.

One of the running battles between my two dads was what a parent should say to a child. My poor dad always said to me, 'Work hard at school so you can get good grades. When you get good grades, you will be able to get a good job. Then you become a good hardworking man.' While Mike and I were in high school, rich dad would snicker at that idea. He used to say, 'Your dad is a good hardworking man but he will never get rich if he continues to think that way. If you boys listen to me, you will work hard for portfolio income and passive income if you want to become rich.'

Back then, I did not fully understand what either man was saying or what the difference in philosophies was all about. At age 25, I was beginning to understand a little better. My dad at age 52 was starting all over again, focused only on earned income, something he had thought was the right thing to do all his life. My rich dad was rich and enjoying life simply because he had lots of all three types of income. I knew now which type of income I was going to work hard for and it was not earned income.

## *Basic Rule Number Two*

'Investment basic rule number two,' said rich dad, 'is to convert earned income into portfolio income or passive income as efficiently as possible.' Rich dad then drew this diagram on his yellow legal tablet:

'And that, in a nutshell, is all an investor is supposed to do,' rich dad summarized with a smile. 'That is about as basic as it can get.'

'But how do I do it?' I asked. 'How do I get the money if I don't already have the money? What happens if I lose the money?' I kept asking.

'How, how, how?' said rich dad. 'You sound like an Indian chief from an old movie.'

'But those are real questions,' I whined.

'I know they are real questions. But for now, I just want you to understand the basics. Later, I'll go into the how. OK? And watch out for the negative thoughts. Look, risk is always part of investing, as it is with life. People who are too negative and avoid risk back themselves out of most opportunities because of their negativity and fear of risk. Got it?'

I nodded. 'I got it. Start with the basics.'

### Basic Rule Number Three

'Investment basic rule number three,' said rich dad, nodding to my last statement, 'is to keep your earned income secure by purchasing a security you hope converts your earned income into passive income or portfolio income.'

'Secure in a security?' I asked. 'I'm confused. What happened to assets and liabilities?'

'Good question,' said rich dad. 'I'm now expanding your vocabulary. It is time for you to go beyond the simple understanding of assets and liabilities – an understanding that most people never achieve, I might add. But the point I am making here is that all securities are not necessarily assets, as many people think they are.'

'You mean a stock or piece of real estate is a security, but it may not be an asset?' I asked.

'That is correct. However, many average investors cannot distinguish between a security and an asset. Many people, including many professionals, do not know the difference. Many people call any security an asset.'

'So what is the difference?' I asked.

'A security is something you hope will keep your money secure. And generally, these securities are bound up tight by government regulations. And that is why the organization that watches over much of the world of investing is called the Securities and Exchange Commission, a.k.a. the SEC. You may notice that its title is not the Assets and Exchange Commission.'

'So the government knows that securities are not necessarily assets,' I stated.

Rich dad nodded and said, 'And neither is it called the Securities and Guarantees Commission. The government knows that all it can do is maintain a tight set of rules and do its best to maintain order by enforcing those rules. It does not guarantee that everyone who acquires a security will make money. That is why securities are not called assets. If you remember the basic definition, an asset puts money in your pocket, or the income column; a liability takes money from your pocket, and that shows up in your expense column. It's simply a matter of basic financial literacy.'

I nodded. 'So it is up to the investor to know which securities are assets and which securities are liabilities,' I stated, beginning to understand where rich dad was going with this.

'That is correct,' said rich dad, again reaching for his legal tablet. He drew this diagram on it:

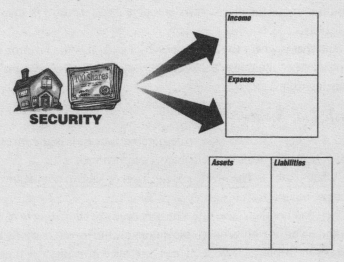

'The confusion begins for most investors when someone tells them that securities are assets. Average investors are nervous about investing because they know that just because they buy a security, it does not mean they will make money. The problem with buying a security is that the investor can also lose money,' said rich dad.

'So if the security makes money, as your diagram shows, it puts money into the income column of the financial statement, and it is an asset. But if it loses money, and that event is recorded in the expense column of the financial statement, then that security is a liability. In fact, the same security can change from being an asset into a liability. For example, I bought a hundred shares of stock in ABC Company in December for which I paid $20 per share. In January, I sold ten shares for $30 per share. Those ten shares of stock were assets because they generated income for me. But in March, I sold ten more shares for only $10, so that same stock had become a liability because it generated a loss (expense).'

Rich dad cleared his throat before speaking. 'So the way I look at this is that there are instruments called securities in which I invest. It is up to me as the investor to determine if each security is an asset or liability.'

'And that is where the risk comes in,' I said. 'It is the investor not knowing the difference between an asset or liability that makes investing risky.'

## Basic Rule Number Four

'And why I say investor basic rule number four is, it is the investor that is really the asset or the liability,' said rich dad.

'What?' I asked. 'The investor is the asset or liability, not the investment or security?'

Rich dad nodded. 'You often hear people say, "Investing is risky." It's the investor who is risky. It is ultimately the investor who is the asset or the liability. I have seen many so-called investors lose money when everyone else is making money. I have sold businesses to many so-called businesspeople and watch the businesses soon go bust. I have seen people take a perfectly good piece of real estate, real estate that is making a lot of money, and in a few years, that same piece of real estate is running at a loss and falling apart. And then I hear people say, investing is risky. It's the investor who is risky, not the investment. In fact, a good investor loves to follow behind a risky investor because that is where the real investment bargains are found.'

'And that is why you love to listen to investors who are crying the blues about their investment losses,' I said. 'You want to find out what they did wrong and see if you can find a bargain.'

'You've got it,' said rich dad. 'I'm always looking for the skipper of the *Titanic*.'

'And that is why you don't like to hear stories about people making a lot of money in the stock market or the real estate market. You hate it when someone tells you that he or she bought a stock at $5 and it went to $25.'

'You have observed me well,' said rich dad. 'Listening to tales of quick money and instant wealth is a fool's game. Such stories draw in only the losers. If a stock is well known or has made a lot of money, the party is often already over or soon to be over. I'd rather hear tales of woe and misery because that is where the bargains are. As a person who operates on the B and I side of the quadrant, I want to find securities that are liabilities and turn them into assets, or wait for someone else to begin turning them into assets.'

'So that would make you a contrarian investor,' I ventured, 'a contrarian being someone who goes against the popular sentiment of the market.'

'That is the lay person's idea of what a contrarian investor is. Most people just think a contrarian investor is anti-social and does not like going along with the crowd. But that is not true. As someone who operates on the B and I side of the Quadrant, I like to think of myself as a repairman. I want to look at the wreck and see if it can be fixed. If it can be fixed, then it would still be a good investment only if other investors also want it fixed. If it cannot be fixed or if no one would want it even after it is fixed, I don't want it either. So a true investor must also like what the crowd likes, and that is why I would not say I am a pure contrarian. I will not buy something just because no one else wants it.'

'So is there an investor basic rule number five?' I asked.

## Basic Rule Number Five

'Yes, there is,' said rich dad. 'Investor basic rule number five is that a true investor is prepared for whatever happens. A non-investor tries to predict what and when things will happen.'

'What does that mean?' I asked.

'Have you ever heard someone say, "I could have bought that land for $500 an acre twenty years ago. And look at it now. Someone built a shopping center right next to it, and now that same land is $500,000 an acre"?'

'Yes, I have heard those stories many times.'

'We all have,' said rich dad. 'Well, that is a case of someone who was not prepared. Most investments that will make you rich are available for only a narrow window of time – a few moments in the world of trading or a window of opportunity that is open for years, as it is in real estate. But regardless of how long the window of opportunity is open, if you are not prepared with education and experience, or extra cash, the opportunity, if it is good, will pass.

'So how does one prepare?'

'You need to focus and keep in mind what others are already looking for. If you want to buy a stock, then attend classes on how to spot bargains in stocks. The same is true for real estate. It all begins with training your brain to know what to look for and being prepared for the moment the investment is presented to you. It is much like the sport of soccer. You play and play, and then all of a sudden the winning kick at the goal appears. You're either prepared or you're not. You're either in position or you're not. But even if you miss the shot in soccer or in investing, there is always another shot at the goal, or an investment "opportunity of a lifetime" right around the corner. The good news is that there are more and more opportunities every day, but first you need to choose your game and learn to play the game.'

'So that is why you chuckle when someone complains about missing out on a good deal or tells you that you must get into this deal or that deal?'

'Exactly. Again there are so many people who come from the mindset that there is scarcity, instead of abundance, in the world. They often cry about missing a deal and hang on to a deal too long thinking that it is the only deal, or they buy thinking that what they are looking at is the only deal. If you are good at the "B" and "I" side of the Quadrant, you have more time and more deals to look at, and your confidence is high because you know you can take a bad deal that most people would reject, and turn it into a good deal. That is what I mean about investing the time to be prepared. If you're prepared, there is a deal of a lifetime being presented to you every day of your life.'

'And that is how you found that big piece of raw land – just walking down the street,' I commented, recalling how rich dad found one of his best pieces of real estate. 'You saw that the "For Sale" sign had fallen down and had been trampled on so no one knew the land was for sale. You called the owner and offered him a low but fair price at your terms and he took it. He took your offer because no one else had made him an offer in over two years. That is what you mean, isn't it?'

'Yes, that is what I mean, and that piece of raw land was a better deal than most. That is what I mean about being prepared. I knew what the land was worth and I also knew what was going to happen in that neighborhood in a few months, so there was very low risk coupled with a very low price. I would love to find ten more pieces of land today in that same neighborhood.'

'And what do you mean by "Don't predict"?' I asked.

'Well have you ever heard someone say, "What if the market crashes? What will happen to my investment then? That is why I am not going to buy. I am going to wait and see what happens"?'

'Many times,' I said.

'I have heard many people, when presented with a good investment opportunity, back away from the investment because their core fears begin to predict the disasters that will occur. They send out their negative vibes and never invest . . . or they sell when they shouldn't sell and they buy something they shouldn't buy based on either optimistic or pessimistic emotional predictions.'

'And that would be handled if they were a little educated, had a little experience, and were prepared,' I said.

'Exactly,' said rich dad. 'Besides, one of the basics of being a good investor is being prepared to profit when the market moves up or if it moves down. In fact, the best investors make more money in a downmarket move simply because the market falls faster than it rises. As they say, the bull comes up the stairs and the bear goes out the window. If you are not covered for either direction, you as the investor are too risky . . . not the investment.'

'That means many people predict themselves right out of being rich investors.'

Rich dad nodded. 'I have heard so many people say, "I don't buy real estate because I don't want calls at midnight to fix toilets." Well I don't either. That is why I have property managers. But I do love the tax advantages that cash flow from real estate offers that stocks do not.'

'So people often predict themselves right out of opportunities, instead of being prepared,' I echoed, beginning to understand why being prepared was so important. 'How do I learn to be prepared?'

'I'll teach you some basic trading techniques that all professional investors should know, techniques such as shorts, call options, put options, straddles, etc. But that will come later. Right now, that is enough about the advantages of preparation over prediction for you.'

'But I have one more question about preparation.'

'And what is that?' asked rich dad.

'What if I find a deal and I don't have any money?' I asked.

## Basic Rule Number Six

'That is investment basic rule number six,' said rich dad. 'If you are prepared, which means you have education and experience, and you find a good deal, the money will find you or you will find the money. Good deals seem to bring out the greed in people. And I don't mean to use the world greed in a negative way. I speak of greed as a general human emotion, an emotion we all have. So when a person finds a good deal, the deal attracts the cash. If the deal is bad, then it is really hard to raise the cash.'

'Have you ever seen a good deal that did not attract the money?' I asked.

'Many times, but it was not the deal that did not attract the cash. The person controlling the deal did not attract the cash. In other words, the deal would have been good if the guy in charge of the deal had stepped aside. It is like having a world-ranked racecar with an average driver. No matter how good the car is, no one would bet on it with an average driver at the wheel. In real estate, people often say the key to success is location, location, location. I think differently. In reality, in the world of investing – regardless of if it is real estate, business, or paper assets – the key is always people, people, people. I have seen the best real estate in the best location lose money because the wrong people were in charge.'

'So, again, if I am prepared, I have done my homework, I have some experience and a track record, and I find something that is a good investment, then finding the money is not that hard.'

'That has been my experience. Unfortunately, all too often, the worst deals, which are deals that investors like me would not invest in, are presented to unsophisticated investors, and the unsophisticated investors often lose their money.'

'And that is why there is the Securities and Exchange Commission,' I said. 'Its job is to protect the average investor from these bad deals.'

'Correct,' said rich dad. 'The primary job of investors is to make sure their money is secure. The next step is to do their best to convert that money into cash flow or capital gains. That is when you find out if you or the person to whom you entrusted your money can turn that security into an asset or if it will become a liability. Again, it is not the investment that is necessarily safe or risky, it is the investor.'

'So is that the last investor basic rule?' I asked.

'No. Not by a long shot,' said rich dad. 'Investing is a subject you can learn the basics of for the rest of your life. The good news is that the better you are at the basics, the more money you make and the less risk you have. But there is one more investor basic rule I would like to leave you with. And that is investor basic rule number seven.'

## Basic Rule Number Seven

'And what is number seven?'

'It is the ability to evaluate risk and reward,' said rich dad.

'Give me an example,' I requested.

'Let's say your two basic investment plans are in place. Your nest egg is doing well and you happen to have, let's say, an extra $25,000 you can invest on something more speculative.'

'I wish I had $25,000 right now,' I commented dryly. 'But tell me more about evaluating the risk and reward.'

'So you have this $25,000 that you can more or less afford to lose – which means that if you lost it all, you would cry a little but you could still put food on the table and gas in the car and save another $25,000. Then you begin to evaluate risk and rewards of the more speculative investments.'

'And how do I do that?'

'Let's say you have a nephew who has an idea for a hamburger stand. The nephew needs $25,000 to start. Would this be a good investment?'

'Emotionally, it could be, but financially it would not be,' I replied.

'Why not?' asked rich dad.

'Too much risk and not enough reward,' I replied. 'On top of that, how would you get your money back? The most important thing here is not return on investment. The most important thing here is return of investment. As you said, security of capital is very important.'

'Very good,' said rich dad. 'But what if I told you that this nephew has been working for a major burger chain for the past 15 years, has been a vice-president of every important aspect of the business, and is ready to go out on his own and build a worldwide burger chain? And what if for a mere $25,000 you could buy 5% of the entire company? Would that be of interest to you?'

'Yes,' I said. 'Definitely, because there is more reward for the same amount of risk. Yet it is still a high-risk deal.'

'That is correct,' said rich dad. 'And that is an example of an investor basic, which is to evaluate risk and reward.'

'So how does a person evaluate such speculative investments?' I asked.

'Good question,' said rich dad. 'That is the rich level of investing, the level of investing that follows the investment plans to be secure and comfortable. You're now talking about acquiring the skills to invest in investments that the rich invest in.'

'So again, it is not the investment that is risky; it is the investor who doesn't have the adequate skills that makes the investment even higher risk.'

### *The Three Es*

'Correct,' said rich dad. 'At this level, the level at which the rich invest in, the investor should have the three Es. And the three Es are:

1. Education
2. Experience
3. Excessive cash

'Excessive cash?' I asked. 'Not just extra cash?'

'No, I use the words "excessive cash" for a reason: Investing in the investments of the rich takes excessive cash, which means you can truly afford to lose and still profit from the loss.'

'Profit from the loss?' I asked. 'What does that mean?'

'We will get into that,' said rich dad. 'In the rich level of investing, you will find out that things are different. At the rich level, you will find out that there are good losses and bad losses. Good debt and bad debt. Good expenses and bad expenses. At the rich level, your educational requirements and experience will need to go up dramatically. If not, you will not be there for long. Got it?'

'I'm getting it,' I replied.

Rich dad went on to explain that if things do not follow the KISS (keep it simple, silly) formula, then the risk is probably high. He said, 'If someone cannot explain the investment to you in less than two minutes, and you understand it, then either you don't understand, he doesn't understand, or you both don't understand. Whatever the case, it is best that you pass on the investment.'

He also said, 'All too often, people try to make investing sound complex, so they use intelligent-sounding jargon. If someone does that, ask him or her to use simple English. If he or she can't explain the investment so a 10-year-old can understand at least the overall concept, chances are he or she does not understand it either. After all, all p/e means is how expensive the stock is. And a cap rate, which is a term used in real estate, just measures how much money the property puts or does not put in your pocket.'

'So if it is not simple, don't do it?' I asked.

'No, I'm not saying that either,' said rich dad. 'All too often, people who lack interest in investing or have a loser's attitude will say, "Man if it's not easy, I won't do it." I often say to that type of person, "Well when you were born, your parents had to work hard and potty train you. So even going to the toilet was at one time difficult. Today, hopefully, you are potty trained, and going to the potty by yourself is just part of the basics."'

## *Mental Attitude Quiz*

I have found that too many people want to invest in the investments of the rich without first having a strong financial foundation under them. All too often, people want to invest at the rich person's level because they are hurting financially and often need money desperately. Obviously, I do not recommend investments at a rich person's level unless you are already rich. Neither did my rich dad. Some people are fortunate enough that their financial plan to be 'comfortable' creates enough excess cash to make them think they are rich. But unless they learn to think as rich people think, they will still be poor people. They will be just be poor people with money.

**So the mental attitude question is:**

1.  If you are going to invest, or intend to invest, in what the rich invest in, are you willing to gain what rich dad called the three Es? They are:

    a.  Education
    b.  Experience
    c.  Excessive cash

Yes _____ No _____

If the answer is no, then the remainder of this book may not be of much value, nor could I in good conscience recommend any of the investments I will be writing about, which are the investments of the rich.

If you are uncertain or are curious about some of the requirements involved in the education and experience that can lead to acquiring excessive cash, then read on. At the end of this book, you can decide whether or not you want to go after the three Es, if you do not already have them.

Along the way, you may discover that your plans to be financially safe, and then financially comfortable, will allow you to 'raise the bar.' Just as a high jumper or pole-vaulter raises the bar after succeeding at each level, you can succeed financially at the safety and comfort levels. You can then 'raise the bar' — and your goals — and focus more of your time on becoming rich.

As rich dad said, 'Investing is a subject where you can study the basics for the rest of your life.' What he meant was that it sounds complex at the start and then it gets simple. The more simple you can make this subject, or the more basics you learn, the richer you can become while reducing risk. But the challenge for most people is to invest the time.

## Chapter 15
### Investor Lesson #13:

# Reduce Risk Through Financial Literacy

It was still early in the spring of 1974. I had but a couple of months to go before I was discharged from my military contract. I still did not know what I was going to do once I drove off the base for the last time. President Nixon was in trouble with Watergate and the trials were about to begin, so I realized that he had larger concerns than I did at that moment. We all knew the war in Vietnam was over and we had lost. I still had a very short military haircut and I stood out each time I went into the civilian world, where long hippie hair was the style. I began to wonder what I would look like in shoulder-length hair. I had worn a military hair cut since 1965, ever since I entered the military academy for college. It was the wrong period of time to have short hair.

The stock market had been going down for the past four days and people were nervous. Even in the pilots' ready room on base, the few pilots that did play the market were nervous and edgy. One had sold all his stock to stand aside with cash. I was not invested in the stock market at the time, so I could watch the effect of the ups and downs of the market had on people without emotion.

Rich dad and I met for lunch at his favorite beachside hotel. He was happy as ever. The market was falling and he was making even more money. I thought it strange that he would be calm and happy and everyone else, even the commentator on the radio, was nervous.

'How is it that you are happy and everyone else I meet who is in the stock market is nervous?'

'Well, we talked about it earlier,' said rich dad. 'We talked about one of the basics of being an investor is to be prepared for whatever happens, rather than attempt to predict what is about to happen. I doubt if anyone can predict the market, although there are many people who claim they can. A person can predict something happening maybe once, maybe even twice, but I have never seen anyone predict anything regarding the market, three times in a row. If there is such a person, he or she must have a high-powered crystal ball.'

'But isn't investing risky?' I asked.

'No,' said rich dad.

'Most people I talk to believe that investing is risky, so they keep their money in the bank, in money market funds or CDs.'

'As they should,' said rich dad, pausing for a moment and then continuing. 'For most people, investing is risky, but always remember that it is not necessarily investing that is risky, it is the investor who is risky. Many people who think they are investors are not really investors. In reality, they are speculators, traders, or — even worse — gamblers. There are fine lines of distinction between those characters and a true investor. Don't get me wrong, there are speculators, traders, and gamblers who do very well financially. But they are not what I would categorize as investors.'

'So how does an investor become less risky?' I asked.

'Good question,' said rich dad. 'Or maybe a better question might be, how do I become an investor who makes a lot of money with very little risk? And then hang on to the money I make?'

'Yes. That is definitely a more accurate question,' I replied.

'My answer is the same. It is to keep things simple and understand the basics. Begin with having your investment plans for security and comfort in place. Those plans are often handled by someone else you hope is competent and following an automatic no-brainer formula. Then you have to pay the price to become an investor who wants to make more money with less risk.'

'And what is that price?' I asked.

'Time,' said rich dad. 'Time is your most important asset. If you are not willing to invest your time, then leave your investment capital with people who are following the investment plan of your choice. Many people dream of getting rich but most will not pay the price of the investment of their time.'

I could tell that rich dad was still very much into the mental preparation mode of our lessons. But by now, I was ready to go. I really wanted to learn to invest following his investment formula. Yet he was still testing my determination to invest my time and effort to learn what I needed to learn. I therefore raised my voice so the tables around me could hear and said, 'I want to learn. I am willing to invest my time. I will study. I won't quit on you. You are not wasting your time teaching me. Just tell me what the basics are to becoming a successful investor with very low risk.'

'Good,' said rich dad. 'I've been waiting for some fire. I got concerned this morning when you came in concerned about the market going down. If you let the ups and downs of the stock market run your life, you should not be an investor. The number one control you must have to be an investor is control over yourself. If you cannot control yourself, the highs and lows of the market will run you and you will lose during one of those ups or downs. The number one reason people are not good investors is that they lack control over themselves and their emotions. Their desire for security and comfort takes control of their heart, their soul, their mind, their view of the world, and their actions. As I said, a true investor does not care which direction the market goes. A true investor will make money in either direction. So "control over yourself" is the first and most important control. Got it?'

'I got it,' I said as I backed up in my chair a little. I had come in a little wimpy and concerned. Yet I had been studying with rich dad for years and I knew that his intensity was letting me know that the lessons on investing were just about to begin.

Rich dad continued at a rapid-fire pace. 'So if you want to invest with very low risk and high returns, you have to pay the price. And the price involves study, lots of study. You need to study the basics of business. So to be a rich investor, you also have to either be a good business owner, or know what a business owner knows. In the stock market, investors want to invest in successful Bs. If you possess the skills of a B, you can either create your own business as a B or analyze other businesses as potential investments as an I. The problem is, most people are trained to be Es or Ss in school. They do not have the skills needed by a B. That is why so few people become very rich investors.'

'And that is why so many people say or think that investing is risky.'

'Exactly,' said rich dad as he reached for his legal tablet. 'This is what fundamental investing is. This is a simple diagram of the basic formula I follow as well as many ultra-rich investors.'

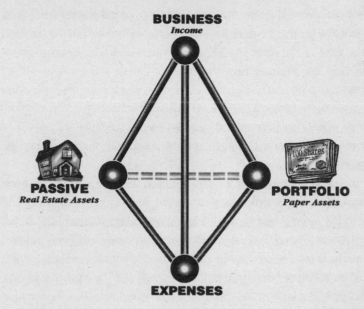

BUSINESS
*Income*

PASSIVE
*Real Estate Assets*

PORTFOLIO
*Paper Assets*

EXPENSES

'In the world of investing, there are three basic asset classes you can invest in. We already covered the idea of earned income, passive income, and portfolio income. Well, the big difference between the really rich and the average rich is the tetrahedron I drew here.'

'You mean building a business is an investment?' I asked.

'Probably the best investment of all, if you want to become a rich investor. Roughly 80% of the very rich became rich through building a business. Most people work for people who build businesses or invest in businesses. Then they wonder why the person who built the business is so rich. The reason is that the builder of a business will always trade money for the asset.'

'You mean the builder or owner of the business values the asset more than the money?' I asked.

'That is part of the picture because all an investor really does is trade time, expertise, or money for a security that they hope or intend will become an asset. So just as you trade money to buy an investment piece of real estate, like a rental house, or pay money for a share or stock, a business owner will pay people money to build a business asset. One of the main reasons the poor and middle class struggle is that they value money over true assets.'

'So the poor and the middle class value money and the rich don't really value it. Is that what you're saying?'

'Partially,' said rich dad. 'Always remember Gresham's Law.'

'Gresham's Law?' I replied. 'I've never heard of Gresham's Law. What is that?'

'Gresham's Law is an economic law that states that bad money will always drive out good money.'

'Good money, bad money?' I asked, shaking my head.

'Let me explain,' said rich dad. 'Gresham's Law has been in effect since humans began valuing money. Back in Roman times, people used to clip silver and gold coins. Clipping coins meant that people would shave a little bit off the coin before handing it to someone else. So the coin began to lose value. The Roman people were not stupid and soon noticed that the coins were lighter. Once the Roman people knew what was happening, they hoarded the coins with high silver and gold content and spent only the lighter coins. That is an example of bad money driving good money out of circulation.

'To combat this clipping of coins, the government began reeding coins, which is why coins of value have the tiny grooves on the edge. If a coin had the groves filed down, a person knew the coin had been tampered with. Ironically, it is the government that does the most clipping of the value of our money.'

'But that was back in Roman times. How does that law apply today?' I asked.

'In 1965, less than ten years ago, Gresham's Law began working in the United States when the government stopped producing coins with silver in them. In other words, the government began producing bad coins, or coins without any real value to them. Immediately, people began hoarding the real silver coins and spending the debased or fake coins.'

'In other words, people somehow intuitively know that government money is not worth much,' I stated.

'It seems that way,' said rich dad, 'which may be why I think people save less and spend more. Unfortunately, the poor and middle class buy things that have even less value than their money. They turn cash into trash. Meanwhile, the rich buy things like businesses, stocks, and real estate with their money. They are looking for secure securities in a time when money has an ever-decreasing real value. That is why I've constantly said to you and Mike, "The rich do not work for money." If you want to be rich, you have to know the difference between good money and bad money . . . assets and liabilities.'

'Good securities and bad securities,' I added.

Rich dad nodded. 'That is why I have always said to you, "The rich don't work for money." I say that because the rich are smart enough to know that money is worth less and less. If you work hard for bad money and do not know the difference between assets and liabilities, good securities, and bad securities, you may struggle financially all your life. It is truly a shame that those who work the hardest and are paid the least suffer the most from this constant erosion of money's value. People who do the hardest work have the hardest time getting ahead due to the effects of Gresham's Law. Since money has ever-declining value, a financially wise person must constantly seek things that do have value and can also produce more and more debased money. If you don't do that, you fall behind financially over time rather than get ahead.'

Rich dad then pointed to the sketch on his legal tablet:

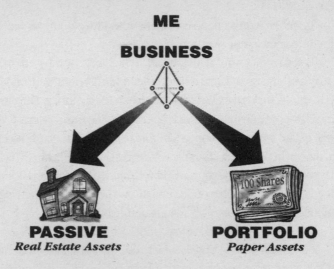

**ME**

**BUSINESS**

**PASSIVE**
*Real Estate Assets*

**PORTFOLIO**
*Paper Assets*

'I am more secure today than your dad because I worked hard to acquire all three of these basic assets or securities. Your dad has chosen to work hard for job security. So what he has worked hard for looks like this:'

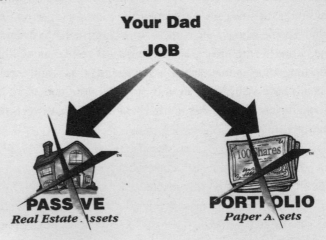

**Your Dad**

**JOB**

**PASSIVE**
*Real Estate Assets*

**PORTFOLIO**
*Paper Assets*

Rich dad then crossed out job security:

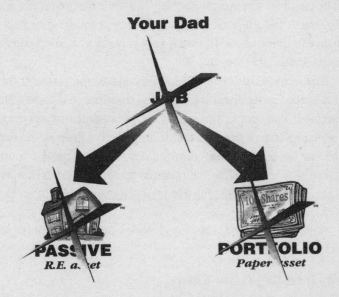

'So when he lost his job, he found out that he had worked hard for nothing. And worst of all, he was successful. He worked himself all the way to the top of the state education system but then he bucked the system. There goes his job security with the state government. I feel for your dad almost as much as you do. But you cannot talk to someone who has very set core values and is not willing to change. He is out looking for another job rather than asking himself if a job will get him what he really wants.'

'So he clung to job security and false assets. However, he failed to convert his earned income into real assets so he could have a rich person's income, which is passive income or portfolio income,' I said. 'He should have done that, converting his paycheck into real securities, before taking on the system.'

'Your dad is a brave man, highly educated, but not financially well educated. And that was his downfall. If he were rich, he could influence the system with campaign contributions, but since he had no money, all he could do was protest and defy the government. Protest is effective, but it takes a heck of a lot of people protesting to make any change in government. Just look at how many protesting people it is taking to stop this Vietnam War.'

'The irony is that he was protesting against the power of the rich to influence government by campaign contributions,' I said. 'He saw the power that people with money had over politicians and the favors the rich receive or the laws that were passed in favor of the rich. My dad saw the money involved in politics and so he ran for lieutenant governor to try and stop that financial abuse. Now it has cost him his position in the government. He knows the laws are written in favor of the rich.'

'Well, that is another subject on money. But not our subject today,' said rich dad.

## Why Investing Is Not Risky

'I've already made up my mind,' I said. 'I have not followed up on any of the jobs for pilots. I will soon begin looking for a job with a company that has sales training, so I can overcome my fear of rejection and learn to sell, or communicate, as you recommended.'

'Good,' said rich dad. 'Both IBM and Xerox have excellent sales training programs. If you're going to be in the B quadrant, then you must know how to sell as well as market. You also have to have a very thick skin and not mind people saying "No" to you. But you also have to be able to change their mind if it is appropriate to do so. Selling is a very necessary, basic skill for anyone who wants to become rich, especially in the B quadrant and very often in the I quadrant.'

'But I have one burning question,' I said.

'Ask it,' said rich dad.

'How can you say investing is not risky when most people say investing is risky?'

'Easy,' said rich dad. 'I can read financial statements and most people cannot. Do you remember me saying to you years ago that your dad was word literate but not financially literate?'

I nodded, saying, 'I remember you saying that very often.'

'Financial literacy is one of the most important investor basics, especially if you want to be a safe investor, an inside investor, and a rich investor. Anyone who is not financially literate cannot see into an investment. Just as a doctor uses X-rays to look at your skeletal system, a financial statement allows you to look into an investment and see the truth, the facts, the fiction, the opportunities, and the risk. Reading a financial statement of a business or individual is like reading a biography or an autobiography.'

'So one of the reasons many people say investing is risky is simply that they have never been taught to read financial statements?' I asked in surprise. 'And that is why you began by teaching Mike and me to read financial statements starting when we were 9?'

'Well, if you remember, you told me when you were just 9 years old that you wanted to be rich. When you told me that, I began with the basics: never work for money, learn to spot opportunities not jobs, and learn to read financial statements. Most people leave school looking for jobs, not opportunities; they have been taught to work hard for earned income rather than passive income or portfolio income; and most have never been taught how to balance a checkbook, much less read and write a financial statement. Small wonder they say investing is risky.'

Rich dad again took his legal tablet and drew the following diagram:

**You**

| Income |
| --- |
| Expense |

| Assets | Liabilities |
| --- | --- |

**Your Business**

| Income |
| --- |
| Expense |

| Assets | Liabilities |
| --- | --- |

**Real Estate**

| Income |
| --- |
| Expense |

| Assets | Liabilities |
| --- | --- |

**Stock**

| Income |
| --- |
| Expense |

| Assets | Liabilities |
| --- | --- |

'A business has a financial statement, a stock certificate is a reflection of a financial statement, each piece of real estate has a financial statement, and each of us as an individual human being has a financial statement attached to us,' said rich dad.

'Every security and human being?' I asked. 'Even my dad? Even my mom?'

'Sure,' said rich dad. 'Everything – regardless of if it is a business, real estate, or human being – that transacts money has an income statement and balance sheet, whether or not they know it. People who are not aware of the power of a financial statement often have the least money and the biggest financial problems.'

'You mean like my dad is having right now,' I said.

'Unfortunately that is true,' said rich dad. 'Not knowing the simple difference between assets and liabilities, earned income from passive and portfolio income, and not knowing where they all appear and how they flow on a financial statement has been a costly oversight for your dad.'

'So when you look at a business, you look at the financial statement, not the price of its stock that day?' I asked, doing my best to move the discussion away from my dad.

'That is correct,' said rich dad. 'That is called fundamental investing. Financial literacy is fundamental to fundamental investing. When I look at the financials of a business, I look at the guts of a business. When I look at the financials, I can tell if the business is fundamentally strong or weak, growing or declining. I can tell if the management is doing a good job or wasting a lot of the investors' money. The same is true with an apartment building or office building.'

'So by reading the financials, you can tell for yourself if the investment is risky or safe,' I added.

'Yes,' said rich dad. A person's, a business's, or a piece of real estate's financials will tell me much more than that. But a cursory look at a financial does three more important things.'

'And they are?'

'For one thing, being financially literate gives me a checklist of what is important. I can look at each line and determine what is not being done right, or what I can do to improve the business and make things right. Most investors look at the price and then the stock's p/e, or price/earnings ratio. The p/e of a stock is an outsider's indicator of the business. An insider needs other indicators, and that is what I will teach you. Those indicators are part of a safety checklist to make sure all the parts of the business are functioning well. If you are not financially literate, you cannot tell the differences. Then, of course, investing is risky for that person.'

'And the second thing?' I asked.

'The second thing is when I look at an investment, I also overlay it on my personal financial statement, and see where it fits. As I said, investing is a plan. I want to see how the business, the stock, mutual fund, bond, or real estate's financial statement impacts my personal financial statement. I want to know that this investment will get me to where I want to go. I can also analyze how I can afford the investment. By knowing my numbers, I know what will happen if I borrow money to buy an investment and the long-term impact balanced with income and outflow due to debt payments.'

'And the third thing?'

'I want to know that this investment is safe and will make me money. I can tell if it is going to make money or lose money in a very short period of time. So if it does not make me money, or I cannot fix the reason why it will not make me money, why should I buy it? That would be risky.'

'So if you do not make money, you don't invest?' I asked.

'In most instances,' said rich dad. 'Yet as simple as that sounds, it always amazes me when I meet people who are losing money or making no money and they think they are investors. Many people who invest in real estate lose money every month and then say, "But the government gives me a tax break for my losses." That is like saying, "If you lose a dollar, the government will give you 30 cents back." A few very sophisticated businesspeople and investors know how to use that government ploy to their advantage, but very few people really do. Why not make a dollar and get an additional 30 cent bonus from the government? That is what a real investor does.'

'People actually do that? They actually lose money and think it is investing?'

'On top of that, they think losing money for tax advantages is a good idea. Do you know how easy it is to find an investment that loses money?' asked rich dad.

'I imagine it would be pretty easy,' I said. 'The world is filled with stocks, mutual funds, real estate, and businesses that do not make any money.'

'So a real investor first wants to make money, and then after making money, they want an additional bonus from the government. So a real investor will make a dollar as well as get a 30 cent bonus from the government. An unsophisticated investor will lose a dollar and be thrilled to get 30 cents from the government in the form of a tax write-off.'

'Just because that person cannot read a financial statement?' I asked.

'That is one of the basics. Financial literacy is definitely an important investor basic at the rich investment level. The other basic is to invest to make money. Never invest with the intent to lose money and then be happy with a tax write-off. You invest for one reason only: to make money. Investing is risky enough without investing to lose money.'

## Your Report Card

As we ended the lesson for the day, rich dad said, 'Now do you realize why I had you do your personal financial statements so often?'

I nodded and said, 'As well as analyze the financial statements of businesses and real estate investments. You kept saying you wanted me to think in financial statements. Now I understand why.'

'While you were in school, you got a report card once a quarter. A financial statement is your report card once you leave school. The problem is that since most people have not been trained to read financial statements or how to keep a personal financial statement, they have no idea how they are doing once they leave school. Many people have failing marks on their personal financial statements but think they are doing well because they have a high-paying job and a nice home. Unfortunately, if I were handing out the grades, anyone who was not financially independent by age 45 would receive a failing grade. It is not that I want to be cruel. I just want people to wake up and maybe do a few things differently . . . before they run out of their most important asset: time.'

'So you reduce risk by being able to read financial statements,' I replied. 'A person needs to get his or her own personal financial statement under control before investing.'

'Definitely,' said rich dad. 'This whole process I have been talking to you about is the process of taking control of yourself, which also means your financial statement. So many people want to invest because they are deep in debt. Investing in the hopes of making more money so you can pay bills or buy a bigger house or a new car is a fool's investment plan. You invest for one reason: to acquire an asset that converts earned income into passive income or portfolio income. That conversion of one form of income into another form of income is the primary objective of a true investor. And to do that requires a higher degree of financial literacy than simply balancing a checkbook.'

'So you're not concerned about the price of a stock or piece of real estate. You're more concerned with the operating fundamentals, the fundamentals that you can see with a financial statement?'

'Right,' said rich dad. 'That is why I got upset with your being

concerned about the prices on the stock market. While price is important, it is far from the most important thing in fundamental investing.
Price is more relevant in technical investing, but technical investing
is another lesson. Now do you understand why I had you do so many
personal financial statements and analyze businesses and real estate
investments?'

I nodded. 'I hated it at the time, but now I'm glad you had me do
so many of them. I realize now how much I think and analyze things
using mental photos of my financial statement and how what I do
with my money affects my financial statement. I did not realize that
most people do not think with the same photo references.'

## *The Magic Carpet*

'You are far ahead of the game,' said rich dad, 'the game of getting
rich. I have a term for the income statement and the balance sheet,
the two primary reports that make up financial statements: the magic
carpet.'

'Why do you call them the magic carpet?' I asked.

'Because they seem to magically take you behind the scenes into
any business, any piece of real estate, and any country in the world.
It is much like taking a diving mask and suddenly looking below the
surface of the water. The mask, symbolizing the financial statement,
lets you see clearly what is going on beneath the surface. Alternatively,
a financial statement is like having Superman's X-ray vision. Instead
of trying to jump over the tall building, a financially literate person
can see right through the building's concrete walls. Another reason I
call them the magic carpet is because they free you to see and do so
many things in so many parts of the world, all the while sitting at your
desk. You can invest in so many parts of the world or just in your
backyard with so much more knowledge and insight. Improving my
financial literacy ultimately reduces my risk and improves my investment returns. A financial statement lets me see what the average

investor cannot see. It also gives me control over my personal finances, and that allows me to go where I want to go in my life. Having control over financial statements also allows me to operate multiple businesses without being in the business physically. Truly understanding financial statements is one of the keys still necessary for an S quadrant person to move to the B quadrant. And that is why I call the income statement and balance sheet the magic carpet.'

## Mental Attitude Quiz

If we were going to buy a used car, we would probably want a mechanic to look it over and hook it up to an electronic analyzer before deciding if it was worth the asking price. If we were going to buy a house, we would ask a home inspector to go through a checklist and check out such things as the condition of the foundation, plumbing, electricity, roof, etc., before buying the house. If we were going to marry someone, we would probably want to know what was really going on beneath the pretty face before deciding to spend a lifetime with that pretty face.

Yet, when it comes to investing, most investors never read the financial statements of the company they are investing in. Most investors would rather invest on a hot tip or a low price or high price, depending upon the momentum of the market. Most people get their cars tuned up and checked out annually, or have an annual health physical, but most people have never have their financial statements analyzed for flaws or potential future problems. The reason is that most people leave school unaware of the importance of a financial statement, much less how to control one. Small wonder why so many people say investing is risky. Investing is not risky. But not being financially literate is.

## *How to See Investment Opportunities*

If you have plans on becoming rich by being an investor, I would say that having a good working knowledge of a financial statement is a minimum requirement. Not only will it improve your safety factor, it will also allow you to make much more money in a shorter period of time. The reason I say this is because being able to read a financial statement will allow you to see investment opportunities that the average investor misses. The average investor looks primarily to price as the opportunity to buy or sell. The sophisticated investor has trained his or her brain to see opportunities other than price. The sophisticated investor knows that most of the best investment opportunities are not visible to the untrained eye.

Rich dad taught me that you make the most money as an investor by being financially literate as well as knowing the internal strengths and weaknesses of the investment. He said, 'Where you find the best investment opportunities is from understanding accounting, the tax code, business law, and corporate law. And it is in these invisible realms where the real investors shop for the biggest investment bargains. That is why I call the income statement and balance sheet the magic carpet.'

**So the mental attitude question is:**

1.  If you plan to become wealthy as an investor and invest in the investments of the rich, are you willing to keep an updated personal financial statement and practice reading other financial statements on a regular basis?

    Yes _____ No _____

# *Financial Literacy*
# *Made Simple*

'Your dad struggles financially because he is word literate, but not financially literate,' rich dad often said to me. 'If he just took the time to learn how to read numbers and the vocabulary of money, his life would change dramatically.'

Financial literacy was one of rich dad's six lessons in *Rich Dad Poor Dad*. To rich dad, financial literacy was crucial for anyone who was sincere about being a business owner or a professional investor. In later sections of this book, Sharon and I will be going into greater detail on the importance of financial literacy as it pertains to business and investing, and how to find investment opportunities that the average investor misses. But for now, I think it best to quickly review financial literacy and how to make it simple and easier to understand.

## *The Basics*

A sophisticated investor should be able to read many different financial documents. At the center of all the documents are the income statement and the balance sheet.

Income Statement

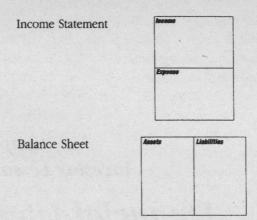

Balance Sheet

I am not an accountant, yet I have attended several classes on accounting. In most of those classes, what struck me was how the instructors focused on one of the documents, but not the relationship between the two documents. In other words, the instructors never explained why one document was important to the other.

Rich dad thought the relationship between the income statement and the balance sheet was everything. He would say, 'How can you understand one without the other?' or, 'How can you tell what an asset or liability really is without the income column or the expense column?' He would go on and say, 'Just because something is listed under the asset column does not make it an asset.' I think that statement was the single most important point he made. He would say, 'The reason most people suffer financially is because they purchase liabilities and list them under the asset column. That is why so many people call their home an asset when it is really a liability.' If you understand Gresham's Law, you may know why such a seemingly minor oversight can cause a lifetime of financial struggle instead of financial freedom. He would also say, 'If you want to be rich for generations, you and the ones you love must know the difference between an asset and a liability. You must know the difference between something of value and something of no value.'

After *Rich Dad Poor Dad* was published, many people asked, 'Is he saying that a person should not buy a house?' The answer to that question is 'No, he was not saying do not buy a house.' Rich dad was only emphasizing the importance of being financially literate. He was saying, 'Don't call a liability an asset, even though it is your house.' The next most asked question was, 'If I pay off the mortgage on my house, will that make it an asset?' Again, the answer in most cases is 'No, just because you have no debt on your home, it does not necessarily make it an asset.' The reason for that answer is again found in the term 'cash flow.' For most personal residences, even if you have no debt, there still are expenses and property taxes. In fact, you never truly own your real estate. Real estate will always belong to the government. That is why the word is 'real' (meaning 'royal' in Spanish), not physical or tangible. Property has always belonged to the royals. Today it belongs to the government. If you doubt that statement, just stop paying your property taxes and you will find out who really owns your property, with a mortgage or without a mortgage. The non-payment of property taxes is where tax-lien certificates come from. In *Rich Dad Poor Dad*, I wrote about the high interest that investors obtained from tax liens. Tax liens are the government's way of saying, 'You may control your real estate, but the government will always own it.'

Rich dad was very much in favor of home ownership. He thought that a home was a secure place to put your money but it was not necessarily an asset. In fact, once he had acquired enough real assets, he lived in a big beautiful home. Those real assets generated the cash flow that allowed him to buy his big beautiful home. The point he was making was that a person should not call a liability an asset, or buy liabilities that he or she thinks are assets. He thought that was one of the biggest mistakes a person could make. He would say, 'If something is a liability, you'd better call it a liability and watch it closely.'

## The Magic Words Are Cash Flow

To rich dad, the most important words in business and investing were cash flow. He would say, 'Just as a fisherman must watch the ebb and flow of the tides, an investor and businessperson must be keenly aware of the subtle shifts in cash flow. People and businesses struggle financially because they are out of control of their cash flow.'

## Financial Literacy for a Child

Rich dad may not have been formally educated but he had a way of taking complex subjects and making them simple enough for a 9-year-old child to understand, because that is how old I was when he began explaining these things to me, even though my wealth has increased. And I must confess that I have not progressed much beyond the simple line drawings rich dad drew for me. Yet rich dad's simple explanations allowed me to better understand money and its flow as well as guided me to a financially secure life.

Today, my accountants do the hard work and I continue to use rich dad's simple diagrams as my guides. So if you can understand the following diagrams, you have a better chance of acquiring great wealth. Leave the technical accounting work to the accountants who are trained to do such important work. Your job is to take control of your financial numbers and guide them to increasing your wealth.

## Rich Dad's Basics of Financial Literacy

**Literacy Lesson #1:** It is the direction of cash flowing that determines if something is an asset or a liability, at that moment. In other words, just because your real estate broker calls your house an asset does not mean it is an asset.

This is the cash flow pattern of an asset. Rich dad's definition of an asset was: 'An asset puts money in your pocket.'

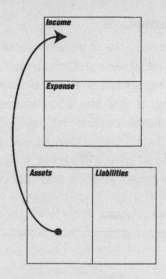

This is the cash flow pattern of a liability. Rich dad's definition of a liability was: 'A liability takes money from your pocket.'

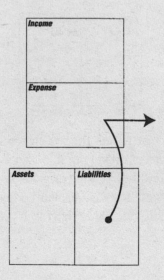

## A Point of Confusion

Rich dad also said to me, 'The confusion occurs because the accepted method of accounting allows us to list both assets and liabilities under the asset column.' He would then draw a diagram to explain what he had just said and say, 'This is why it is confusing.'

He would say, 'In this diagram, we have a $100,000 house that someone has put $20,000 cash down on and now has an $80,000 mortgage. How do you know if this house is an asset or a liability? Is the house an asset just because it is listed under the asset column?

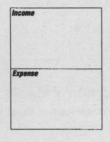

The answer of course is 'No.' The real answer is: 'You need to refer to the income statement to find out if it is an asset or a liability.'

Rich dad then drew the following diagram, saying, 'This is a house that is a liability. You can tell it is a liability because its only line items are under the expense column; nothing is in the income column.'

```
┌─────────────────────────┐
│ Income                  │
│                         │
│                         │
│                         │
├─────────────────────────┤
│ Expense                 │
│         Mortgage        │
│         Real estate taxes│
│         Insurance       │
│         Utilities       │
│         Maintenance     │
└─────────────────────────┘
┌────────────┬────────────┐
│ Asset      │ Liability  │
│ $100,000   │ $80,000    │
│            │            │
│            │            │
│            │            │
└────────────┴────────────┘
```

## Changing a Liability to an Asset

Rich dad then added to the diagram a line that read, 'Rental Income and Net Rental Income,' the key word being 'net.' 'That change to

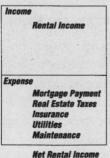

the financial statement changed this house from a liability to an asset.'

After understanding the concept, rich dad would add the numbers, just so I could understand the concept better. 'Let's say all the expenses associated with this house add up to $1,000. That includes, the mortgage payment, real estate taxes, insurance, utilities, and maintenance. And you now have a tenant paying you $1,200 a month. You now have a net rental income of $200.00 a month, which makes it an asset because this house is now putting money in your pocket, as verified by the $200.00 income. If your expenses stayed the same, and you collected only $800.00 a month in rent, you would now be losing $200.00, and even though you had gross rental income of $800.00 a month, the property would become a liability. So even with rental income, the property could still be a liability instead of an asset. And then I hear people say, "But if I sell it for more than I paid for it then it becomes an asset." Yes that would be true but only when that event occurs sometime in the future. And contrary to popular belief, the price of real estate does go down on occasion. So the saying "Don't count your chickens before they hatch," is a wise bit of financial wisdom.'

## *The Government Changed the Rules*

Literally billions of dollars were lost on real estate after the 1986 Tax Reform Act. So many speculators lost money because they were willing to buy high-priced real estate and lose money on the assumption that the price of real estate would always go up and the government would give them a tax break for their passive real estate losses. In other words, the government would subsidize the difference between rental income and rental expenses, which were higher. As they say, 'Someone changed the rules.' After the tax law change, the stock market crashed, savings and loans went broke, and a huge transfer of wealth occurred between 1987 and 1995. Investment property flowed from primarily the S quadrant – the high-income professionals, such as doctors, lawyers, accountants, engineers, and architects – to the investors in the I quadrant. That single tax law change forced millions of people out of investing in real estate and into the paper asset market known as the stock market. Could another transfer of wealth from one side of the Quadrant to the other be ready to occur soon? This time, could it be paper assets instead of real estate? Only time will tell, and history does tend to repeat itself. When it does repeat itself, some people will lose, but many others will win.

In Australia today, the government still has laws that allow investors to 'negatively gear' their investment real estate. In other words, you are encouraged to lose money on your rental real estate, with the idea of gaining a tax break from the government. We in the United States had the same tax rules until 1986. When I speak in Australia about investing, I often hear howls of protest about my warnings that the government could change the laws just as they did in the United States. I hear things such as 'The government won't change the rules,' and I just shake my head. They just don't realize how painful the law change was to millions of investors in the United States. Several of my friends had to declare bankruptcy and lost everything they had worked years or decades to acquire.

The point I make is: Why subject yourself to the risk? Why not find a property that makes money? Any person can find a property or investment that loses money. You don't have to look too far to find an investment that loses money. You don't have to be smart or financially literate to find an investment that loses money. The problem I have and rich dad had with the idea that losing money was a good idea because of the tax breaks was that such ideas often caused people to be sloppy. I often hear people say even here in America, 'It's OK that I am losing money. The government gives me a tax break for losing money.' That means for every dollar you lose, the government gives you back approximately 30 cents (depending on your tax bracket). To me, there is something missing in that logic. Why not invest so you can have it all, which is security, income, appreciation, and tax breaks?

The idea behind investing is to make money, not to lose money. You can still gain many tax breaks and make money if you are a sophisticated investor. A friend of mine, Michael Tellarico, a real estate broker in Sydney, Australia, says, 'People come into this real estate office every day and say, "My accountant told me to come in here and look for property that I can negatively gear."' In other words, my accountant told me to buy a property to lose money on. Michael then says, 'You don't need my help to find a property that loses money. There are thousands of them all around you. What I can help you find is a property that will make you money and you will still get your tax breaks.' The reply often is, 'No. No. I want to find a property to lose money on.' The same thing was going on in America just before 1986.

There are several important lessons from this example:

1.  The idea that losing money is OK because of tax breaks often causes people to become sloppy in choosing investments.

2.  These people do not look as hard for real investments. They do not look at the financials as closely when analyzing an investment.

3.  Losing money destabilizes your financial position. In other words, there is enough risk involved with investing as it is. Why make it any more risky? Take the extra time and look for solid investments. You can find them if you can read the numbers.

4.  The government does change the rules.

5.  What might be an asset today could be a liability tomorrow.

6.  While millions of investors lost money in 1986, there were other investors that were prepared for the change. Those who were prepared made the millions that the unprepared investors lost.

## *The Biggest Risk of All*

Rich dad said, 'The riskiest investor of all is a person who is out of control of his or her personal financial statement. The riskiest of all investors are those who have nothing but liabilities they think are assets, have as much in expenses as they have in income, and whose only source of income is their labor. They are risky because they are often desperate investors.'

In my investment classes, I still have people come up to me and argue that their home is an asset. Recently one man said, 'I bought my house for $500,000 and today it's worth $750,000.' I then asked him, 'How do you know that?' His reply was, 'Because that is what my real estate broker said it was worth.'

To which I asked, 'Will your broker guarantee you that price for 20 years?'

'Why no,' he said. 'He just said that was the comparable average price of houses in the neighborhood being sold today.'

And that is exactly why my rich dad said the average investor does not make much money in the market. Rich dad said, 'The average investor has the count your chickens before they hatch mentality. They buy items that cost them money each month, yet call them assets based upon opinions. They count on their house going up in value in the future, or they act like their house can be sold immediately for what their real estate broker told them it is worth. Have you ever ended up selling your home for less than what your broker, or banker thought it was worth? I have. As a result of basing financial decisions on these opinions and expectations, people lose control over their personal finances. That to me is very risky. If you want to be rich, you must take control over your education as well as your personal cash flow. There is nothing wrong with hoping the price of something goes up in the future as long as you do not lose control of your finances today.' He would also say, 'If you're so certain the price is going up why not buy 10 of those houses?'

This mentality also applies to people who say, 'My retirement account is worth $1 million today. It will be worth $3 million when I retire.' Again, I would ask, 'How do you know that?' What I learned from my rich dad was that the average investor often 'Counts their chickens before they hatch.' Or they bet everything on one event which means they literally 'Wait for their ship to come in,' sometime in the future. In most cases, many eggs do hatch and most ships do eventually come in. Yet the professional investor does not want to take that chance. The sophisticated investor knows that being financially educated gives you more control today and if you keep studying, greater financial control tomorrow. The sophisticated investor knows that sometimes eggs get eaten or stepped on and sometimes the ship people are waiting for is the *Titanic*.

I meet many investors who are new to the world of investing. They have been investing for less than 20 years. Most have never been through a market crash or owned real estate worth much less than they paid for it where they still must make the monthly payments. These new investors come up to me and spout off industry averages such as, 'The market on average has been going up since 1974.' Or 'Real estate over time has averaged over 4% per year for the last 20 years.'

As rich dad said, 'Averages are for average investors. A professional investor wants controls. And that control begins with yourself, your financial education, your sources of information, and your own cash flow.' That is why rich dad's advice to the average investor was, 'Don't be average.' To him being an average investor was being a risky investor.

## *Why People Don't Have Control Over Their Personal Finances*

People leave school not even knowing how to balance a checkbook much less how to prepare a financial statement. They never learned how to control their finances. And the only way you can tell if people are in control of themselves is by looking at their financial statements. Just because people have high-paying jobs, big houses, and nice cars does not necessarily mean they are in control financially. If people knew how a financial statement worked, they would be more financially literate and more in control of their money. By understanding financial statements, people can better see how their cash is flowing.

For example, this is the cash flow pattern of writing a check:

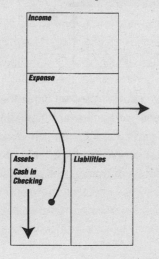

This is the cash flow pattern of using a credit card:

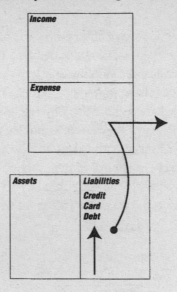

When people write checks, they are depleting an asset. And when people use their credit cards, they are increasing their liabilities. In other words, credit cards make it so much easier to get deeper and deeper into debt. Most people cannot see it happening to them simply because they have not been trained to fill out and analyze a personal financial statement.

Today, many individuals' financial statements look like this:

| Income | |
|---|---|
|    Paycheck | |

| Expense | |
|---|---|
|    Taxes | |
|    Mortgage payment | |
|    Real estate taxes | |
|    Car payment | |
|    School loan payment | |
|    Credit card payment | |
|    Food | |
|    Clothing | |
|    Other expenses | |

| Asset | Liability |
|---|---|
| | Mortgage |
| | School Loans |
| | Car loan |
| | Credit Card |
| |    Balances |

Unless something changes inside this person, chances are that this person will live a life of financial servitude. Why do I say financial servitude? Because each payment this person makes is making a rich person richer.

*AUTHOR'S NOTE: Many people ask me: 'What is my first step to financial freedom?' My response is, 'Take control of your financial statement.' I asked my tax strategist and accountant, Diane Kennedy, to put together an audiotape program and workbook to:*

*1. Learn how a personal financial statement works*

*2. Take control of your own financial statement*

*3. Get on track to become financially free*

*4. Learn how to manage money like the rich do by paying less in taxes*

*Diane and I produced these tapes, and we walk you through the process of getting out of debt. More importantly, however, you will learn how to manage your money like the rich do. This is important because most people think that making more money will*

*solve their money problems. In most instances, it does not.*
*Learning to manage the money you do have like a rich person*
*does is how you can solve your short-term money problems. Doing*
*so also gives you the opportunity to possibly become financially*
*free. The audiotape set and workbook are contained in a program*
*titled 'Your First Step to Financial Freedom.' The information*
*found in this educational package is simple, easy to understand,*
*and essential to start building a strong financial foundation. You*
*can find out more information about this audiotape package in*
*the back of this book or from our website at www.richdad.com.*

## Who Are You Making Rich?

**Literacy Lesson #2:** It takes at least two financial statements to see
the entire picture.

Rich dad said, 'Sophisticated investors must see at least two financial statements simultaneously if they want a true picture.'

During one of my lessons, rich dad drew this diagram:

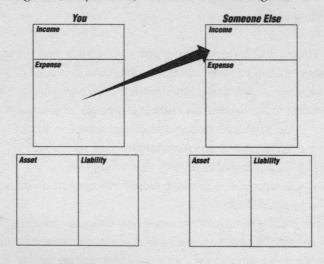

'Always remember that your expense is someone else's income.

People who are out of control of their cash flow make the people who are in control of their cash flow rich.'

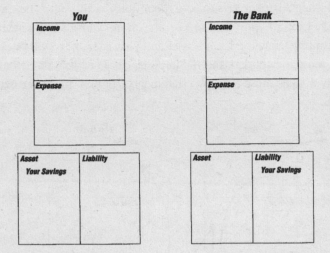

## *What an Investor Does*

He then drew this diagram, saying, 'Let me show you what an investor does, using a home owner and banker as an example':

I sat there looking at the diagram for a moment and then said, 'The person's mortgage appears on two financial statements. The difference is that this same mortgage appears under two columns: the asset column and the liability column.'

Rich dad nodded. 'Now you are seeing a true financial statement.'

'That is why you say it takes at least two different financial statements to see the entire picture,' I added. 'For every one of your expenses, it is someone else's income, and each one of your liabilities is someone else's asset.'

Rich dad nodded, saying, 'And that is why people leaving school who have not been trained to think in terms of financial statements often fall prey to those who do. That is why each time people use their credit card, they are actually adding to their own liability column and simultaneously adding to the bank's asset column.'

'And when a banker says to you, "Your home is an asset," they are not really lying to you. They're just not saying whose asset it really is. Your mortgage is the bank's asset and your liability,' I said, beginning to more fully understand the importance of financial statements and why it takes more than two statements to gain a more accurate picture.

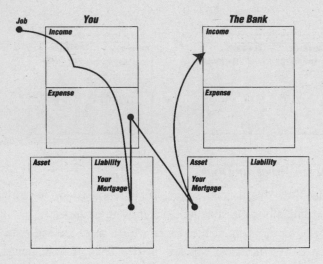

Rich dad nodded and said, 'Now let's add cash flow to this picture and we begin to see how an asset, in this example a mortgage, really works:

'In this example, the mortgage takes money from your pocket and puts it in the bank's pocket. That is why the mortgage is a liability to you and an asset to the bank. The point I am making is that it is the same legal document.'

'So the bank has created an asset that for you is a liability,' I added. 'What an investor does is acquire an asset that someone else pays for. That is why investors own apartment houses. Every month, cash flows into the investors' income statements from the rent, just as their mortgage payments flow into the bank's income statement.'

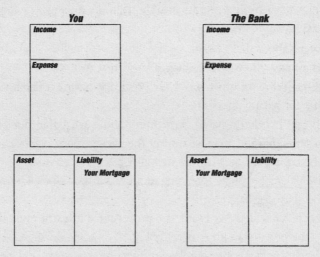

Rich dad nodded and grinned. 'You're beginning to get it. You definitely want to be on one side of the equation more than the other. But it is a two-way street,' he said.

'Oh,' I said. 'My savings are my asset and the bank's liability. Again, it takes a minimum of two financial statements to see the complete picture.'

'Yes,' said rich dad. 'And what else do you notice about these diagrams?'

I stared at the diagrams for a while, looking at the examples of the mortgage and the savings. 'I don't know,' I said slowly. 'I just see what you have drawn there.'

Rich dad smiled and said, 'This is why you need to practice reading financial statements. Just as you learn more the second and third time you read or listen to someone, you learn more and more the more you practice being financially literate. More things come into your mind that your eyes often miss.'

'So what have I missed? What have I not seen?' I asked.

'What is not visible from my diagrams is that the government gives you a tax incentive to acquire liabilities. That is why it gives you a tax break for buying a house.'

'I forgot about that,' I said.

'And it taxes you for your savings,' said rich dad.

'The government gives me a tax break for having a liability and taxes me for having an asset?' I asked.

Rich dad nodded, saying, 'Now think about what that does to a person's thinking and financial future. The average person gets excited about being in debt and not excited about acquiring assets.'

'People get a tax break for losing money?' I asked in bewilderment. 'Why do they do that?'

Rich dad chuckled, 'As I said, the professional investor must think beyond the price of an investment going up or going down. A sophisticated investor reads the numbers to get the true story and begins to see things that the average investor does not see. A sophisticated investor must see the impact of government regulations, tax codes, corporate law, business law, and accounting law. One reason it is hard to find accurate investment information is that to gain a full picture requires financial literacy, an accountant, and an attorney. In other words, you needed two different professionals to get the real picture. The good news is that if you take your time and invest the time to learn the ins and outs of what goes on behind the scenes, you will find investment opportunities and great wealth, wealth that very few people ever find. You will find out the truth about why the rich get richer, and the poor and middle class work harder, pay more in taxes, and get deeper in debt. Once you know the truths, you can then decide which side of the Quadrant you want to operate from. It's not hard; it just takes some time . . . time that people who just want a hot investment tip do not want to invest.'

I did not have to think about which side of the Quadrant I wanted to operate from. I knew I wanted to invest legally from the inside, not the outside. I wanted to know what the truths were, regardless of if I became rich or not. I now wanted to know how and why the rich got richer.

## *The Need for Financial Education*

In the early 1980s, I began teaching entrepreneurship and investing to adults as a hobby. One of the problems I ran into immediately was that most people who wanted to start businesses or invest with greater confidence lacked the basics of financial literacy. I believe that this lack of financial education is why nine out of ten new businesses fail in the first five years, and why most investors think investing is risky and do not make or keep much money.

When I recommended that people take classes in accounting, finance, and investing before starting a business or investing, most groaned and did not want to go back to school. That is when I began to search for a way that individuals could gain the basic knowledge in an easy and fun way. In 1996, I created *CASHFLOW, Investing 101*, a game that teaches the basics of financial literacy, accounting, and investing.

## *Teaching Versus Learning*

*CASHFLOW* is a board game because investing and financial analysis are subjects that you cannot learn by reading. My poor dad the schoolteacher often said, 'A teacher must know the difference between what can be taught and what must be learned.' He would go on to say, 'You can teach a child to memorize the word "bicycle" but you cannot teach a child to ride one. A child needs to learn how to ride a bicycle by doing.'

In the past three years, I have observed thousands of people learning to be investors by playing *CASHFLOW, Investing 101* and *202*. They learn by doing things I could never teach by writing or by lecturing, just as I could never teach you to ride a bicycle. The games teach in a few hours what my rich dad took 30 years guiding me to learn. And that is why this book is titled *Rich Dad's Guide to Investing* because that is what he did. He guided me because that was the best he could do. Investing and accounting are subjects that he could not teach me. I had to want to learn. The same is true for you.

## *Improving Your Results*

The more you read financial statements, annual reports, and prospectuses, the more your financial intelligence, or financial vision, increases. Over time you will begin to see things that the average investor never sees.

We all know that repetition is how we really learn and retain what we learn. Recently, I was listening to an audiotape of an interview of Peter Lynch. I had listened to that audiotape a dozen times before. Each time I listen to it, I hear something new. For over 30 years, rich dad had me review financial statements. Today, I think automatically in financial statements.

When we learn to ride a bicycle, we train our subconscious mind to ride our bike. Once that is done, we don't have to think or remember how to ride a bike as we ride. When we learn to drive a car, we also train our subconscious mind. And that is why, once we have trained our subconscious mind to drive, we can drive and talk to someone else, eat a hamburger, think about problems at work, or listen to the radio and sing along. Driving is (hopefully) automatically handled. The same can happen with reading financial statements.

What takes the longest time in finding a good investment is analyzing the numbers. Learning to read financial statements is a tedious process, especially when you first begin to learn. The good news is that it gets easier and faster as you practice. Not only does it get easier, but you can also review many more investment opportunities almost automatically without thinking . . . just like riding a bike, or driving a car.

## *Mental Attitude Quiz*

We as humans learn to do many things subconsciously. If you are serious about becoming a more successful investor, an investor who makes more money with less and less risk, I recommend training your brain to analyze financial statements. Analyzing financial statements is basic to the world's best fundamental investors, investors such as Warren Buffet.

The way this is done is by a term called 'deal flow.' Every professional investor has a continuous number of potential business or real estate investments that need investment capital. Rich dad had Mike and me read, study, and analyze these investments regardless of if we were interested in them or not. Even though it was slow and painful at first, over the years, the process became faster, easier, more fun, and more exciting. So we learned by repetition, and that repetition has paid off by allowing me to retire early, feel more financially secure, and make even more money.

**So the mental attitude question is:**

Are you willing to practice filling out your own financial statement and keep it up to date as well as read those of other business and real estate investment financial statements?

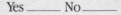

Yes _____ No _____

You will note that it is very similar to the question at the end of Chapter 15. It is repeated to emphasize the importance of financial literacy. This question is very important because one of the costs of becoming a rich investor and investing in investments of the rich is the price of investing time in continual improvement of your own financial literacy. If your answer is 'No' to this question, then most of the investments that the rich invest in are far too risky for you. If you are financially literate, then you will be better prepared to find the very best investments in the world.

# *The Magic of Mistakes*

My real dad came from the world of academics, a world where mistakes are perceived as bad and to be avoided. In the world of education, the more mistakes a person makes, the less intelligent that person is thought to be.

My rich dad came from the streets. He had a different view on mistakes. To him, mistakes were opportunities to learn something new, something he did not know before. To him, the more mistakes a person made, the more the person learned. He often said, 'There is a bit of magic hidden in every mistake. So the more mistakes I make and I take the time to learn from, the more magic I have in my life.'

My rich dad constantly used the example of learning to ride a bicycle to reinforce the idea of the magic found inside of mistakes. He would say, 'Just remember the frustration you went through as you struggled to learn how to ride a bicycle. All your friends are riding but all you are doing is climbing on the bike and immediately falling off. You make mistake after mistake. Then suddenly, you stop falling off, you begin to pedal, the bike begins rolling, and then suddenly like magic, a whole new world opens to you. That is the magic found in mistakes.'

## Warren Buffet's Mistake

Warren Buffet, America's richest investor, is known and respected for his company Berkshire Hathaway. Today, Berkshire Hathaway's share price is one of the highest priced company shares in the world. While many investors value Berkshire Hathaway's stock, few people realize that acquiring Berkshire Hathaway was one of Warren Buffet's biggest investment mistakes.

When he acquired the company, Berkshire Hathaway was a shirt-manufacturing company that was slowly going out of business. Warren Buffet thought his team could turn the company around. Well as most of us know, textile manufacturing was dying in America and moving to other countries. It was a trend that even Warren Buffet could not go against, and the company eventually failed as a manufacturing company, even with Warren Buffet behind it. Yet, inside of this company failure, Warren Buffet found the gems that ultimately made him extremely rich. For those who are interested in this story, the book *The Warren Buffet Way*, by Robert Hagstrom, is most enlightening, giving the reader insights into one of the greatest investor minds in the world.

## Other Mistakes

Another company, Diamond Fields, was formed to look for diamonds, which were never found. The company's head geologist had made a mistake. Yet, instead of finding diamonds, they struck one of the largest nickel deposits in the world. Their stock price soared upon the discovery. Today, although the name remains Diamond Fields, they make their money in nickel.

Levi Strauss headed for the gold fields of California to strike it rich in mining. However, he was not a good miner, so he instead began sewing pants out of canvas for the miners who were successful. Today, I think most of the world has heard of Levi's jeans.

It is said that Thomas Edison would never have invented the light bulb if he had been an employee for the company he ultimately founded – General Electric. It is said that Edison failed over 10,000 times before finally inventing the light bulb. If he had been an employee of a major corporation, he would most likely have been fired for making so many mistakes.

Christopher Columbus's big mistake was that he was looking for a trade route to China and accidentally bumped into America, the richest, most powerful country in the world.

## Street Smarts Versus School Smarts

My rich dad was so very successful financially for many reasons. At the top of the list was his attitude towards making mistakes. Like most of us, he hated making them, yet he was not afraid of making them. He would take risks simply to make a mistake. He would say, 'When you come to the boundaries of what you know, it's time to make some mistakes.'

Several times, one of his businesses failed to get off the ground and he lost money. I have also seen him launch a new product only to have it be rejected by the marketplace. Yet each time he made a mistake, instead of being depressed, he often seemed happier, wiser, more determined, and even richer from the experience. He would say to his son and me, 'Mistakes are how we learn. Every time I make a mistake, I always learn something about myself, I learn something new, and I often meet new people I would never have met.'

In one of his failed ventures, a plumbing distribution company, he met one of his future business partners. And from that failed plumbing business, they formed a friendship and partnership that went on to make tens of millions of dollars. He said, 'If I had not taken the risk to form that business, I would never have met Jerry. And meeting Jerry is one of the most important events in my life.'

My poor dad was an excellent student in school. He rarely made mistakes, which was why he had such high grades. The problem was that at age 50, he seemed to have made one of the biggest mistakes in his life and he could not recover from it.

As I watched my real dad struggle financially and professionally, my rich dad said, 'To be successful in the real world of business, you have to be school smart as well as street smart. Your dad entered school at the age of 5. Because he had good grades, he stayed in school, eventually becoming the top man in the school system. Now at age 50, he is hitting the streets . . . and the streets are a very tough teacher. In school, you're given the lesson first. On the street, you're given the mistake first and then it's up to you to find the lesson, if you ever find it. Since most people have not been taught how to make mistakes and learn from them, they either avoid mistakes altogether, which is a bigger mistake, or they make a mistake but fail to find the lesson from the mistake. That is why you see so many people making the same mistake over and over again. They make the same mistake over and over again because they have never been taught how to learn from their mistakes. In school, you are considered smart if you don't make mistakes. On the street, you're smart only if you make mistakes and learn from them.'

### The Biggest Failure I Know

Rich dad said to Mike and me, 'I am so rich because I've made more financial mistakes than most people. Each time I made a mistake, I learned something new. In the business world, that something new is often called "experience." But experience is not enough. Many people say they have a lot of experience because they keep making the same mistake over and over again. If a person truly learns from a mistake, his or her life changes forever, and what that person gains instead of experience is "wisdom."' He went on to say, 'People often avoid making financial mistakes, and that is a mistake. They keep saying to themselves, "Play it safe. Don't take risks." People may be struggling financially because they have already made mistakes and have not learned from the mistakes. So they get up every day, go to work, and repeat the mistake and avoid new mistakes, but they never find the lesson. These people often say to themselves, "I'm doing everything right, but for some reason, I'm not getting ahead financially."' Rich dad's comment to that statement was, 'They may be doing all the right things but the problem is that they are avoiding the wrong things – wrong things such as taking more risks. They are avoiding their weaknesses instead of confronting them. They are not doing something they may be afraid of doing, and consciously choosing to avoid making a mistake rather than make one.' He also said, 'Some of the biggest failures I know are people who have never failed.'

### The Art of Making a Mistake

Instead of instructing his son and me to avoid mistakes, rich dad taught us the art of making a mistake and gaining wisdom from it.

During one of those lessons, rich dad said, 'The first thing that happens after you make a mistake is that you become upset. Everyone I know gets upset. That is the first indication of a mistake,' said rich dad. 'At this point of upset, you find out who you really are.'

'What do you mean, "Who you really are?"' asked Mike.

'Well at a moment of upset, we become one of these characters,' rich dad said, going on to describe the cast of characters who are brought to center stage when upsets from mistakes occur:

1. **The Liar.** The liar will say such things as: 'I didn't do that.' Or 'No, no, no. It wasn't me.' Or 'I don't know how that happened.' Or 'Prove it.'
2. **The Blamer.** The blamer will say such things as: 'It's your fault, not mine.' Or 'If my wife didn't spend so much money, I would be better off financially.' Or 'I would be rich if I didn't have you kids.' Or 'The customers just don't care about my products.' Or 'Employees just aren't loyal anymore.' Or 'You weren't clear in your instructions.' Or 'It's my boss's fault.'

3.  **The Justifier.** The justifier says things such as: 'Well, I don't have a good education so that is why I don't get ahead.' Or 'I would have made it if I had had more time.' Or 'Oh, I really didn't want to be rich anyway.' Or 'Well, everyone else was doing it.'

4.  **The Quitter.** The quitter says things such as: 'I told you that it would never work.' Or 'This is too hard and it's not worth it. I'm going to do something else easier.' Or 'Why am I doing this? I don't need this hassle.'

5.  **The Denier.** Rich dad often called this person 'the cat in the litter box,' which means this person tends to bury his or her mistakes. The person who denies that he or she has made a mistake often says things such as: 'No, there is nothing wrong. Things are fine.' Or 'Mistake? What mistake?' Or 'Don't worry. Things will work out.'

Rich dad said, 'When people are upset due to a mistake or accident, one or more of these characters will take over their mind and body. If you want to learn and gain wisdom from this priceless mistake, you have to let The Responsible You eventually take control of your thinking. The Responsible You will eventually say, 'What priceless lesson can I learn from this mistake?'

Rich dad went on to say, 'If a person says, "What I learned is that I'll never do this again," he or she probably has not learned much. Too many people live in a diminishing world because they continue to say, "I'll never do that again" instead of saying, "I'm glad that happened because I learned this or that from the experience." Besides, people who avoid mistakes or waste mistakes never see the other side of the coin.'

## *I Slept Like a Baby*

For example, after I lost my nylon and Velcro wallet business, I was upset for about a year. I slept like a baby during that year, which meant

I woke up crying every two hours. I could hear my mind saying, 'I should never have started the business. I knew it would fail. I'll never start a business again.' I also blamed a lot of people and found myself justifying my actions a lot, saying things such as, 'It was Dan's fault' and 'Well, I didn't really love the product.'

Instead of run from my mistake and get a job, rich dad had me face the mess I had made and begin to work my way out from under the pile of rubble that was once my business. Today, I say to people, 'I learned more about business by failing than I ever did by being successful. Working through the wreckage and rebuilding the company made me a much better businessman.' Today, instead of saying, 'I'll never do that again,' I say, 'I'm glad I did fail and learn because I am grateful for the wisdom I gained.' And then I say, 'Let's start another business.' Instead of fear and resentment, there is excitement and fun. Instead of being afraid of failing, I now know that making mistakes is the way we were all designed to learn. If we fail to make mistakes, or make them and do not learn from them, the magic goes out of life. Life goes backward and gets smaller, instead of expansive and filled with magic.

I failed in high school twice because I could not write. To have my books on bestseller lists such as those of *The New York Times*, *Sydney Morning Herald*, and *The Wall Street Journal* is magical. It is ironic that I am well known for subjects I initially failed at: writing, business, selling, speaking, accounting, and investing. I am not known for the subjects that were easy and enjoyable for me: surfing, economics, rugby, and painting.

## *What Is the Lesson?*

Whenever I hear people saying, 'Investing is too risky' or 'I don't like taking risks with my money' or 'What if I fail?' or 'What if I lose my money?' I am often reminded of my poor dad because what he was really saying was 'I don't want to make a mistake.' As I said, in his world, the world of academics, people who made mistakes were considered stupid.

In rich dad's world, he viewed risk, mistakes, and failure as an integral part of human development. So instead of avoiding risk and mistakes, he learned to manage risk and mistakes. His view on mistakes was that a mistake was simply a lesson with emotions attached to it. He said, 'Whenever we make a mistake, we become upset. An upset is our maker's way of telling us that we need to learn something. It is a tap on our shoulder saying, "Pay attention. You have something important to learn. If you lie, blame, justify, or deny the upset, you waste the upset and will waste a precious gem of wisdom."'

Rich dad taught me to count to ten if I was angry or to a hundred if I was very angry. After cooling off, I simply say, 'I apologize' and never blame the other person, no matter how angry I am. If I blame, I give power to the other person. If I take responsibility for whatever happened, I will learn a precious lesson that I obviously needed to learn. If I lie, blame, justify, or deny, I learn nothing.

Rich dad also said, 'Unsuccessful people blame the other person. They often want the other person to change, and that is why they stay upset for so long. They are upset because they fail to learn their personal lesson. Instead of being upset, such people should be grateful for the other person being there to teach them something they needed to learn.

'People come together to teach each other lessons. The problem is, we often do not know what lesson we are teaching. To be upset or hold a grudge against the other person is like being upset with your bicycle because you fell off once or twice while trying to learn something new,' rich dad would say.

## Mistakes Today

As I write, the stock market and real estate markets are climbing. Individuals who have never invested before are climbing into the market, most saying the same things. They say things like, 'I have made so much money in the market.' Or 'I'm in early and the price has gone up 20%.' Those are often enthusiastic words of new investors, investors who have never lost in a down market. I am afraid that in a short while, many of these new investors who are now winning will find out what it feels like to make a mistake in the market. At that moment, we will see who the real investors are. As rich dad said, 'It's not how much your investment goes up that matters, it's how much it can come down that is most important. Real investors must be prepared to profit as well as learn when things do not go as they want them to in the market. The best thing a market can teach you is how to learn from your mistakes.'

For me, learning to control my temper has been a lifelong process. So has the process of being willing to take risks, make mistakes, and be grateful for the other person – even though I may no longer speak to or do business with that person. When I reflect back on my life, I would say that it is this mental attitude that has made me the most money, has brought me the most success, and has ultimately allowed me to have the most magic in my life.

## *Mental Attitude Quiz*

I learned from both dads that both school smarts and street smarts are important. Being intelligent is recognizing the differences between the two, or as rich dad said, 'School smarts are important but street smarts make you rich.'

### So the mental attitude questions are:

1. What are your attitudes to risk, making mistakes, and learning?

2. What are the attitudes of the people around you to risk, making mistakes, and learning?

3. Are there still some financial, professional, or business upsets that remain unresolved?

4.   Are you still angry with someone else in regards to money?

5.   And if you are upset with someone else or yourself, what lesson can you learn and be grateful for because you were courageous enough to have taken a risk and maybe learned something?

I always remember my rich dad saying, 'I have so much money because I was willing to make more mistakes than most people and learn from them. Most people have not made enough mistakes or continue to make the same mistakes over and over again. Without mistakes and learning, there is no magic in life.'

**ADDITIONAL NOTE:**
This subject of the magic of mistakes is one of rich dad's most important lessons, especially in this brave new world we enter. It is the people who fear mistakes who will be left behind financially and professionally as the Information Age continues to pick up speed.

— *I recently created an educational program on audiotape with Nightingale Conant titled 'Rich Dad Secrets to Money, Business, and Investing,' which covers this very important lesson from rich dad. In my opinion, this educational product is for anyone wanting to learn how to overcome the fear of failing, the fear of making mistakes, or the fear of taking risks.*

*If you are interested in this product, you may order it from us or directly from Nightingale Conant. As Winston Churchill said, 'Success is the ability to go from one failure to another with no loss of enthusiasm.'*

# Chapter 18
## Investor Lesson #16:

# What Is the Price of Becoming Rich?

Rich dad would tell me that there are many ways a person can become rich, and each one has a price.

1. **You can become rich by marrying someone for his or her money.** And we all know what that price is. Rich dad would scrunch up his face and say, 'Both men and women marry for money, but can you imagine spending your life with someone you don't love? That is a very high price.'

2. **You can become rich by being a crook, a cheat, or an outlaw.** He would say, 'It is so easy to become rich legally. Why would people want to break the law and risk going to jail unless they really enjoyed the thrill of it all? To risk going to jail is much too high a price for me. I want to be rich for my freedom, so why risk going to jail? I would lose my self-respect. I could not face my family and friends if I were doing something illegal. Besides, I am a bad liar. I have a poor memory,

and I could not keep track of all my lies, so it is best to just tell the truth. In my opinion, honesty is the best policy.'

3. **You can become rich through inheritance.** Rich dad would say, 'Mike often feels like he did not earn his keep. He wonders if he could have become rich on his own. I have therefore given him very little. I have guided him as I guide you, but it is up to him to create his own wealth. It is important for him to feel he has earned it. Not everyone fortunate enough to inherit money feels that way.'

As Mike and I had grown up together, both our familes were relatively poor. By the time we were adults, however, Mike's dad had become very rich, while my real dad was still poor. Mike stood to inherit a fortune from his dad, the man I call my rich dad. I was starting with nothing.

4. **You can become rich by winning the lottery.** All rich dad could say to that was, 'It's OK to buy a ticket now and then, but to bet your financial life on winning the lottery is a fool's plan on becoming rich.'

Unfortunately, winning the lottery is how many Americans say they plan on becoming rich. Living your life with odds of one in a hundred million is a very high price to pay.

And if you do not have a plan on how to handle the problem of too much money, you will go back to being poor. Recently, there was a story in the paper of a man who won the lottery. He had a great time but was soon so deeply in debt that he considered filing bankruptcy. He was doing fine financially before he won the lottery. So to solve his problem, he went out and played the lottery again – and won. This time, he has financial advisors helping him with his money. So the moral of the story is: If you win the lottery once have a plan for the money. Not too many people win it twice.

5.  **You can become rich by being a movie star, a rock star, a sports star, or someone outstanding in one field or another.** Rich dad would say, 'I am not smart, talented, good looking, or entertaining. So becoming rich by being outstanding is not realistic for me.'

    Hollywood is filled with actors who are broke. Clubs are filled with rock bands dreaming of cutting a gold record. The golf courses are filled with golfers dreaming of becoming a pro like Tiger Woods. However, if you look closely at Tiger Woods, you will notice that he paid a high price to get to where he is today. Tiger started playing golf at the age of 3 and did not turn pro until he was 20. His price was 17 years of practice.

6.  **You can become rich by being greedy.** The world is filled with people like this. Their favorite saying is: 'I got mine and I am going to keep it.' Greedy with their money and assets usually means they are also tight with other things. When asked to help other people, or to teach other people, they often do not have the time.

    The price for being greedy is that you have to work even harder to keep what you want. Newton's Law states, 'For every action there is a reaction.' If you're greedy, people will respond to you in kind.

    When I meet people who are having a tough time with money, I ask them to start giving money away on a regular basis – to their church or favorite charity. Following the laws of economics and physics, give what you want. If you want a smile, first give a smile. If you want a punch, first throw a punch. If you want

money, first give some money. For greedy people, opening up
their fist or wallet can be very hard to do.

7. **You can become rich by being cheap.** This is the one that
set rich dad's blood boiling. He said, 'The problem with
becoming rich by being cheap is that you are still cheap. The
world hates rich people who are cheap. That is why people
hated the character Scrooge in Charles Dickens' famous story,
"A Christmas Carol."' Rich dad would say, 'It is people who
become rich like Scrooge that give the rich a bad name. To
live poor and die poor is a tragedy. But to live poor and die
rich is insanity.'

After he calmed down, he would say, 'I think money is meant
to be enjoyed, so I work hard, my money works hard, and I
enjoy the fruits of our labor.'

## *Affording the Good Life*

A recent article reinforces my rich dad's point of view. The article,
'Affording the Good Life in an Age of Change,' was in the *Strategic
Investment Newsletter*, published by James Dale Davidson and Lord
William Rees-Mogg. These two men have also co-authored several
best-selling books: *Blood in the Streets*, *The Great Reckoning*, and
*The Sovereign Individual*. These books have dramatically affected the
way I invest and how I look to the future. Davidson is the founder of
the National Taxpayers Union, and Rees-Mogg is a financial advisor to
some of the world's wealthiest investors, a former editor of *The Times*
of London, and vice-chairman of the British Broadcasting Corporation.

My rich dad would say, 'There are two ways to become rich. One
way is to earn more. The other way is to desire less. The problem is
that most people are not good with either way.' The article and this
book are about how you can earn more so you can desire more. Here
are excerpts from the article 'Affording the Good Life in an Age of
Change' as published in the *Strategic Investment Newsletter*.

> *'Being frugal is the cornerstone of wealth-building.'*
> *Thomas J. Stanley & William Danko*
> *The Millionaire Next Door 1996*

This reminds me of my complaint with the reasoning of the popular books, such as *The Millionaire Next Door*, by Stanley and Danko, and *Getting Rich In America: 8 Simple Rules for Building a Fortune and a Satisfying Life* by my friend Dwight Lee. Both books define success downward by suggesting that anyone who lives an abstemious lifestyle and pinches pennies will become 'rich.' . . .

Yes. If you never earn more than $50,000 a year, you may become a millionaire by pinching pennies. But there is a limit to the amount of wealth you can acquire by living as though you were poor. Even eating Spam or canned spaghetti from Chef Boyardee at every meal would not save enough money to make you a multimillionaire. This helps explain why only one-in-10 millionaires reaches a net worth of $5 million . . . Simply penny pinching, per se, is only a preliminary step that would permit someone without inherited capital or a significant annual cash flow to make the kind of investment that would lead to riches. For Americans, becoming a 'millionaire' is a necessary step to allow you to participate as an 'accredited investor' in private placements for private, high growth companies. This is the main route to riches. I was a millionaire in my early 20s. But I quickly recognized even then that a few millions did not amount to much. I could not afford my preferred lifestyle on such a small fortune.

. . . My conclusion is that the best way to make real money is to undertake private stage investments in private companies.

'Affording the Good Life in an Age of Change' discusses why being cheap is not a way to really become wealthy. Davidson's point is that while it is possible to become rich by being cheap, there is a huge price to pay. In fact, there are many prices to pay. One such price is that being cheap and scrimping money will get you only so far. Being cheap does not necessarily mean that you have the competence to become richer. All you know how to do is to be cheap, and that is an expensive price to pay.

Davidson disagrees and I disagree with the popularity of ideas such as cut up your credit cards and live below your means. That may be a good idea for some people, but it is not my idea of becoming rich and enjoying the bounties of the good life.

### The Importance of Being Frugal

In contrast to Davidson's article, however, I did enjoy *The Millionaire Next Door*. It makes many fundamental points about frugality. There are differences between being cheap and frugal. Rich dad was more concerned with being frugal than being cheap. He said, 'If you want to be really rich, you need to know when to be frugal and when to be a spendthrift. The problem is that too many people know how to be cheap only. That is like having only one leg to walk on.'

### A Million Dollars Is the Starting Point

Davidson also said it is best to acquire wealth with financial competence. Being a millionaire today does not mean that much. Today, $1 million is just the starting point to beginning to invest like the rich. So Davidson is in reality recommending choice #8 as the means to becoming rich. To rich dad, being financially smart included knowing when to be frugal and when not to be.

8. **You can become rich by being financially smart.** It was learning to be financially smart where I began to harness the same investing power I had witnessed at the age of 12 standing on the beach looking at rich dad's new piece of ocean front land. Many people become rich by being very smart with

knowledge from the B and I quadrants. Many of these individuals operate behind the scenes and manage, control, and manipulate the world's business and financial systems.

Millions of people faithfully place their retirement savings and other monies into the market. However, the decision-makers of the marketing and distribution system of the underlying investments actually make the large sums of money, not necessarily the individual investor or retiree. As rich dad taught me years ago, 'There are people who buy tickets to the game, and there are people who sell tickets to the game. You want to be on the side that is selling the tickets.'

## *Why the Rich Get Richer*

When I was younger, my rich dad said to me, 'The rich get richer partly because they invest differently than others; they invest in investments that are not offered to the poor and the middle class. Most importantly, however, they have a different educational background. If you have the education, you will always have plenty of money.'

Davidson points out that the dollar has lost 90% of its value in the last century. Being a cheap millionaire is therefore not enough. To qualify to invest in the investments of the rich, the price is at least $1 million of net worth. Even then, you may not be competent enough to safely invest in what the rich invest in.

Rich dad said, 'If you want to invest in the same investments the rich invest in, you need:

1. Education,
2. Experience, and
3. Excessive cash.'

At each level of what rich dad called the three Es, you find a different type of investor with a different level of education, experience, and excessive cash.

The price of being financially free requires time and dedication to gain the education, experience, and excessive cash to invest at those levels. You know you are financially smarter or increasing in sophistication when you can tell the differences between:

1. Good debt and bad debt
2. Good losses and bad losses
3. Good expenses and bad expenses
4. Tax payments versus tax incentives
5. Corporations you work for versus corporations you own
6. How to build a business, how to fix a business, and how to take a business public
7. The advantages and disadvantages of stocks, bonds, mutual funds, business, real estate, and insurance products as well as the different legal structures and when to use which product

Most average investors know only of:

1. Bad debt, which is why they try and pay it off
2. Bad losses, which is why they think losing money is bad
3. Bad expenses, which is why they hate paying bills
4. Taxes they pay, which is why they say that taxes are unfair
5. Job security and climbing the corporate ladder instead of owning the ladder
6. Investing from the outside, and buying shares of a company rather than selling shares of a company they own
7. Investing only in mutual funds, or picking only blue chip stocks

9. **You can become rich by being generous.** This was the way rich dad became rich. He often said, 'The more people I serve, the richer I become.' He also said, 'The problem with being on the E and S side of the Quadrant is that you can serve only so

many people. If you build large operating systems in the B and I quadrants, you can serve as many people as you want. And if you do that, you will become richer beyond your dreams.'

### Serving More and More People

Rich dad shared this example on how to become rich by serving more and more people, 'If I am a doctor and I know how to work with one patient at a time only, there are just two ways for me to make more money. One is to work longer, and the other is to raise my rates. But if I keep my job and work in my spare time to find a drug that cures cancer, then I will become rich by serving many more people.'

### The Definition of Rich

*Forbes* magazine defines rich as $1 million in income and $10 million in net worth. Rich dad had a tougher definition: a consistent $1 million in passive income, which is income that comes in regardless of if you work or not, and $5,000,000 in assets, not net worth. Net worth can be an elusive and much-manipulated figure. He also felt that if you could not maintain a 20% return from capital invested, you were not really an investor.

The price to reach rich dad's goal, starting from nothing, is actually measured in rich dad's three Es: education, experience, and excessive cash.

When I returned from Vietnam in 1973, I had very little of all three. I had to make a choice: Was I willing to invest my time to attain all three of the Es? Rich dad did, his son Mike did, and many of my friends are still investing their time to gain the three Es. That is why they got richer and richer.

### It Starts with a Plan

To be a rich investor, you must have a plan, be focused, and play to win. An average investor does not have a plan, invests in hot tips, and chases the hot investment products of the day, flitting from technology stocks to commodities to real estate to starting his or her own business. It's OK to invest on a hot tip now and then, but please do not delude yourself that one hot tip will make you rich forever.

In addition to the three Es, rich dad had a list of what he called the five Ds that were required to become very rich, especially when you start with nothing. They are:

1. Dream          4. Data
2. Dedication     5. Dollars
3. Drive

Most people focus on the last two, data and dollars. Many people go to school and think that the education or data they gain there will get them the dollars. Alternatively, if they don't have a formal education, they say, 'I can't be rich because I don't have a college education' or 'It takes money to make money' or 'If I work harder and make more money, then I'll be rich.' In other words, many people use the lack of education or money as their excuse for not being rich as investors.

Rich dad concluded his discussion on the five Ds by saying, 'In reality, it is the focus on the first three Ds that ultimately gains you the data and dollars you need to become very, very rich.' In other words, the data and the dollars are derived from having a dream, being dedicated, and having the drive to win. In my classes, I often find people who want more data before they begin doing anything, or think that first earning more money will make them rich. In most cases, exclusively trying to get more data or more dollars does not make a person rich. While data and dollars are important, it really takes just getting out there and doing it, especially if you are starting with nothing.

### *End of Phase One*

This completes Phase One, which is, in my opinion, the most important phase. Money is just an idea. If you think money is hard to get and you'll never be rich, then it will be true for you. If you think that money is abundant, then that can be true.

The remaining four phases cover the specifics of rich dad's plan and how they were similar to the plans of some of the richest people in the world. As you read, consider how rich dad's plan conflicts, adds to, subtracts from, or agrees with your personal financial plan.

I caution you to use the information provided as a guide and not as hard data. Much of it is subject to legal interpretation and should be considered based on your individual circumstances. Its application is not always black and white and should be carefully reviewed. We advise you to consult with your legal and financial advisors to make sure you develop the plan most appropriate for your needs and goals.

# Chapter 19

# The 90/10 Riddle

In February of the year 2000, I was working with a group of very bright graduate students at Thunderbird University, The American School of International Management. During the three hour session I asked one of the young students, 'What is your investment plan?'

Without hesitation he replied, 'When I graduate I will find a job that pays me at least $150,000 a year and begin putting aside at least $20,000 a year to buy investments.'

I thanked him for his willingness to share his plan with me. Then I said, 'Do you remember me discussing my rich dad's 90/10 principle of money?'

'Yes,' said the young man with a smile, knowing that I was about to challenge the way he was thinking. He was enrolled in the entrepreneurship program of this very prestigious school where I was a guest instructor. By now, he knew my style of teaching was not to give students answers. My style was to challenge core beliefs and ask students to evaluate old thought patterns. 'What does the 90/10 principle of money have to do with my investment plan?' he asked cautiously.

'Everything,' I replied. 'Do you think your plan of finding a job and investing at least $20,000 a year will put you in the category of the 10% of investors that make 90% of the money?'

'I don't know,' he replied. 'I never really thought about my plan with that benchmark in mind.'

'Most people don't,' I replied. 'Most people find an investment plan and think it is the only investment plan or the best investment plan, but few compare their plans to other plans. And the problem is, most people will not find out if their plan was the right plan until it's too late.'

'You mean the average investor is investing for retirement and will not find out if their plan worked or not until they retire?' asked another student in the class. 'They'll find out when it is too late.'

'For many people my age that will be true,' I replied. 'Sad but true.'

'But isn't the idea of finding a high paying job and putting $20,000 a year away a pretty good plan?' asked the student. 'After all, I'm only 26 years old.'

'A very good plan,' I replied. 'Definitely putting away more money than the average person and starting young with that much money will probably make you a very rich man. But my question is, "Will your plan put you in the 90/10 league of investors?"'

'I don't know,' said the young man. 'What would you advise?'

'Do you remember me telling you the story of walking along the beach with my rich dad at the age of 12?' I asked.

'You mean the story of you wondering how he could afford such an expensive piece of real estate,' another student replied. 'Your rich dad's first big investment and his first move into the world of bigger investments?'

I nodded my head and replied, 'That's the story.'

'And that story has to do with the 90/10 rule of money?' asked the student.

'Yes it does. It applies because I always wondered how my rich dad could acquire an asset so big even though he had very little. So after asking him how he did it, he gave me what he called the 90/10 riddle.'

'The 90/10 riddle?' replied one of the students. 'What is the 90/10 riddle and what does it have to do with my investment plan?'

With that question, I turned, walked to the chalk board, and drew the following diagram. 'This is the 90/10 riddle.' I said.

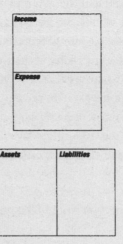

'That's the 90/10 riddle?' asked the student. 'All it looks like is a financial statement without any assets in it.'

'And it is. So this is the question that completes the riddle,' I said with a grin, watching the students' faces to see if they were still with me.

After a long pause on my part, one of the students finally demanded, 'So give us the question.'

'The question is,' I said slowly, 'How do you fill your asset column without buying any assets?'

'Without buying any assets,' replied the student. 'You mean without any money?'

'More or less,' I replied. 'Your investment plan for putting $20,000 a year aside to invest with is a good idea. But my challenge to you is: Is the idea of buying assets with money a 90/10 idea, or is it an average investor idea?'

'So you're saying to create assets in the asset column instead of buying the assets with money, which is what most people do.'

I nodded my head. 'You see, this diagram, the diagram I call the 90/10 riddle, is the riddle that my rich dad would challenge me with on a regular basis. He would ask me for my ideas on how I could create assets in the asset column without buying them with money.'

The students were silent looking at the riddle on the chalk board. Finally one turned and said, 'Is that why you often say, "It doesn't take money to make money?"'

I nodded my head and replied, 'You're catching on. Most people in the 90% who own the 10% often say, "It takes money to make money." Many often give up on investing if they do not have any money.'

'So your rich dad's 90/10 riddle was to give you a blank asset column and ask you how you would fill it with assets without having to buy the assets.'

'Constantly. After I came back from Vietnam, he would routinely have a lunch or dinner with me and ask me for new ideas on how to fill the asset column by creating assets instead of buying assets. He knew that is how many of the ultra-rich got rich in the first place. That is how Bill Gates, Michael Dell, Richard Branson all became billionaires. They did not become billionaires by looking for a job and putting a few dollars aside.'

'So you're saying the way to become rich is by being an entrepreneur?'

'No, I am not saying that. I just use those examples because you are all in the entrepreneurship program at Thunderbird University. The Beatles became ultra-rich by creating a different kind of asset, none-the-less they created assets that still pay them money today. All I am saying is that rich dad put this financial statement with a blank asset column in front of me on a regular basis and asked me how I would create assets inside the asset column without having to spend money to acquire them. He began giving me this 90/10 quiz when I asked him how he found the power to acquire a piece of the most expensive beachfront land without any money.'

'So he said his business bought the land,' another student chimed in.

'As I said, that is one way but there are many ways you can create assets inside an asset column without buying them. Inventors do it by inventing something of great value. Artists paint paintings that are priceless. Authors write books that pay them royalties for years. Creating a business is the way an entrepreneur does it, but you don't have to be an entrepreneur to create an asset inside the asset column. I've done it with real estate without using any money. All you have to do is be creative and you can be rich for life.'

'You mean I can invent something with new technology and become rich?' asked one of the students.

'You could, but it does not have to be an invention or new technology,' I said, pausing for a while. 'It is a way of thinking that creates assets and once you have that way of thinking you will be richer than you ever dreamed possible.'

'What do you mean it doesn't have to be a new invention or technology? What else could it be?'

I said, doing my best to make my point, 'Do you remember the story in my book, *Rich Dad Poor Dad*, the story of the comic books?'

'Yes,' said one of the students. 'The story of your rich dad taking away your 10 cents an hour and asking you to work for free after you asked for a raise? He took away the 10 cents because he did not want you to spend your life working for money.'

'Yes, that story,' I replied. 'That is a story about filling the asset column with an asset without buying the asset.'

The students stood quietly for a while thinking about what I had just said. Finally one spoke up and said, 'So you took old comic books and turned them into assets.'

I nodded my head. 'But were the comic books the asset?' I asked

'Not until you turned them into an asset,' replied another student. 'You took something that was being thrown out as trash and turned it into an asset.'

'Yes but were the comic books the asset or were the comic books merely the part of the asset you could see?'

'Oh,' another one of the students jumped in. 'It was the invisible thought process that created the comic book into the asset that was the real asset.'

'That is how my rich dad saw it. He later told me that the power he had was his thinking process. It was a thinking process that he often jokingly called, "Turning trash into cash." He also said, "Most people do exactly the opposite and turn cash into trash. That is why the 90/10 rule holds true."'

'He was like the ancient alchemists,' said one of the students. 'The alchemists who searched for the formula to turn lead into gold.'

'Exactly,' I said. 'The people who are in the 90/10 grouping of money are modern day alchemists. The only difference is that they are able to turn nothing into assets. Their power is the ability to take ideas and turn them into assets.'

'But as you say, many people have great ideas. They are just not able to turn them into assets,' said a student.

I nodded my head. 'And that was my rich dad's secret power I saw that day on the beach. It was that mental power or financial intelligence that allowed him to acquire such an expensive piece of real estate, while the average investor would walk away from it, saying "I can't afford it," or "It takes money to make money."'

'How often did he give you the 90/10 quiz?' asked a student.

'Very often,' I replied. 'It was his way of exercising my brain. Rich dad often said that our brains are our most powerful asset and, if used improperly, they can be our most powerful liability.'

The students were silent, I assume contemplating and questioning their own thoughts. Finally the original student, the student whose plan it was to put the $20,000 dollars a year away, said, 'So that is why in your book *Rich Dad Poor Dad*, one of rich dad's lessons was that the rich invent their own money.'

I nodded my head and said, '"And lesson number one of the six lessons was "the rich don't work for money."'

Again there was silence from the young students before one then said, 'So while we are planning on getting a job and saving money to buy assets, you were taught that your job was to create assets.'

'Well said,' I replied. 'You see the idea of a "job" was created in the Industrial Age and ever since 1989, we have been in the Information Age.'

'What do you mean the idea of a job is an Industrial Age idea?' one student asked with a start. 'Humans have always had jobs, haven't they?'

'No, at least not in the way we know of a job today. You see, in the Hunter-Gatherer period of humanity, humans lived in tribes and each person's job was to contribute to the communal survival of the tribe. In other words, it was all for one and one for all. Then came the Agrarian Age, the era when there were kings and queens. A person's job during that period was to be a serf or a peasant who paid the king to work the land the king owned. Then came the Industrial Age and serfdom or slavery was abolished and human beings began selling their labor on the open market. Most people became employees or self-employed, doing their best to sell their labor to the highest bidder. That is the modern concept of the word "job."'

'So the moment I said I'm going to get a job and put $20,000 away a year, you see that kind of thinking as Industrial Age thinking.'

I nodded my head. 'Just as today there are still Agrarian Age workers that are known as farmers and ranchers. Today there are still hunter gatherers, commercial fishermen for example. Most people are working with Industrial Age ideas and that is why so many people have jobs.'

'So what would an Information Age idea of work be?' asked a student.

'People who do not work because their ideas are at work. Today, there are students who are much like my rich dad who are going from school to becoming rich without a job. Look at many of the Internet billionaires. Some of them dropped out of college to become billionaires without ever having a formal job.'

'In other words, they started with an empty asset column and filled it with a very big asset, an Information Age asset,' added one of the students.

'Many built multi-billion dollar assets,' I said. 'They went from students to billionaires and soon there will be high school students who will go from high school students to billionaires without ever applying for a job. I already know of one that is a millionaire without ever having a job. After reading my book and playing my games, he bought a large piece of real estate, sold off a section of vacant land, kept the apartment house, and paid off his loan with the money from the land. He now owns the apartment house which is worth a little over a million dollars and has cash flow of $4,000 a month income without working. He will graduate from high school in about a year.'

The students stood silently again thinking about what I just said. Some had a hard time believing my story about the high school student, yet they knew the story of college drop outs becoming billionaires was true. Finally one spoke up, 'So in the Information Age people are getting rich with information.'

'Not just in the Information Age,' I replied. 'It has been this way throughout the ages. It is the people who do not have assets who work for, or are controlled by, those people who create, acquire, or control the assets.'

'So you're saying a high school kid could beat me financially even though he does not have a great education from a prestigious school, or a high paying job,' said the first student.

'That is exactly what I am saying. It's a matter of the way you think more than your education. Bestselling author of *The Millionaire Next Door* Thomas Stanley in his latest book *The Millionaire Mind* states that his research found no correlation between high SAT scores, good grades and money.'

The student with the $20,000 a year investment plan then said, 'So if I want to join the 90/10 club I am better off to practice creating assets instead of buying assets. I should be creative rather than do what everyone else does, when it comes to acquiring assets.'

'That is why billionaire Henry Ford said, "Thinking is the hardest work there is. That is why so few people engage in it,"' I replied. 'It also explains why if you do what the 90% of investors do you will join them in sharing only 10% of the wealth.'

'Or why Einstein said, "Imagination is more important than knowledge,"' added another student.

'Or why my rich dad gave me this tip when hiring an accountant. He said, when you're interviewing an accountant ask him or her, "What is 1+1?" If the accountant answers "3" don't hire the person. They're not smart. If the accountant answers "2" you also don't hire them because they are not smart enough. But if the accountant answers, "What do you want 1+1 to be?" You hire them immediately.'

The students laughed as we began packing up our materials. 'So you create assets that buy other assets and liabilities. Is that correct?' asked a student.

I nodded my head.

'Do you ever use money to buy other assets?' asked the same student.

'Yes, but I like to use money generated by the asset I create, to buy other assets,' I replied, picking up my briefcase. 'Remember that

I don't like working for money. I'd rather create assets that buy other assets and liabilities.'

A young student from China gave me a hand with my bags and said, 'And is that why you recommend network marketing so much? For very little money and risk, a person can build an asset in their spare time.'

I nodded my head, 'A worldwide asset they can pass on to their kids if their kids want it. I don't know of too many companies that will let you pass on your job to your kids. That is one test of an asset, the test if you can hand it on down to the people you love. My dad, the man I call my poor dad, worked very hard to climb the government ladder. Even if he had not been fired, he would not have been able to pass on his years of hard work to his kids, not that any of us wanted the job or were qualified to take the job anyway.'

The students gave me a hand out to my car. 'So think about creating assets rather than working hard and buying assets,' said the $20,000 student.

'If you want to get into the 90/10 club,' I replied. 'That is why my rich dad constantly challenged my creativity to create different types of assets in the asset column without buying them. He said it was better to work years at creating an asset rather than to spend your life working hard for money to create someone else's asset.'

The $20,000 student then said as I climbed into my car, 'So all I have to do is take an idea and create an asset, a big asset, that makes me rich. If I do that I will solve the 90/10 riddle and join the 10% of all investors that control 90% of the wealth.'

Laughing, I pulled my door shut and replied to his last comment, 'If you solve the 90/10 riddle in real life, you will have a good chance of joining the 10% that control 90% of the money. If you don't solve the 90/10 riddle in real life, you will probably join the 90% that control just 10% of the money.' I thanked the students and drove away.

## *Mental Attitude Quiz*

As Henry Ford said, 'Thinking is the hardest work there is. That is
why so few people engage in it.' Or as my rich dad said, 'Your brain
can be your most powerful asset and if not used properly, it can be
your most powerful liability.'

My rich dad had me repeatedly create new assets in an empty asset
column. He would sit down with his son and me and ask us how we
could create a new and different asset. He really did not care if the
idea was crazy and zany, he just wanted us to be able to substantiate
how this idea could be turned into an asset. He would ask us to
defend our thoughts and challenge his challenges. In the long run, it
was a lot better than him telling us to work hard, save money, and
live frugally, which is what my poor dad recommended.

### So the mental attitude quiz question is:

'Are you willing to consider creating your own assets rather than buying
them?'

Yes _____   No _____

There are many books and educational programs written on how
to buy assets wisely. For most people, buying assets is the best plan
for them. I would also recommend that for the secure and comfortable levels of your investment plan that those assets be assets you
buy. Invest in such assets as blue chip stocks and well managed mutual
funds for the secure and comfortable level. But if you have dreams
of becoming a very rich investor, the question is 'Are you willing to
create your assets rather than buy someone else's assets?' If not, then
as I said, there are many books and educational programs about how
to purchase assets.

If you are willing to consider how to create assets, then the
remainder of this book will be valuable, maybe priceless. It is about
how to take an idea and turn it into an asset that will acquire other

assets. It is not only about how to make a lot of money in the asset column, it is also about how to keep the money that asset makes and have it acquire even more assets as well as the luxuries of life. It reveals how many of the 10% came to acquire 90% of the money. So if this is of interest to you, then please read on.

Again, this is the 90/10 riddle:

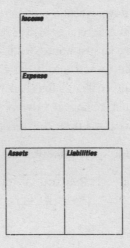

The riddle is, 'How do you create an asset in the asset column without spending money to acquire it?'

### Robert's Note:

My first big business was the nylon and Velcro surfer wallet business in 1977. It was created as a very big asset in the asset column. The problem was, the size of the asset created was big, but my business skills were small. So while I was technically a millionaire in my twenties, I also lost it all in my twenties. I repeated the same process three years later in the rock and roll business. When MTV hit, our little company was in the perfect position to capitalize on the craze. Again, the asset created was bigger than the people that created it. We went up like a rocket ship and came down like a rocket ship without gas. The rest of this book is dedicated to creating big assets, having the professional talent to match the size of the asset, and how to keep the money made by investing in other, often more stable, assets. As my rich dad said, 'What good is making a lot of money if you don't keep it?' Investing is the way smart people keep their money.

# What Type of Investor Do You Want to Become?

## Chapter 20

# *Solving the 90/10 Riddle*

My rich dad said, 'There are investors who buy assets and there are investors who create assets. If you want to solve the 90/10 riddle for yourself, you need to be both types of investor.'

In the introduction, I told the story of rich dad, Mike and me walking along a beach looking at a very expensive piece of beach front real estate he had just purchased. You may recall me asking rich dad how he could afford such an expensive piece of real estate when my poor dad could not. Rich dad's reply was, 'I can't afford this land either, but my business can.' All I could see was a piece of land with old abandoned cars, a building half falling down, lots of brush and debris, and a large 'For Sale' sign sticking up from the middle of the property. At the age of 12, I could not see any business on this land, but my rich dad could. The business was being created in his head and that ability to create businesses in his head was the reason he would go on to be one of the richest men in Hawaii. In other words, rich dad solved his 90/10 riddle by creating assets that in turn purchased other assets. That plan was not only rich dad's investment plan, it is the investment plan for most of the 10% who make 90% of the money, in the past, in the present, and into the future.

For those of you who read *Rich Dad Poor Dad*, you may recall the story of Ray Kroc saying to my friend's MBA class that McDonald's, the company he founded, was not in the business of hamburgers. Their business was the business of real estate. Again the formula is to create an asset that buys other assets and that formula is the reason why McDonald's owns the most expensive real estate in the world. It was all part of the plan. And that is why rich dad repeatedly said to me once he knew I was serious about becoming rich, 'If you want to solve the 90/10 riddle for yourself, you need to be both types of investor. You need to be a person who knows how to create assets as well as a person who knows how to buy assets. The average investor is not generally aware of the different processes and is not good at either process of investing. The average investor usually does not even have a formally written plan.'

### Making Millions, Maybe Billions from Your Ideas

Much of the second half of this book is about how people create assets. Rich dad spent many hours with me teaching me the process of how a person takes an idea and turns it into a business that creates assets that buys assets. During one of these lessons with rich dad, he said, 'Many people have ideas that could make them rich beyond their wildest dreams. The problem is, most people have never been taught how to put a business structure inside their ideas and so many of their ideas never take shape or stand on their own. If you want to be one of the 10% that makes 90% of the money, you will need to know how to build a business structure inside your creative ideas.' Much of the second half of this book is about what rich dad called the 'B-I Triangle' which is the mental structure that can give life to your financial ideas. It is the power of the B-I Triangle that takes an idea and turns it into an asset.

Rich dad often said, 'More than just knowing how to create assets that buy assets, one of the main reasons the richest of investors are able to become richer is becuase they know how to turn their ideas into millions and maybe even billions of dollars. The average investor may have excellent ideas, but they often lack the skills to turn their ideas into assets that buy assets.' The remainder of this book is dedicated to how ordinary people are able to turn their ideas into assets that buy assets.

## 'You Can't Do That'

While teaching me how to turn my ideas into assets, rich dad often said, 'When you first set out to turn your ideas into your personal fortune, many people will say, "You can't do that." Always remember that nothing kills your great ideas more than people with small ideas and limited imaginations.' Rich dad gave me two reasons he thought people tended to say, 'You can't do that.'

1.  They say, 'You can't do that' even if you are doing what they say you cannot do, not because you can't do it but because they can't do it.
2.  They say, 'You can't do it' because they cannot see what you are doing.

Rich dad explained that the process of making a lot of money is a mental process more than a physical process.

One of rich dad's favorite quotes came from Einstein, which went, 'Great spirits have often encountered violent opposition from mediocre minds.' Commenting on Einstein's quote, rich dad said, 'We all possess both a great spirit and a mediocre mind. The challenge in turning our ideas into a million dollar or even billion dollar asset is often the battle between our own great spirits and our own, often mediocre, minds.

When I explain the B-I Triangle, which is the business structure that gives life to business ideas and is explained in the second part of this book, some people become overwhelmed by the amount of knowledge required to make the B-I Triangle work for them. When that happens I often remind them of the battle between their great spirits and mediocre minds. Whenever a person's mediocre mind begins to oppose their own great spirits, I always remind them of what my rich dad said to me. He said, 'There are many people with great ideas but very few people with great amounts of money. The reason the 90/10 rule holds true is because it does not take a great idea to become rich but it does take a great person behind the idea to become rich. You must be of strong spirit and strong in your convictions to turn your ideas into fortunes. Even if you understand the process via which your ideas can become millions, even billions of dollars, always remember that great ideas only become great fortunes if the person behind the idea is also willing to be great. It is often difficult to keep going when everyone around you is saying, "You can't do it." You must have a very strong spirit to withstand the doubt of those around you. But your spirit must be even stronger when you are the person saying to yourself "You can't do that." This does not mean that you plough blindly on not listening to the good and bad ideas of your friends or yourself. Their thoughts and input should be listened to and often used when their ideas are better than yours. But at this moment, I am not talking to you about mere ideas or advice.

'What I am talking to you about is more than just ideas. I am talking about your spirit and the will to go on even when filled with doubt and out of good ideas. No one can you tell you what you can or cannot do in your life. Only you can determine that. Your own greatness is often found at the end of the road, and when it comes to turning your ideas into money, there are many times when you come to the end of the road. The end of the road is when you are out of ideas, out of money, and filled with doubt. If you can find in yourself the spirit to go on, you will find out what it really takes to turn your ideas into great assets. Turning an idea into a great fortune is more a matter of human spirit rather than the power of the human mind. At the end of every road, the entrepreneur finds his or her spirit.

Finding your entrepreneurial spirit and making it strong is more important than the idea or business you are developing. Once you find your entrepreneurial spirit, you will forever be able to take very ordinary ideas and turn them into extraordinary fortunes. Always remember the world is filled with people with great ideas and very few people with great fortunes'.

The remainder of this book is dedicated to you finding your entrepreneurial spirit and developing your ability to turn ordinary ideas into extraordinary fortunes. Phase Two gives you insight into rich dad's different types of investors and allows you to choose the path that may be best for you. Phase Three analyzes rich dad's B-I Triangle and how it can provide the structure for you to make an asset out of your good idea.

Phase Four goes into the mind of the sophisticated investor and how he or she analyzes investments as well as the pathway of the ultimate investor who takes his or her idea and B-I Triangle and creates fortunes. The last phase is Phase Five, Giving It Back, the most important phase.

## Chapter 21

# *Rich Dad's Categories of Investors*

This book is an educational story about rich dad guiding me from having no money and no job when I left the Marines to well down my path to becoming the ultimate investor – a person who becomes a selling shareholder rather than a buying shareholder, a person who is on the inside of the investment rather than on the outside. Other investment vehicles in which the rich invest that the poor and middle class do not include initial public offerings of stock (IPOs), private placements, and other corporate securities. Whether you are on the inside of an investment or on the outside, it is important to understand the basics of the securities regulations.

By reading *Rich Dad Poor Dad*, you have learned about financial literacy, which is imperative for a successful investor. From reading *CASHFLOW Quadrant*, you have learned about the four different quadrants and the ways people make money as well as how the different tax laws affect the different quadrants. By just reading the first two books and possibly playing our educational board game *CASHFLOW*, you already know more about the fundamentals of investing than many people who actively invest.

Once you understand the fundamentals of investing, you can better understand rich dad's categories of investors and the ten investor controls he said were important to all investors:

## *The Ten Investor Controls*

1. The control over yourself
2. The control over income/expense asset/liability ratios
3. The control over the management of the investment
4. The control over taxes
5. The control over when you buy and when you sell
6. The control over brokerage transactions
7. The control over the ETC (entity, timing, and characteristics)
8. The control over the terms and conditions of the agreements
9. The control over access to information
10. The control over giving it back, philanthropy, redistribution of wealth

Rich dad often said, 'Investing is not risky, not being in control is risky.' Many people find investing risky because they are not in control of one or more of these ten investor controls. This book will not go into all of these controls. As you read this book, however, you may gain some insights on how you can gain greater control as an investor – especially control number 7, the control over entity, timing, and characteristics. This is where many investors lack control, need more control, or simply lack any basic understanding about investing.

The first phase of this book was dedicated to rich dad's most important investor control – CONTROL OVER YOURSELF. If you are not mentally prepared and committed to becoming a successful investor, you should turn your money over to a professional financial advisor or team trained to help you choose your investments.

## *I Was More Than Ready*

At this point in my financial education, rich dad knew I had made the choice:

> *I was mentally prepared to become an investor.*
> *I wanted to become a very successful investor.*

I knew I was mentally prepared and that I wanted to be rich. However, rich dad now asked me, 'What kind of investor do you want to become?'

'A rich investor' was my answer. This is when rich dad brought out his yellow pad again and wrote down the following categories of investors:

1. The accredited investor
2. The qualified investor
3. The sophisticated investor
4. The inside investor
5. The ultimate investor

'What is the difference?' I asked.

Rich dad added a description to each type of investor:

1. The accredited investor earns a lot of money and/or has a high net worth.
2. The qualified investor knows fundamental and technical investing.
3. The sophisticated investor understands investing and the law.
4. The inside investor creates the investment.
5. The ultimate investor becomes the selling shareholder.

When I read the definition of the accredited investor, I felt pretty hopeless. I had no money and no job.

Rich dad saw my reaction, took the yellow pad back, and circled inside investor.

## Start As an Insider

'This is where you'll start, Robert,' rich dad said as he pointed to inside investor.

'Even if you have very little money and very little experience, it is possible to start at the inside level of investing,' rich dad continued. 'You need to start small and keep learning. It does not take money to make money.'

At this point, he listed his three Es on the tablet:

1. Education
2. Experience
3. Excessive cash

'Once you have all three Es, you will have become a successful investor,' rich dad said. 'You've done well with your financial education, but now you need the experience. When you have the right experience combined with good financial literacy, the excessive cash will come.'

'But you have inside investor listed fourth. How can I start as an inside investor?' I said, still confused.

Rich dad wanted me to start as an insider because he wanted me to be a person who created assets that eventually bought other assets.

## Start by Building a Business

'I am going to teach you the fundamentals of building a successful business,' rich dad continued. 'If you can learn to build a successful B quadrant business, your business will generate excessive cash. Then you can use the skills you learned becoming a successful B to analyze investments as an I.'

'It is like coming in through the back door, isn't it?' I asked.

'Well, I would rather say it is the opportunity of a lifetime!' rich dad replied. 'Once you learn to make your first million, the next ten are easy!'

'OK, so how do I get started?' I asked impatiently.

'First let me tell you about the different categories of investors,' rich dad answered, 'so you can understand what I'm saying.'

## Overview – You Get to Choose

In this phase of *Rich Dad's Guide to Investing*, I share rich dad's descriptions of each one of his categories of investors. The following mini-chapters explain the distinctions (the advantages and disadvantages) of each category because the path I chose may not be the right path for you.

## The Accredited Investor

The accredited investor is someone with high income or high net worth. I knew I could not qualify as an accredited investor.

A long-term investor who has chosen to invest for security and comfort may very well qualify as an accredited investor. There are many Es and Ss who are very content with their financial position. They recognized early on the need to provide for their financial future through the I quadrant and adopted a plan for investing with their income earned as Es and Ss. Their financial plans, whether to be secure or comfortable, have been met.

In *CASHFLOW Quadrant*, we discussed this 'two-legged' approach to building financial security. I applaud these individuals for their foresight and discipline in developing a financial plan and providing for their financial future. For them, the path I took will sound like either an impossible mission or a lot of hard work.

There are also many highly paid Es and Ss who qualify as accredited investors based on their income alone.

If you can qualify as an accredited investor, you will have access to investments that most people do not. To be successful in choosing your investments, however, you still need financial education. If you choose not to invest your time in your financial education, you should turn your money over to competent financial advisors who can assist you with your investment decisions.

Aa a statistic of interest, in America today there are reportedly just 6 million people who meet the qualifications of an Accredited Investor. In a country of approximately 250 million people, and if this number is true, then there are only 2.4% of the population that meet this minimum requirement. If this statistic is true, then there are even fewer people who will meet the following levels of investors. This means there are many unqualified investors investing in high risk speculative investments they should not be investing in.

Again, the SEC definition of an Accredited Investor today is:

1.  $200,000 or more annual income for an individual
2.  $300,000 or more for a couple, or
3.  $1 million net worth.

Realizing that there are only 6 million people who qualify as Accredited Investors indicates to me that working hard for money is a very difficult way to qualify to invest in the investments of the rich. As I sit and ponder the idea of needing a $200,000 minimum income, I realize that my dad, the person I call my poor dad, would never have come close to qualifying, no matter how hard he worked and how many pay raises his government job provided.

If you have played *CASHFLOW 101*, you may note that the Fast Track of the game is the track that represents where the Accredited Investor meets the minimum requirements as an investor. In other words, technically, less than 2.4% of the U.S. population meets the requirements to invest in the investments found on the game's Fast Track. That means 97% of the population invests in the Rat Race.

## *The Qualified Investor*

The qualified investor understands how to analyze publicly traded stock. This investor would be considered an 'outside' investor as opposed to an 'inside' investor. Generally, qualified investors include stock traders and analysts.

## *The Sophisticated Investor*

The sophisticated investor typically has all three of rich dad's 'three Es.' In addition, the sophisticated investor understands the world of investing. He or she utilizes the tax, corporate, and securities laws to maximize both earnings and to protect the underlying capital.

If you want to become a successful investor but do not wish to build your own business to do so, your goal should be to become a sophisticated investor.

From the sophisticated investor on, these investors know that there are two sides of the coin. They know that on one side of the coin, the world is a world of black and white and they also know that the other side of the coin is a world of different shades of gray. It is a world where you definitely do not want to do things on your own. On the black and white side of the coin, some investors can invest on their own. On the gray side of the coin, an investor must enter with their team.

## *The Inside Investor*

To build a successful business is the goal of the inside investor. The business may be a single piece of rental real estate or a multi-million-dollar retail company.

A successful B knows how to create and build assets. Rich dad would say, 'The rich invent money. After you learn to make your first million, the next ten will be easy.'

A successful B will also learn the skills needed to analyze companies for investment from the outside. Therefore, a successful inside investor can learn to become a successful sophisticated investor.

### *The Ultimate Investor*

To become the selling shareholder is the goal of the ultimate investor. The ultimate investor owns a successful business in which he or she sells ownership interest to the public; hence, he or she is a selling shareholder. This is my goal. Although I have not achieved it yet, I continue to educate myself and learn from my experiences, and I have committed to doing so until I can become a selling shareholder.

### *Which Investor Are You?*

The next few chapters will go into each type of investor in greater detail. After you have studied each type of investor, you may be better prepared to choose your own goal for investing.

## Chapter 22

# The Accredited Investor

Who Is an Accredited Investor?

Most developed countries have laws written to protect the average person from bad and risky investments. The problem is that these very same laws can also prevent the masses from being able to invest in some of the best investments.

In America, we have the Securities Act of 1933, the Securities Exchange Act of 1934, SEC Regulations under these laws and the Securities and Exchange Commision (SEC). These laws and regulations were designed to protect the public from misrepresentations, manipulation, and other fraudulent practices in the buying and selling of securities. They limit certain investments only to accredited and sophisticated investors as well as require detailed disclosure of such investments. The SEC was created to be the watchdog for the laws.

In fulfilling its role as a watchdog over securities, the SEC defined the accredited investor as a person who has earned at least $200,000 or more as an individual (or $300,000 as a couple) in each of the last two years and who expects to earn the same amount in the current year. The individual or couple may also qualify with a net worth of at least $1 million.

Rich dad said, 'An accredited investor is simply a person who earns significantly more money than the average person. It does not necessarily mean the person is rich or knows anything about investing.'

The problem with this rule is that less than 3% of all Americans qualify under the $200,000 to $300,000 annual income requirement. This means that only this 3% can invest in these stock issues regulated by the SEC. The other 97% are not allowed to invest in the same investments because they are not accredited investors. The SEC's test for sophisticated investors has to do with the investor's level of financial intelligence.

I remember when rich dad was offered an opportunity to invest in a company called Texas Instruments before it went public. Not having the time to look into the company and do his analysis, he turned the opportunity down, a decision he regretted for years. Yet, he did not turn down other opportunities to invest in companies before they went public. He became even wealthier from those investments, investments not available to the general public. Rich dad qualified as an accredited investor.

When I asked to invest in the next pre-public offering of a company, rich dad informed me that I was not rich enough or wise enough to invest with him. I still remember him saying, 'Wait until you're rich, and the best investments will come to you first. The rich always get first pick of the best investments. In addition, the rich can buy at very low prices as well as in volume. That is one of the reasons why the rich get richer.'

My rich dad agreed with the SEC. He thought it a smart idea to protect the average investor from the risks of these types of investments although he had made a lot of money investing as an accredited investor himself.

However, rich dad cautioned me, 'Even if you are an accredited investor, you still may not get the opportunity to invest in the best investments. To do that requires a completely different type of investor with the right knowledge and access to the information about new investment opportunities.'

## The Investor Controls of the Accredited Investor

None

Rich dad believed that an accredited investor, without financial education, had none of the ten investor controls. The accredited investor might have a lot of money but usually didn't know what to do with it.

## The Three Es Possessed by the Accredited Investor

Excessive cash — maybe

Rich dad would clarify that although you might qualify as an accredited investor, you still needed the education and experience to progress to the qualified, sophisticated, inside, or ultimate investor. In fact, he knew many accredited investors who didn't actually have any excessive cash. They met the income thresholds but didn't know how to manage their cash very well.

## Sharon's Notes

Just about anyone can open a brokerage account to buy and sell stocks of companies that are considered 'public companies.' The stock of a public company is traded freely as well as bought and sold by the public, usually through an exchange. The stock market is truly a free market in action. Without government or outside intervention, individuals can decide for themselves whether the price of a stock is fair or not. They can decide to buy it and therefore purchase an ownership interest in the company.

In the last decade, mutual funds have become increasingly popular. They are professionally managed portfolios in which each share of the mutual fund represents ownership of partial shares in many different individual securities. Many individuals invest in mutual funds because of the professional management as well as the appeal of owning a small piece of many different securities rather than stock in a single company. If you do not have the time to study investing (so you can make informed investment decisions), choosing a mutual fund or hiring an investment advisor to handle your investments may be wise.

One way to true wealth from securities comes from participating in the initial public offering (IPO) of a company's stock. Typically, the company's founders and initial investors already own blocks of stock. To attract additional funding the company can offer an IPO. This is when the Securities and Exchange Commission (SEC) steps in – with detailed filing and disclosure requirements – in its attempt to prevent fraud and protect the investor from misrepresentation. This does not mean, however, that the SEC prevents IPOs from being poor deals. An IPO can be legal and still be a poor investment or an outright liability (it goes down in value).

The Securities Act of 1933 and the Securities Exchange Act of 1934 were adopted to regulate this type of investment and to protect the investor from fraudulent or high-risk investments, as well as broker mismanagement. The SEC was formed to oversee the issuance of securities as well as the securities industry.

The regulations for stock issues apply to public issues as well as certain private issues of stock. There are certain exemptions from the regulations that we have not covered. For now, it is important to understand the definition of accredited investor. The accredited investor may invest in certain types of securities that a non-accredited, non-sophisticated investor cannot because the 'accredited' status implies that the investor can withstand a higher level of monetary risk than the non-accredited investor.

Robert has discussed the accredited investor requirements of an individual or couple related to income or net worth. Any director, executive officer, or general partner of the issuer of the stock will also be considered an accredited investor even if that person does not meet the income or net worth requirements. This will become a very important distinction when we discuss the 'inside investor.' In fact, this is the path often taken by the inside and ultimate investor.

## Chapter 23

# The Qualified Investor

Rich dad defined the qualified investor as a person who has money as well as some knowledge about investing. A qualified investor is usually an accredited investor who has also invested in financial education. As it relates to the stock market, for example, he said qualified investors would include most professional stock traders. Through their education, they have learned and understand the difference between fundamental investing and technical investing.

1.  **Fundamental investing:** Rich dad said, 'A fundamental investor reduces risk looking for value and growth by looking at the financials of the company.' The most important consideration for selecting a good stock for investment is the future earnings potential of the company. A fundamental investor carefully reviews the financial statements of any company before investing in it. The fundamental investor also takes into account the outlook for the economy as a whole as well as the specific industry in which the company is involved. The direction of interest rates is a very important factor in fundamental analysis.

    *Warren Buffet has been acknowledged as one of the best fundamental investors.*

2. **Technical investing:** Rich dad said, 'a well-trained technical
   investor invests on the emotions of the market and invests with
   insurance from catastrophic loss. The most important consideration for selecting a good stock for investment is based on
   the supply of and demand for the company's stock. The technical investor studies the patterns of the sales price of the
   company's stock. Will the supply of the shares of stock being
   offered for sale be sufficient based on the expected demand
   for those shares?

The technical investor tends to buy on price and market sentiment
. . . just like a shopper shops for sales and discounted items. In fact, many
technical investors are like my Aunt Doris. Aunt Doris goes shopping for
bargains and sales with her lady friends, buying items because they are
cheap, marked down, or because her friends are buying them. Then she
gets home, wonders why she bought the item, tries it on and then takes
it back for a refund so she can have money to go shopping again.

The technical investor studies the pattern of the history of the
company's stock price. A true technical investor is not concerned with
the internal operations of a company as a fundamental investor would
be. The primary indicators the technical investor is concerned with
are the mood of the market and the price of the stock.

One of the reason so many people think the subject of investing
is risky is because most people are technically operating as 'technical
investors' but don't know the difference between a technical investor
and a fundamental investor. The reason investing seems risky from
the technical side is because stock prices fluctuate with market
emotions. Here are just a few examples of things that can cause fluctuations in stock prices:

*   *one day a stock is popular and in the news, next week it isn't, or
    the company manipulates supply and demand by splitting the
    stock, diluting the pool with additional shares being created*

*through such things as secondary offerings, or cutting back the number of shares by buying them back; or*

*an institutional buyer (like a mutual fund or pension fund) buys or sells the shares of a certain company in such volume that it disturbs the market.*

Investing seems risky to the average investor because they lack the basic financial education skills to be a fundamental investor and do not have adequate technical investor skills. If they are not on the board of the company changing the supply side of the shares they have no management control over the fluctuations of supply and demand of the stock's price on the open market. They remain at the whim of the market's emotions.

Many times a fundamental investor will find an excellent company with great profits but, for some reason, the technical investors will not be interested in it so the price of the company's shares will not go up, even though it is a profitable well managed company. In today's market, many people are investing in IPOs of Internet companies which have no sales or profits. That is a case of technical investors determining the value of a company's stock.

Since 1995, people operating strictly as fundamental investors have not done as well as investors who also consider the technical side of the market. In this wild market where the people who take the most risk win, people with more cautious and value oriented views lost out on this market mania. In fact, many of these risk takers frightened many technical investors as well with their high prices of stock without any value. But in a crash, it is those investors with the strong fundamental investments and technical trading skills who do well. The amateur speculators rushing into the market as well as all the new start up IPOs flush with money will be hurt in the downturn. Rich dad said, 'The trouble with getting rich quickly without a parachute is that you fall farther and faster. Lots of easy money makes people think they are

financial geniuses when in fact, they become financial fools.' Rich dad
believed that both technical as well as fundamental skills were important to survive the ups and downs of the world of investing.

> *Charles Dow of Dow-Jones fame was a technical investor. That is
> why* The Wall Street Journal, *the paper he helped found, is pri-
> marily a paper written for technical investors, and not neces-
> sarily for fundamental investors.*

> *George Soros is often recognized as one of the best technical
> investors.*

The difference between the two investment styles is dramatic. The
fundamental investor analyzes the company from its financial statements to assess the company's strength and potential for future
success. In addition, the fundamental investor tracks the economy
and the industry of the company.

A technical investor invests from charts that track the price and
volume trends and patterns of the company's stock. The technical
investor may review the put/call ratio for the stock as well as the short
positions taken in the stock. While both investors invest from the
facts, they find their facts from different sources of data. Also, both
types of investors require different skills and different vocabulary. The
frightening thing is that most of today's investors are investing without
technical or fundamental investor skills. In fact, I'll bet most new
investors today do not know the difference between a fundamental
and technical investor.

Rich dad used to say, 'Qualified investors need to be well versed
in both fundamental analysis as well as technical analysis.' He would
draw the following diagrams for me. These diagrams are why we developed our products the way we did. We want people to be able to
learn to be financially literate and to teach their children to be financially literate at a young age, as rich dad taught me.

**Fundamental Investing**

ABC Corporation

**Technical Investing**

ABC Corporation Stock Prices

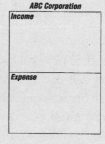

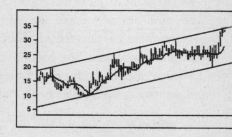

Financial Statement

**Important Skills:**
* Financial Literacy
* Basics of Financials
* Economic Forecasts

**Important Skills:**
* Stock Price and Sales History
* Puts/Calls Options Techniques
* Short Selling

**Educational Tools:**
*CASHFLOW, Investing 101*
*CASHFLOW for Kids*

**Educational Tool:**
*CASHFLOW, Investing 202*

I am often asked, 'Why does a qualified investor need to understand both fundamental investing as well technical investing?' My answer is found in one word: 'confidence.' Average investors feel that investing is risky because:

1. They are on the outside trying to look into the inside of the company or property they are investing in. If they do not know how to read financial statements, they are totally dependent on others' opinions. If only at an unconscious level, people know that insiders have better information and therefore lower risk.

2. If people cannot read financial statements, their personal financial statements are often a mess. And as rich dad said, 'If a person's financial foundation is weak, his or her self-confidence is also weak.' A friend of mine, Keith Cunningham, often says, 'The main reason people do not want to look at their personal financial statements is that they might find out they have financial cancer.' The good news is that once they cure the financial disease, the rest of their lives also improves — and sometimes even their physical health too.

3. Most people know how to make money only when the market is going up, and they live in terror of the market coming down. If a person understands technical investing, he or she has the skills to make money when the market goes down as well as when it goes up. The average investor without technical skills makes money only in a rising market, often losing all he or she has gained in a falling market. Rich dad said, 'a technical investor invests with insurance from huge losses. The average investor is like a person flying a plane without a parachute.'

As rich dad often said about technical investors, 'The bull comes up by the stairs and the bear goes out the window.' A bull market will rise slowly, but when it crashes, the market is like a bear going out the window. Technical investors are excited about market crashes because they position themselves to make money quickly when average investors are losing their money, money that often increased very slowly.

So the chart of various investors and their returns often looks like this:

|                     | Market | |
| ------------------- | ----- | ----- |
|                     | UP    | DOWN  |
| Losing investor     | loses | loses |
| Average investor    | wins  | loses |
| Qualified investor  | wins  | wins  |

Many investors often lose because they wait too long to get into the market. They are so afraid of losing that they wait too long for proof that the market is going up. As soon as they enter, the market peaks and crashes and they end up losing on the way down.

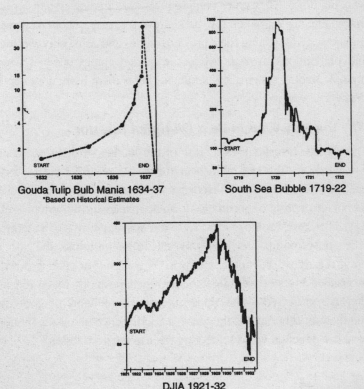

Gouda Tulip Bulb Mania 1634-37
*Based on Historical Estimates

South Sea Bubble 1719-22

DJIA 1921-32

Nikkei 1950-????

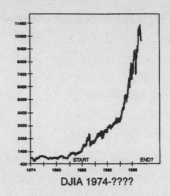
DJIA 1974-????

Qualified investors are less concerned about the market going up or going down. They enter confidently, with a trading system for an uptrending market. When the market reverses, they will often change trading systems, exiting their previous trades and using short selling, and put options to profit while the market comes down. Having multiple trading systems and strategies helps them have more confidence as investors.

## *Why You May Want to Be a Qualified Investor*

The average investor lives in fear of the market crashing or prices coming down. You can often hear them say, 'What if I buy a stock and the price comes down?' Hence many average investors fail to take advantage of profit opportunities in an up market and a down market. A qualified investor looks forward to the ups and downs of a market. When prices go up, they have the skills to minimize risk and earn a profit regardless of whether the price is going up or coming down. A qualified investor will often 'hedge' their positions which means they are protected if the price goes down suddenly or goes up suddenly. In other words they have a good chance of making money in either direction while protecting themselves from losses.

## The Problem with New Investors

Today, with such a hot market, I often hear new investors say with confidence, 'I don't have to worry about a market crash because this time, things are different.' A seasoned investor knows that all markets go up and all markets come down. Today as I write, we are in one of the biggest bull markets in the history of the world. Will this market come crashing down? If history holds any stories, then we should be in for one of the biggest crashes the world has ever seen. Today people are investing in companies without any profits . . . which means a mania is on. The diagrams on the previous page are diagrams of past bubbles, manias, or booms and busts the world has gone through.

Sir Isaac Newton who lost most of his fortune in the South Sea Bubble is quoted as saying, 'I can calculate the motions of heavenly bodies, but not the madness of people.' Today, in my opinion, there is madness. Everyone is thinking about getting rich quick in the market. I am afraid that we may soon see millions of people lose everything simply because they invested in the market, some borrowed money to invest, instead of first investing in their education and experience. At the same time, I am excited because many people will soon be selling in a panic and that is when the qualified investor really becomes wealthy.

It is not the crash that is so bad but the emotional panic that occurs at the times of such financial disasters/opportunities. The problem with most new investors is that they have not yet been through a real bear market . . . since this current bull market started in 1974. Many mutual fund managers were not yet born or barely born in 1974 so how would they know what a market crash and bear market feels like, especially if it goes on for years, such as the Japanese market has done.

Rich dad simply said, 'It is not possible to predict the market, but it is important that we be prepared for whichever direction it decides to go.' He also said, 'Bull markets seem to go on forever, which causes people to become sloppy, foolish, and complacent. Bear markets also seem to go on forever causing people to forget that bear markets are often the best times to become very, very rich. That is why you want to be a qualified investor.'

## Why Markets Will Crash Faster in the Information Age

In his book, *The Lexus and the Olive Tree*, a book I strongly recommend for anyone wanting to understand the new era of global business we are in, author Thomas L. Friedman often makes reference to The Electronic Herd. The electronic herd is a group of several thousand, very often young, people who control great sums of electronic money. They are the individuals who work for large banks, mutual funds, hedge funds, insurance companies, and the like. They have the power with the click of their mouse to move literally trillions of dollars from one country to another country in a split second. That power gives the electronic herd more power than politicians.

I was in South East Asia in 1997 when the electronic herd moved their money out of countries like Thailand, Indonesia, Malaysia, and Korea, virtually sinking those countries' economies over night. It was not a pretty sight nor was it pleasant to be physically present in those countries.

For those of you who invest globally, you may recall how most of the world, even Wall Street, was singing praises to the new Asian Tiger Economies. Everyone wanted to invest in these countries. Then suddenly, literally over night, their world changed. There were murders, suicides, riots, looting, and a general feeling of financial sickness everywhere. The electronic herd did not like what it saw in those countries and moved their money out in a matter of seconds.

Quoting from Thomas Friedman's book, he states:

'Think of the Electronic Herd as being like a herd of wildebeests grazing over a wide area of Africa. When a wildebeest on the edge of the herd sees something move in the tall, thick brush next to where it's feeding, that wildebeest doesn't say to the wildebeest next to it, "Gosh, I wonder if that's a lion moving around there in the brush." No way. That wildebeest just starts a stampede, and those wildebeests don't stampede for a mere hundred yards. They stampede to the next country and crush everything in their path.'

That is what happened to the Asian Tigers in 1997. The electronic herd did not like what they saw going on in the area and moved out literally overnight. It went from high optimism to riots and murder in a matter of days.

That is why I predict that market crashes will come faster and more severely in the Information Age.

## How Does One Protect Oneself from These Crashes?

The way some of these countries are protecting themselves from the power of the electronic herd is by cleaning up and tightening up their national financial statements and increasing their financial requirements and standards. In his book Thomas Friedman writes:

Standards: 'If you were writing a history of the American capital markets,' Deputy Treasury Secretary Larry Summers once observed, 'I would suggest that the single most important innovation shaping that capital market was the idea of generally accepted accounting principles. We need that internationally. It is a minor, but not insignificant, triumph of the IMF that in Korea somebody who teaches a night school class in accounting told me that he normally has 22 students in his Winter term, and this year (1998) he has 385. We need that at the corporate level in Korea. We need that at the national level.'

Years ago rich dad said a similar thing, but he was not referring to an entire country as Larry Summers is in this quote. Rich dad was referring to any individual who wanted to do well financially. Rich dad said, 'The difference between a rich person and a poor person is much more than how much money they make. The difference is found in their financial literacy and the standards of importance they put on that literacy. Simply put, poor people have very low financial literacy standards, regardless of how much money they make.' He also said, 'People with low financial literacy standards are often unable to take their ideas and create assets out of them. Instead of creating assets, many people create liabilities with their ideas just because of low financial literacy standards.'

## Getting Out Is More Important than Getting In

Rich dad often said, 'The reason most average investors lose money is because it is often easy to invest into an asset, but it is often difficult to get out. If you want to be a savvy investor you need to know how to exit an investment as well as how to get into the investment.' Today when I invest, one of the most important strategies I must consider is what is called my 'exit strategy.' Rich dad put the importance of an exit strategy in these terms so I could understand its importance. He said, 'Buying an investment is often like getting married. In the beginning things are exciting and fun. But if things do not go well, then the divorce can be much more painful than all that initial excitement and fun. That is why you must really think about an investment almost like a marriage. Because getting in is often a lot easier than getting out.'

Both my dads were very happily married men. So when rich dad talked about divorce, he was not encouraging people to get divorced, he was just advising me to think long term. He said, 'The odds are 50% of all marriages will end in divorce and the reality is nearly 100% of all marriages think they will beat those odds.' And that may be why so many new investors are buying IPOs, buying shares from the more seasoned investors. Rich dad's best words on this subject were, 'Always remember that when you are excitedly buying an asset there is often someone who knows more about the asset who is excitedly selling it to you!'

When people learn to invest by playing the *CASHFLOW* games, one of the technical skills they learn is when to buy and when to sell. Rich dad said, 'When you buy an investment you should also have an idea of when to sell it, especially investments offered to Accredited Investors and above. In the more sophisticated types of investments, your exit is often more important than the entry strategy. When getting into such investments you should know what will happen if the investment goes well and what will happen if the investment goes bad.'

## *The Financial Skills of a Qualified Investor*

For people who want to learn the basic financial skills, we developed *CASHFLOW 101*. We recommend playing it at least six to twelve times. By playing *101* repeatedly, you begin to understand the basics of fundamental investment analysis. After playing *101* and gaining an understanding of the financial skills it teaches, you may want to move on to playing *CASHFLOW 202*. The advanced game uses the very same game board as *101*, but it goes to another level, using a different set of cards and scoring sheets. In *202*, you begin to learn the complex skills and vocabulary of technical trading. You learn to use trading techniques such as short selling, which is selling shares you do not own, in anticipation of the price coming down. You also learn to use call options, put options, and straddles. All of these are very sophisticated trading techniques, which all qualified investors need to know. The best thing about these games is that you learn by playing and using play money. That same education in the real world could be very expensive.

## *Why Games Are Better Teachers*

In 1950 a nun, who was a history and geography teacher in Calcutta, was called on to help the poor and to live amongst them. Instead of just talking about caring for the poor she chose to say very little and helped the poor with her actions not her words. It was because of her actions that when she did speak, people listened. She had this to say about the difference between words and actions, 'There should be less talk. A preaching point is not a meeting point. There should be more action on your part.'

I chose to use games as the means of teaching the investment skills my rich dad taught me because games require more action than lecture in the teaching and learning process. As Mother Teresa said, 'A preaching point is not a meeting point.' Our games are meeting points. Games provide a social interaction for learning and helping someone else to learn. When it comes to investing, there are too many people trying to teach investing by preaching. We all know that there are certain things that are not best learned by simply reading and listening. Some things require action to be learned and games provide this elementary action step to learning.

There is an old aphorism that goes:

'I hear and I forget. I see and I remember. I do and I understand.'

My purpose in going beyond just writing books about money and investing, and creating games as learning tools, is to create more understanding. The more understanding people have, the more they can see the other side of the coin. Instead of seeing fear and doubt, the players begin to see opportunities they never saw before because their understanding increases each time they play the game.

Our web site is filled with stories of people who have played our games and have had their lives suddenly changed. They have learned a new understanding about money and investing, an understanding that pushed out some old thoughts and gave them new possibilities for their lives.

At the back of this book is my edumercial about the games which gives you more information on how these educational tools can assist you in increasing your understanding of money, business, and investing.

Rich dad taught me to be a business owner and investor by playing the game of *Monopoly*. He was able to teach his son and me so much more after the game was over when we visited his businesses and real estate. I wanted to create educational games that taught the same fundamental and technical investing skills that rich dad taught me, far beyond what is taught in *Monopoly*. As rich dad said, 'The ability to manage cash flow and to read financial statements is fundamental to success on the B and I side of the CASHFLOW Quadrant.'

## The Investor Controls Possessed by the Qualified Investor

1. The control over yourself
2. The control over income/expense asset/liability ratios
5. The control over when you buy and when you sell

## The Three Es Possessed by the Qualified Investor

1. Education
3. Excessive cash – maybe

## Sharon's Notes

The qualified investors, both fundamental and technical, are analyzing a company from the outside. They are deciding whether to become 'buying shareholders.' Many very successful investors are happy operating as qualified investors. With the proper education and financial advice, many qualified investors can become millionaires. They are investing in businesses developed and run by others. Because they have studied and gained the financial education, they are able to analyze the company from its financial statements.

### What Does p/e Mean?

The qualified investor understands the price/earnings (p/e) ratio of a stock, which is also referred to as the market multiplier. The p/e ratio is calculated by dividing the current market price of a stock by the previous year's earnings per share. Generally, a low p/e would mean that a stock is selling at a relatively low price compared to its earnings; a high p/e would indicate that a stock's price is high and may not be much of a bargain.

$$\text{p/e Ratio} = \frac{\text{Market's Price (Per Share)}}{\text{Net Income (Per Share)}}$$

The p/e ratio of one successful company may be very different from that of another successful company if the two companies are in different industries. For example, high-tech companies with big growth and high earnings generally sell at much higher p/es than low-tech or mature companies where growth has stabilized. Just look at the stocks being sold in Internet companies today: Many of them are selling at very high prices even when the companies have no earnings. The high prices in these cases reflect the market's expectation for high earnings in the future.

### The Future p/e Is the Key

A qualified investor recognizes that the current p/e is not as important as the future p/e. The investor wants to invest in a company where the company's financial future is strong. In order for the p/e ratio to be helpful to the investor, much more information about the company may be needed. Generally, the investor will compare a company's ratios for the current year with that of previous years to measure the growth of the company. The investor will also compare the company's ratios with those of other companies in the same industry.

### Not All Day Traders Are Qualified

Many people today are participating in 'day trading,' which has become popular due to the convenience and availability of online trading. The day trader is hoping to earn profits through buying and selling securities within a single day. The day trader is very familiar with p/e ratios. What distinguishes a successful day trader from an unsuccessful day trader is often his or her ability to see behind the p/e ratio. For the most part, successful day traders have taken the time to learn the basics of technical or fundamental trading. Day traders without proper financial education and financial analysis skills are operating more like gamblers than traders. Only the most educated and successful day traders would be considered qualified investors.

In fact, it has been said that the majority of new day traders lose some or all of their capital and quit trading within two years. Day trading is an extremely competitive S quadrant activity in which the most knowledgeable and best prepared use everyone else's money.

Remember to get your free audio report 'My Rich Dad said, "Profit Don't Panic,"' available at www.richdadbook3.com. Learning how to keep a cool head and invest wisely during a crash is a very important qualified investor skill. Besides, it is during a crash that many people become very rich.

# Chapter 24

# The Sophisticated Investor

The sophisticated investor knows as much as the qualified investor but has also studied the advantages available through the legal system. Rich dad defined the sophisticated investor as an investor who knows what the qualified investor knows and who is familiar with the following specialties of law:

1. Tax law
2. Corporate law
3. Securities law

While not a lawyer, the sophisticated investor may base as much of his or her investment strategy on the law as well as the investment product and potential returns. The sophisticated investor often gains higher returns with very low risk by using the different disciplines of law.

## Knowing the E-T-C

By knowing the basics of the law, the sophisticated investor is able to use the advantages of E-T-C, which stand for entity, timing, and characteristic:

Rich dad would describe the E-T-C as follows: 'The E stands for control over the entity, which means the choice of business structure.' If you are an employee, this is not usually in your control. A person from the S quadrant usually can choose from the following entities: a sole proprietorship, partnership (which is the worst structure because you are entitled to your share of income but are responsible for all the risk), an S-Corporation, an LLC (limited liability corporation), an LLP (limited liability partnership), or a C-Corporation.

Today, if you are an attorney, doctor, architect, dentist, etc., and choose the C-Corporation as your entity of choice in the United States, your minimum tax rate is 35% versus 15% for someone like me because my business is a non-licensed professional services business.

That additional 20% tax rate differential adds up to a lot of money, especially when measured over years. It means a non-professional would have a 20% financial head start over a professional at the start of each year within a C-Corporation.

Rich dad would say to me, 'But just think about people in the E quadrant who cannot elect their choice of entity. For them, regardless of how hard they work and how much they make, the government always gets paid first through income tax withholding. And the harder you work to make more money, the more the government takes. That's because the people in the E quadrant have virtually no control over entity, expenses, and taxes. Again, people in the E quadrant cannot pay themselves first because of the Current Tax Payment Act of 1943, which started withholding of income taxes from employees. After the passage of that act, the government always got paid first.'

### Sharon's Notes

In America, partnerships, S-Corporations, LLPs, and LLCs are often called 'pass-through' entities because the income passes through the entities' returns and shows up on the owner's return. Consult a tax advisor for applicability of which entity is appropriate for your situation.

## C-Corporations

'And you always try to operate via a C-Corporate entity, don't you?' I would ask rich dad.

'In most cases,' he replied. 'Remember that it is the plan before the product or in this case the corporate entity. The point is that those who operate from the B quadrant tend to have more choices and hence more control over the best entity to best make their plan work. Again, those fine points should be discussed with both your tax attorney and your tax accountant.'

'But why a C-Corporation?' I asked. 'What is the difference that is so important to you?'

'This is the one big difference,' he said, having waited a long time to explain it. 'A sole proprietorship, a partnership, and an S-Corporation are all part of you. They are, in simple terms, an extension of you.'

'And what is a C-Corporation?' I asked.

'A C-Corporation is another you. It is not just an extension of you. A C-Corporation has the ability to be a clone of you. If you are serious about doing business, then you do not want to do business as a private citizen. That is too risky, especially in this day and age of lawsuits. When you do business, you want a clone of you actually doing the business. You do not want to do business or own anything as a private citizen,' rich dad guided me. 'If you want to be a rich private citizen, you need be as poor and penniless as possible on paper.' Rich dad also said, 'The poor and the middle class, on the other hand, want to own everything in their name. "Pride of ownership," they call it. I call anything with your name on it "a target for predators and lawyers."'

The main point rich dad was trying to make was 'The rich do not want to own anything but want to control everything. And they control via corporations and limited partnerships.' That is why control of the E in E-T-C is so important to the rich.

Within the last two years, I have seen a devastating example of how the choice of entity could have helped prevent the financial destruction of a family.

A very successful local hardware store was owned as a family partnership. The family had been in town forever, knew everyone, had become wealthy, and was quite involved in civic and charitable organizations. You could not have asked for a more wonderful, caring, and giving couple. One night, their teenage daughter was drinking and driving, had an accident, and killed a passenger in the other car. Their lives were dramatically altered. Their 17-year-old daughter was sent to an adult prison for seven years and the family lost everything they owned, including the business. In sharing this example, I am not trying to make any moral or parenting statements; I'm simply pointing out that proper financial planning for both the family and the business might – through the use of insurance, trusts, limited partnerships, or corporations – have prevented this family from losing its livelihood.

### *What about Double Taxation?*

I am often asked, 'Why do you recommend C-Corporations instead of S-Corporations or LLC corporations? Why do you want to be subject to double taxation?'

Double taxation occurs when a corporation is taxed on its income and then when it declares a dividend to its shareholders they are taxed on the dividend. The same thing can occur when an improperly structured sale of a corporation occurs and a liquidity dividend is declared. The dividend is not deductible to the corporation but is taxable to the shareholder. Therefore, that income is taxed at both the corporate and individual level.

Business owners often increase their own salaries to reduce or wipe out corporate profits and thereby eliminate the possibility of having those profits taxed twice. Alternatively, as the corporation continues to grow, the retained profits are used to expand the business and help it grow. (In the United States, a C-Corporation must justify this accumulation of earnings or it will become subject to the Accumulated Earnings Tax.) There is no double taxation unless dividends are declared.

I personally like C-Corporations because I believe they provide the maximum flexibility. I always look at the big picture. When I start a business, I expect it to become a big business. Most big businesses today are C-Corporations (or the equivalent in other countries). I grow businesses because I want to sell them or take them public, not receive dividends.

Sometimes, I choose a different entity for a business. For example, I just formed an LLC with partners so that I could buy a building.

You should consult with your financial and tax advisors to determine the appropriate structure for your situation.

## *Timing*

Rich dad would describe the T as timing. 'Timing is important because ultimately, we all need to pay taxes. Paying taxes is an expense of living in a civilized society. The rich want to control how much they pay in taxes as well as when they have to pay them.'

Understanding the law helps in controlling the timing of paying taxes. For instance, Section 1031 of the U.S. Tax Code allows you to 'roll over' your gain in investment real estate if you buy another property at a greater price. This allows you to defer paying taxes until the second property is sold (or you may choose to roll it over repeatedly – perhaps forever!).

Another important timing issue is provided by the C-Corporation status. C-Corporations can elect a different year-end for tax and accounting purposes (such as June 30, for instance) than December 31, which is required for most individuals, partnerships, S-Corporations, and LLC Corporations. This allows for a certain amount of strategic tax planning as to the timing of distributions between corporations and to individuals.

## Sharon's Notes

Although Robert discusses the entity and timing issues as simple tax planning vehicles, it is important to understand that all decisions related to entity selection as well as income timing issues should have legitimate business purposes and be thoroughly discussed with your legal and tax advisors. Although Robert uses these tax-planning opportunities personally, he does so with the careful guidance and planning of his legal and tax advisors.

The chart on page 274 describes the various forms of business entities and related issues that you need to consider when choosing the entity right for your individual needs. It is imperative that you carefully review your individual financial and tax situation with your legal and tax advisors in choosing the right entity for your business.

## Character of Income

Regarding the third component of the E-T-C, rich dad would say, 'Investors control. Everyone else gambles. The rich are rich because they have more control over their money than the poor and middle class. The moment you understand that the game of money is a game of control, you can focus on what is important in life, which is not making more money but gaining more financial control.'

Reaching for his yellow pad, rich dad would write:

1. Earned income
2. Passive income
3. Portfolio income

'These are the three different kinds of income.' Rich dad would stress that I should know the difference between these three different types of income. The C of the E-T-C stands for the character of the income.

'Is there a lot of difference?' I would ask.

'Very much so,' he would reply. 'Especially when combined with the E (entity) and T (timing) of the E-T-C. Controlling the characteristics of your income is the most important financial control of all. But you may first want to control the E and the T.'

It took me awhile to fully appreciate and understand why controlling the characteristics of these three different types of income is so important.

'It's important because the characteristic of the income is what separates the rich from the working class,' rich dad analyzed. 'The poor and middle class focus on earned income, also called wages or paycheck income. The rich focus on passive income and portfolio income. That is the fundamental difference between the rich and the working class, which explains why control of the C (characteristic) is a fundamental control, especially if you plan on being rich.'

'In America and other advanced economies, even the first dollar of earned income is taxed at higher rates than passive and portfolio income. The higher rates are necessary to provide various forms of "social insurance,"' rich dad would further explain. Social insurance stands for payments the government makes to various people. (In the United States, this would include Social Security, Medicare, and unemployment insurance, just to name a few.) Income taxes are then calculated on top of social insurance taxes. Passive and portfolio income are not subject to social insurance taxes.

'So every day that I get up and focus on working hard to earn money, I am focusing on earned income, which means I pay more in taxes,' I would say. 'That is why you have been encouraging me to change my focus on what kind of income I want to earn.'

I realized rich dad was back to Lesson #1 of *Rich Dad Poor Dad*.

**LEGAL ENTITIES FOR BUSINESSES**

| ENTITY | CONTROL | LIABILITY | TAX | YEAR END | CONTINUITY |
|---|---|---|---|---|---|
| SOLE PROPRIETORSHIP | You have complete control | You are completely liable | You report all income and expense on your personal tax return | Calendar year end | Business terminates with your death |
| GENERAL PARTNERSHIP | Each partner, including you, can enter into contracts and other business agreements | You are totally liable for all business debts including your partners' share | You report your share of partnership income on your personal tax return | Must be same as the majority interest tax year, or principal partners. If neither, must be calendar | Partnership terminates on death or withdrawal of any partner |
| LIMITED PARTNERSHIP | General partners control the business | General partners are totally liable – Limited partners are liable for only the amount of their investment | Partnership files annual tax returns – General & Limited partners report their income or loss on their personal tax returns. Losses may be subject to limitations | Must be same as the majority interest tax year, or principal partners. If neither, must be calendar | Partnership does not dissolve with death of a limited partner but may dissolve with death of a general partner unless the partnership agreement states otherwise |
| LIMITED LIABILITY COMPANY | Owners or members have the authority | Owners or members are not liable for business debts | Rules vary dependent on the State – 'Check the box' allows election of treatment | Rules vary dependent on the State – 'Check the box' allows election of treatment | Rules vary depending on the State – In some States the company will dissolve upon the death of an owner or member |
| CORPORATION C Corp | Shareholders appoint Board of Directors which appoints Officers who have the most authority | Shareholders risk only the amount of their investment in the corporation's stock | Corporation pays its own taxes – Shareholders pay tax on dividends received | Any month end. Personal service corp must use calendar | The Corporation stands alone as a legal entity – It can survive the death of owner, officer or shareholder |
| SUBCHAPTER S | Shareholders appoint Board of Directors which appoints Officers who have the most authority | Shareholders risk only the amount of their investment in the corporation's stock | Shareholders report their share of the corporate profit or loss on their personal tax returns | Calendar year | The Corporation stands alone as a legal entity – It can survive the death of owner, officer or shareholder |

WARNING: Please consult your financial and tax advisors to determine the entity best suited for you

'The rich don't work hard for money. They have their money work hard for them.' It suddenly all made sense. I needed to learn how to convert earned income into passive and portfolio income so my money could start working for me.

### The Investor Controls Possessed by the Sophisticated Investor

1. The control over yourself
2. The control over income/expense and asset/liability ratios
4. The control over taxes
5. The control over when you buy and when you sell
6. The control over brokerage transactions
7. The control over the E-T-C (entity, timing, characteristic)

### The Three Es Possessed by the Sophisticated Investor

1. Education
2. Experience
3. Excessive cash

### Sharon's Notes

The SEC test of a 'sophisticated investor' is a non-accredited investor who either alone or with his purchasing representative has enough knowledge and experience in financial and business matters to be able to evaluate the merits and risks of the prospective investment. The SEC presumes that accredited investors (as defined earlier as the well-to-do, who can afford to hire advisors) are capable of watching out for their own interests.

In contrast, we believe many accredited and qualified investors are not sophisticated. Many wealthy individuals have not learned the basics of investing and the law. Many of them rely on investment advisors who they hope are sophisticated investors to do the investing for them.

Our sophisticated investor understands the impact and advantages of the law and has structured his or her investment portfolio to take maximum advantage of entity selection, timing, and characteristic of income. In doing so, the sophisticated investor has sought the advice of his or her legal and tax counsel.

Many sophisticated investors are often content investing in other entities as outside investors. They may not possess control over the management of their investments, which distinguishes them from the inside investor. They may invest in management teams without possessing a controlling interest in the company. Alternatively, they may invest as partners in real estate syndications or as shareholders in large corporations. They study and invest prudently but lack control over the management of the underlying asset and therefore have access only to public information of the company's operations. This lack of management control is the defining difference between a sophisticated investor and an inside investor.

However, the sophisticated investor still uses the advantages provided by the E-T-C analysis for his or her own financial portfolio. In Phase Four, we will discuss how the sophisticated investor applies these principles to obtain the maximum advantage provided by the law.

### Good Versus Bad

In addition to the three characteristics of income Robert discusses, three other general principles distinguish a sophisticated investor from an average investor. A sophisticated investor knows the difference between:

> Good debt and bad debt
> Good expenses and bad expenses
> Good losses and bad losses

As a general rule, good debt, good expenses, and good losses all generate additional cash flow for you. For instance, debt taken to acquire a rental property, which has a positive cash flow each month, would be good debt. Likewise, paying for legal and tax advice are good expenses if they save you thousands of dollars in reduced taxes from tax planning. An example of a good loss is the loss generated by depreciation from real estate. This good loss is also called a phantom loss because it is a paper loss and does not require an actual outlay of cash. The end result is a savings in the amount of tax paid on the income offset by the loss.

Knowing the difference between good and bad debt, expenses, and losses is what distinguishes the sophisticated investor from the average investor. When average investors hear the words 'debt, expense, and loss,' they usually react negatively. Generally, their experiences with debt, expenses, and losses result in additional cash flowing 'out of their pockets' instead of into their pockets.

The sophisticated investor enlists the advice of accountants, tax strategists, and financial advisors to structure the most beneficial financial organization for his or her investments. He or she looks for and invests in those deals that include the E-T-C features that support his or her personal financial plan – the map he or she is following to become rich.

## How Can You Identify a Sophisticated Investor?

I remember a story my rich dad once told me about risk. While part of it has been covered in other parts of the book, it is worth repeating here. The average investor views risk from a completely different point of view than the sophisticated investor. And it is this view of risk that truly differentiates the sophisticated investor.

## Why Being Secure Is Risky

One day, I went to my rich dad and said, 'My dad thinks that what you do is far too risky. He thinks that one financial statement is secure but you think that controlling only one financial statement is risky. It seems like such a contradiction in points of view.'

Rich dad just chuckled. 'It is,' said rich dad, continuing to chuckle. 'Almost exactly opposite and contradictory.' Rich dad paused for a moment to gather his thoughts. 'If you want to become really rich,' he said, 'then one of the things you will have to change is your point of view on what you think is risky and what is secure. What the poor and middle class think is secure, I think is risky.'

I thought about that statement for a brief moment, letting the idea that what my dad thought was secure, my rich dad thought was risky sink in. 'I don't fully understand.' I finally asked. 'Can you give me an example?'

'Sure,' said rich dad. 'Just listen to our words. Your dad always says, "Get a safe, secure job." Is that correct?'

I nodded my head. 'Yes, he thinks that is a secure way to run your life.'

'But is it really secure?' asked rich dad.

'I guess for him it is,' I replied. 'But you see it differently?'

Rich dad nodded his head and then asked, 'What often happens when a public company announces a large layoff of employees?'

'I don't know,' I replied. 'You mean what happens when a company fires a lot of employees?'

'Yes,' said rich dad. 'What often happens to the price of their stock?'

'I don't know,' I replied. 'Does the share price go down?'

Rich dad shook his head. Quietly he said, 'No, unfortunately when a publicly listed company announces a large layoff of employees, the share price of that company often goes up.'

I thought about that statement for a moment and then said, 'And that is why you have often said there is a big difference between people on the left side of the CASHFLOW Quadrant and people on the right.'

Rich dad nodded his head. 'A big difference. What is secure for one side is risky to the other.'

'And that is why so few people become really rich?' I asked.

Again rich dad nodded his head and repeated, 'What seems secure to one side seems risky to the other side. If you want to be rich and keep your wealth for generations, you must be able to see both sides to risk and security. The average investor only sees one side.'

## What Seems Secure Is Really Risky

As an adult, I now see what my rich dad saw. Today, what I think is secure most people think is risky. The following are some of the differences.

| AVERAGE INVESTOR | SOPHISTICATED INVESTOR |
|---|---|
| Only one financial statement. | Multiple financial statements. |
| Wants everything in their name. | Wants nothing in their name. Uses corporate entities. Often personal residence and automobile are not in their names. |
| Does not think of insurance as an investment. Uses words such as 'diversify.' | Uses insurance as an investment product to hedge against exposed risk. Uses words such as 'covered,' 'exposure' and 'hedge.' |
| Holds only paper assets, which includes cash and savings. | Has both paper assets and hard assets such as real estate and precious metals. Precious metals are a hedge against government mismanagement of the money supply, also know as fiat money. |
| Focuses on job security. | Focuses on financial freedom. |
| Focuses on professional education. Avoids making mistakes. | Focuses on financial education. Understands that mistakes are part of learning. |

| AVERAGE INVESTOR | SOPHISTICATED INVESTOR |
|---|---|
| Does not seek financial information or wants it for free if sought. | Willing to pay for financial information. |
| Thinks in good or bad, black or white, right or wrong. | Thinks in financial gray. |
| Looks at past indicators — such as p/es and CAP rates. | Looks for future indicators — trends, proformas, changes in management & products. |
| Calls brokers 1st and asks for investment advice or invests alone, asking no one for advice. | Calls broker last . . . after consulting with plan and team of financial and legal advisors then calls appropriate broker. Their brokers are often part of team. |
| Seeks external security, such as job, company, government. | Values personal self-confidence and independence. |

In conclusion, what looks secure to some investors seems risky to others.

# Chapter 25

# *The Inside Investor*

The inside investor is someone who is on the inside of the investment and has some degree of management control.

Although an important distinction of the inside investor is the aspect of control over management, the most important distinction rich dad pointed out was that you don't need to have a lot of income or net worth to be considered an inside investor. An officer, director, or owner of 10% or more of the outstanding shares of the corporation is an inside investor.

Most investment books are written for people who are on the outside of the world of investing. This book is written for people who want to invest from the inside.

In the real world, there is legal inside investment activity as well as illegal insider activity. Rich dad always wanted his son and me to be investors on the inside rather than the outside. It is one very important way to reduce risk and increase returns.

Someone with the financial education but not the financial resources of an accredited investor can still become an inside investor. This is where many people enter the world of investing today. By building their own companies, inside investors are building assets that they can run, sell, or take public.

In his book, *What Works on Wall Street*, James P. O'Shaughnessy analyzes the returns by market capitalization of various types of investments. It shows that the small stocks far outperform the other categories. A chart from his book is included for your reference on the next page.

Almost all of the high returns are found in the small microcap stocks with market capitalizations below $25 million. The down side is that these stocks are too small for mutual funds to invest in and hard to find for the average investor. As O'Shaughnessy states, 'tantalizingly out of reach of nearly everyone.' There is very little trading volume in these stocks so the ask price and bid price are usually far apart. This is an example of how 10% of the investors gain control of 90% of the shares.

If you can't find these stocks to invest in, then consider the next best thing. Build your own small cap stock company and enjoy the superior returns as the inside investor.

### How I Did It

I found my financial freedom as an inside investor. Remember that I started small, buying real estate as a sophisticated investor. I learned how to use limited partnerships and corporations to maximize the tax savings and asset protection. I then started several companies to gain additional experience. With the financial education I learned from my rich dad, I built businesses as an inside investor. I did not become an accredited investor until I found success as a sophisticated investor. I have never considered myself a qualified investor. I do not know how to pick stocks and do not choose to buy stocks as an outsider. (Why would I? Being an insider is much lower risk as well as much more profitable!)

I share this with you to give you hope. If I can learn to become an inside investor through building a company, then so can you. Remember that the more controls you possess over your investment, the less risky it is.

## *The Investor Controls Possessed by the Inside Investor*

1. The control over yourself
2. The control over income/expense and asset/liability ratios
3. The control over the management of the investment
4. The control over taxes
5. The control over when you buy and when you sell
6. The control over brokerage transactions
7. The control over the E-T-C (entity, timing, characteristic)
8. The control over the terms and conditions of the agreements
9. The control over access to information

## *The Three Es Possessed by the Inside Investor*

1. Education
2. Experience
3. Excessive cash

## *Sharon's Notes*

The SEC defines an 'insider' as anyone who has information about a company that has not yet been made publicly available. The Securities Exchange Act of 1934 made it illegal for anyone who had non-public information on a company to profit from that information. This includes the insider as well as anyone to whom he or she gives a 'tip' who subsequently profits from the information.

Robert's use of the word 'insider' defines investors who have management control over the operations of the business. The inside investor has control over the direction of the company. An outside investor does not. Robert distinguishes between legal and illegal insider trading, and strongly opposes illegal insider trading. It is too easy to make money legally.

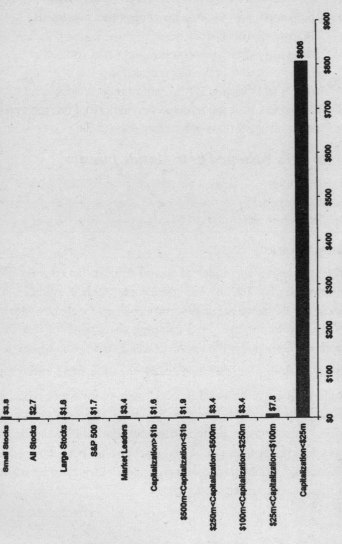

Source: *What Works on Wall Street* by James P. O'Shaughnessy

December 31, 1996 value of $10,000 invested on December 31, 1951 and annually rebalanced by market capitalization (in millions).

| | |
|---|---|
| Small Stocks | $3.8 |
| All Stocks | $2.7 |
| Large Stocks | $1.6 |
| S&P 500 | $1.7 |
| Market Leaders | $3.4 |
| Capitalization>$1b | $1.6 |
| $500m<Capitalization<$1b | $1.9 |
| $250m<Capitalization<$500m | $3.4 |
| $100m<Capitalization<$250m | $3.4 |
| $25m<Capitalization<$100m | $7.8 |
| Capitalization<$25m | $808 |

## *Creating Control*

The money you invest and risk as the owner of a private business is your own. If you have outside investors, you have a fiduciary responsibility to manage their investment well, but you are able to control the management of the investment as well as access to insider information.

## *Buying Control*

In addition to building a business on your own, you may become an inside investor through buying a controlling interest in an existing company. Buying a majority of the stock in a company allows you to acquire the controlling interest. Remember that as you increase the number of investor controls you possess, you continue to reduce your risk in the investment – that is, of course, if you possess the skill to manage the investment properly.

If you already own a business and wish to expand, you may acquire another business through merger or acquisition. The important issues in mergers and acquisitions are far too numerous to explore here. However, it is very important to seek competent legal, tax, and accounting advice before any purchase, merger, or acquisition to make sure such transactions are done properly.

To move from being an inside investor to an ultimate investor, you must decide to sell a portion or all of your business. The following questions may help you in your decision process:

1. Are you still excited about the business?
2. Do you want to start another business?
3. Do you want to retire?
4. Is the business profitable?
5. Is the business growing too rapidly for you to handle it?

6.  Does your company have large capital funding needs that can best be met through selling stock or through selling to another business?
7.  Does your company have the money and time for a public offering?
8.  Can your individual focus be diverted from the daily operations of the company to negotiate a sale or public offering without hurting the operations of the company?
9.  Is the industry your business is in expanding or contracting?
10. What impact will your competitors have on a sale or public offering?
11. If your business is strong, can you pass it on to your children or other family members?
12. Are there well-trained and managerially strong family members (children) to pass it on to?
13. Does the business need managerial skills that you lack?

Many inside investors are extremely happy running their businesses and investment portfolios. They have no desire to sell a portion of their business through a public or private offering, nor do they want to sell the business outright. This is the type of investor that Robert's best friend Mike has become. He is very content running the financial empire that he and his father built.

## Chapter 26

# *The Ultimate Investor*

The ultimate investor is a person such as Bill Gates or Warren Buffet. These investors build giant companies that other investors want to invest in. The ultimate investor is a person who creates an asset that becomes so valuable that the asset they created is worth literally billions of dollars to millions of people.

Both Gates and Buffet became rich not because of their high salaries or their great products but because they built great companies and took the companies public.

While it is not likely that many of us will ever build a Microsoft or Berkshire Hathaway, we all have the possibility of building a smaller business and becoming wealthy by selling it privately or selling it publicly.

Rich dad used to say, 'Some people build houses to sell; others build cars, but the ultimate is to build a business that millions of people want to own a share of.'

## *The Investor Controls Possessed by the Ultimate Investor*

1.  The control over yourself
2.  The control over income/expense and asset/liability ratios
3.  The control over the management of the investment

4.  The control over taxes
5.  The control over when you buy and when you sell
6.  The control over brokerage transactions
7.  The control over the E-T-C (entity, timing, characteristic)
8.  The control over the terms and conditions of the agreements
9.  The control over access to information
10. The control over giving it back, philanthropy, redistribution of wealth

### The Three Es Possessed by the Ultimate Investor

1.  Education
2.  Experience
3.  Excessive cash

### Sharon's Notes

There are advantages and disadvantages of 'going public,' which we will discuss in greater detail later. However, here are a few of the advantages and disadvantages of an initial public offering (IPO):

**Advantages:**

1.  To allow business owners to 'cash in' some of their equity in the business. For example, Gates's original partner, Paul Allen, sold some of his Microsoft shares in order to buy cable TV companies.
2.  To raise expansion capital.
3.  To pay off company debt.
4.  To raise the company's net worth.
5.  To allow the company to offer stock options as benefits to its employees.

**Disadvantages:**

1. Your operations become public. You are forced to disclose information to the public that had previously been private.
2. The IPO is very expensive.
3. Your focus is diverted from running the operations of the business to facilitating and meeting the requirements of being a public company.
4. Compliance with the IPO and ongoing quarterly and annual reporting requirements are extensive.
5. You risk losing control of your company.
6. If your stock does not perform well in the public market, you risk being sued by your shareholders.

For many investors the potential financial reward of taking their company public greatly overshadows any potential disadvantage of an IPO.

## *Starting on My Path*

The rest of this book is about rich dad guiding me as an inside investor and sophisticated investor on my path to becoming the ultimate investor. He no longer had to guide his son Mike. Mike was content being an inside investor. You will gain some insights into what rich dad thought was important, what I needed to learn, and some of the mistakes I made along the way. It is my hope that you can learn from my successes as well as my mistakes on your own path to becoming the ultimate investor.

# Chapter 27

# *How to Get Rich Quick*

Rich dad would regularly review the various levels of investors with me. He wanted me to understand the various ways investors made their fortunes. My rich dad had become wealthy by first investing as an inside investor. He had started small and learned the tax advantages available to him. He quickly gained confidence and became a truly sophisticated investor at an early age. He had built an incredible financial empire. My real dad, on the other hand, had worked hard all his life as a government employee and had little to show for it.

As I got older, the gap between my rich dad and my poor dad was increasingly evident. I finally asked my rich dad why he was becoming wealthier while my real dad was working harder and harder.

In the introduction this book I related the story of walking along the beach with my rich dad looking at the large piece of oceanfront property he had just purchased. During that walk on the beach, I realized that my rich dad had just purchased an investment that only a rich person could acquire. The problem was my rich dad was not really a rich man, yet. That is why I asked him how he could afford such an expensive investment when I knew my real dad, a man who made more money than my rich dad, could not.

It was during this walk on the beach that my rich dad shared the basis of his investment plan. He said, 'I can't afford this land either, but my business can.' As I stated in the introduction, this was when my curiosity about the power of investing began and when I became a student of the profession. During that walk on the beach, at the age of 12, I was beginning to learn the secrets of how many of the very richest people in the world invest and why they are the 10% that control 90% of money.

Again, I refer to Ray Kroc, founder of McDonald's, saying virtually the same thing to my friend's MBA class. Ray Kroc said to the class, 'My business is not hamburgers. My business is real estate.' That is why McDonald's owns the most valuable real estate in the world. Ray Kroc and rich dad understood that the purpose of a business was to buy assets.

### Rich Dad's Investment Plan

When I was a young boy still in elementary school, rich dad was already placing ideas in my head about the differences between being rich, poor, and middle class. During one of our Saturday lessons, he said, 'If you want job security, follow your dad's advice. If you want to be rich, you need to follow my advice. The chances of your dad having both job security and becoming rich are slim. The laws are not written in his favor.'

One of rich dad's six lessons as described in *Rich Dad Poor Dad* was a lesson about the power of corporations. In *CASHFLOW Quadrant*, I wrote about how the different quadrants were governed by different tax laws. Rich dad used these lessons to show me the difference between his investment plan and my real dad's investment plan. These differences greatly affected my life's path after my formal education was complete and my military duty was over.

'My business buys assets with pre-tax dollars,' said rich dad as he drew the following diagram:

'Your dad tries to buy assets with after-tax dollars. His financial statement looks like this,' said rich dad:

As a young boy, I really did not fully comprehend what rich dad was trying to teach me, yet I recognized the difference. Because I was confused, I spent much time quizzing him on what it meant. To help me understand a little better, he drew the following diagram:

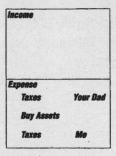

'Why?' I asked rich dad. 'Why do you pay your taxes last and why does my dad pays his taxes first?'

'Because your dad is an employee and I am a business owner,' said rich dad. 'Always remember that we may live in a free country, but everybody does not live by the same laws. If you want to be rich, or get rich quickly, you had best follow the same laws the rich use.'

'How much in taxes does my dad pay?' I asked.

'Well, your dad is a highly paid government employee, so I estimate that he pays at least 50% to 60% of his total income in taxes in one form or another,' said rich dad.

'And how much do you pay in taxes?' I asked.

'Well, that is not really the correct question,' said rich dad. 'The real question is: "How much is my taxable income?"'

I became confused and asked, 'What is the difference?'

'Well,' said rich dad. 'I pay taxes on net income, and your dad's taxes are withheld from his total income. That is one of the biggest differences between your dad and me. I get ahead faster because I get to buy my assets with gross income and pay taxes on net income. Your dad pays taxes on gross income and then tries to buy assets with his net income. That is why it is very, very hard for him to achieve any kind of wealth. He gives a lot of his money to the government first, money that he could be using to buy assets. I pay my taxes on the net, or what is left over, after I buy my assets. I buy assets first and pay taxes last. Your dad pays taxes first and has very little money left over to buy assets with.'

At the age of 10 or 11, I really did not understand exactly what rich dad was saying. I just knew it did not sound fair and I said so. 'That is not fair,' I protested.

'I agree,' said rich dad, nodding. 'It isn't fair, but that is the law.'

## *The Laws Are the Same*

When discussing this issue in my seminars, I often hear, 'That may be a law in the United States but that is not the law in my country.'

Since I teach in many English-speaking countries, I often reply with 'How do you know? What makes you think the laws are different?' The fact is, most people do not know which laws are similar and which laws are different, so I offer a short lesson in economic history and laws.

I point out to my classes that most English-speaking countries' laws are based upon English common law, the law spread throughout the world by the British East India Company. I also point out to them the exact date the rich began to make the rules, 'In 1215, the Magna Carta, the most famous document of British constitutional history, was signed. By signing the Magna Carta, King John yielded part of his power to the rich barons of England. It is now generally recognized that the Magna Carta showed the viability of opposition to the excessive use of royal power.'

I then explain the importance of the Magna Carta just how my rich dad had explained it to me. 'Ever since the signing of the Magna Carta, the rich have been making the rules.' He also said, 'The spiritual golden rule is: "Do unto others as you would have them do unto you." Other people say that the financial golden rule is: "He who has the gold makes the rules." However, I think the real financial golden rule is: "He who makes the rules gets the gold."'

The September 13, 1999 *Wall Street Journal* discussed in the introduction article seems to back up rich dad's view of the real financial golden rule. The article said, 'For all the talk of mutual funds for the masses, of barbers and shoeshine boys giving investment tips, the stock market has remained the privilege of a relatively elite group.

'Only 43.3% of all households owned any stock at all in 1997, the most recent year for which data is available, according to New York University economist, Edward Wolff. Of those, many portfolios were relatively small. Nearly 90% of all shares were held by the wealthiest

10% of households. The bottom line: That top 10% held 73% of the country's net worth in 1997, up from 68% in 1983.'

### Business Buys Your Assets

When I was 25 and almost out of the Marine Corps, rich dad reminded me of the difference in two life paths.

He said, 'This is how your dad tries to invest and acquire assets':

He added, 'This is how I invest':

'Always remember that the rules are different for the different quadrants. Therefore, make your next career decision carefully. While that job with the airlines might be fun in the short term, in the long run, you might not get to be as rich as you want to be.'

## How the Tax Laws Changed

Although rich dad did not finish school, he was an avid student of economics, world history, and laws. When I was attending the U.S. Merchant Marine Academy, at Kings Point, New York (1965 to 1969), studying world trade, rich dad was very excited that my studies included admiralty law, business law, economics, and corporate law. Because I had studied these subjects, it was much easier for me to decide to not take a job as an airline pilot.

## The Reason Is Found in History

One of the differences between America and the rest of the world colonized by the English is that the colonists in America protested excess taxes by organizing the Boston Tea Party. America grew rapidly from the 1800s to the 1900s simply because we were a low-tax country. Being a low tax haven, the United States attracted entrepreneurs from all over the world who wanted to get rich quickly. In 1913, however, we passed the 16th Amendment, which made taxation of the rich possible, and that was the end of the low-tax state. Yet, the rich have always found a way out of the trap, which is why the laws are different for the different quadrants, especially favoring the B quadrant, the quadrant of the ultra-rich of America.

The rich have gotten even for the tax law change of 1913 by slowly changing laws and putting the pressure back on the other quadrants. So the slow creep of taxation has looked like this:

In 1943, the Current Tax Payment Act was passed. Now, instead of just taxing the rich, the federal government was allowed to tax everyone in the E quadrant. If you were an employee, in the E quadrant, you could no longer pay yourself first because the government got paid first. People are always shocked to see how much is taken out in both direct taxes as well as hidden taxes from their paycheck.

In 1986, the Tax Reform Act was passed. This law change dramatically affected anyone who was a professional worker – people such as doctors, lawyers, accountants, architects, engineers, etc. This law change prevented someone in the S quadrant from using the same tax laws used by the B quadrant. For example, if an S quadrant person has the same income as a B quadrant person, the S quadrant worker will have to pay a beginning tax rate of 35% (50% when you include social insurance taxes). On the other hand, the B quadrant person could possibly pay 0% on the same amount of income.

In other words, the golden rule – 'He who makes the rules keeps the gold' – was once again true. The rules are made from the B quadrant and have been made from there ever since 1215, when the barons forced the king to sign the Magna Carta. Maybe the B in the B quadrant stands for baron.

Some of these laws and changes were explained in more detail in *Rich Dad Poor Dad* and in *CASHFLOW Quadrant*.

## *The Decision Is Made*

Even after I had decided to follow rich dad's investment plan instead of my poor dad's plan, rich dad shared with me a simple analysis about my chances for success in life that reinforced my decision. Drawing the *CASHFLOW Quadrant*, he said, 'Your first decision is to figure out in which quadrant you have the most chance of achieving long-term financial success.'

Pointing to the E quadrant, he said: 'You don't have the expertise that employers will pay the big money for, so you'll probably never make enough money as an employee to invest with. Besides, you're sloppy, you get bored easily, you don't have a very long attention span, you tend to argue, and you don't follow instructions well. Therefore, your chances for financial success in the E quadrant don't look very good.'

Pointing to the S quadrant, he said, 'S stands for smart. That is why so many doctors, lawyers, accountants, and engineers are in the S quadrant. You're bright, but you're not that smart. You were never much of a student. The S also stands for star. You'll probably never be a rock star, movie star, or sports star, so your chances of making the big money in the S quadrant are slim.

'That leaves the B quadrant,' rich dad continued. 'This quadrant is perfect for you. Since you lack any special talent or expertise, your

chances for attaining great wealth will be in this quadrant.'

And with that comment, I was certain. I decided that my best chance for great wealth and financial success would be through building a business. The tax laws were in my favor, and my lack of stardom in the other quadrants just made my decision easier.

### The Author's Lesson in Hindsight

I try to pass along the bits of wisdom I learned from my rich dad in the seminars I present today. When I am asked how I invest, I usually tell the group about investing through a business, or as rich dad said, 'My business buys my assets.'

**Invariably, people raise their hands and say things like:**

1. 'But I am an employee and I do not own my own business.'
2. 'Not everyone can own a business.'
3. 'Starting a business is risky.'
4. 'I don't have any money to invest.'

To these types of responses to rich dad's investment plan, I offer these ideas.

To the statement that not everyone can own a business, I remind people that less than 100 years ago, most people did own their own businesses. Just 100 years ago, approximately 85% of the U.S. population were either independent farmers or small shopkeepers. I know that both sets of my grandparents were small-business owners.

Only a small percentage of the population was comprised of employees. I then say, 'It seems that the Industrial Age – with its promise of high-paying jobs, job security for life, and pension benefits – has bred that independence out of us.' I also add that our educational system was designed to create employees and professional people, not entrepreneurs, so it would be only natural for people to feel that starting a business would be risky.

**The points I make are:**

1. Chances are that you all have the potential to be great business owners if you have the desire to develop the skills. Our ancestors developed and depended upon their entrepreneurial skills. If you do not have a business today, the question is: Do you want to go through the process of learning how to build a business? You are the only one who can answer that question.

2.  When people say, 'I have no money to invest,' or 'I need a real estate deal I can buy for no money down,' I reply, 'Maybe you should switch quadrants and invest from the quadrant that allows you to invest with pre-tax dollars. Then you might have a lot more money to invest.'

One of the first considerations in your investment plan should be to decide in which quadrant lies the best opportunity for you to make the most money quickly. That way, you can begin investing for the highest returns, with the least risk, and you'll have the best chance of becoming very, very rich.

## Chapter 28

# Keep Your Day Job and Still Become Rich

Once I decided to build a business, the next problem facing me was that I had no money. First, I did not know how to build a business. Second, I had no money to build a business with, and third, I had no money to live on. Feeling weak in the stomach and lacking confidence in myself, I called rich dad and asked him what I should do.

He immediately said, 'Go get a job.'

His reply shocked me. 'I thought you were telling me to start my own business.'

'Yes I did. But you still have to eat and put a roof over your head,' he said.

What he said to me next I have passed on to countless people. Rich dad said, 'Rule number one in becoming an entrepreneur is to never take a job for money. Take a job only for the long-term skills you will learn.'

The first and only job I got after the Marine Corps was with the Xerox Corporation. I chose it because it had the best sales training program. Rich dad knew I was very shy and terrified of rejection. He recommended I learn to sell, not for the money but to learn to overcome my personal fears. Each day, I had to go from office building to office building knocking on doors trying to sell people a Xerox machine. It was a very painful learning process, yet this process has made me millions of dollars over the years.

Rich dad would say, 'If you cannot sell, you cannot be an entrepreneur.'

For two years, I was the worst salesperson in the Honolulu branch. I took extra classes on selling as well as bought tapes and listened to them. Finally, after nearly being fired several times, I began to make sales. Although I was still painfully shy, the sales training helped me to develop the skills I needed to acquire wealth.

The problem was that no matter how hard I worked and how many machines I sold, I was always short of cash. I had no money with which to invest or to start a business. One day, I told rich dad that I planned to take a part-time job to supplement my income so I could invest. That was the moment he had been waiting for.

Rich dad said, 'The biggest mistake people make is that they work too hard for their money.' He went on to say, 'Most people do not get ahead financially because when they need more money, they take a part-time job. If they really want to get ahead, they need to keep their day job and start a part-time business.'

Rich dad drew this diagram for me once he knew I was learning valuable skills and was serious about becoming a business owner and investor:

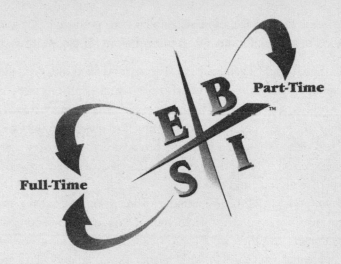

'It is time for you to start your business – part-time,' he said. 'Don't waste your time with a part-time job. A part-time job keeps you in the E quadrant, but a part-time business puts you in the B quadrant. Most big companies are started as part-time businesses.'

In 1977, I started my nylon and Velcro wallet business part-time. Many of you are familiar with that product line today. From 1977 to 1978, I worked very hard at Xerox, eventually becoming one of the top sales representatives in the branch. In my spare time, I was also building a business that would soon become a worldwide, multi-million-dollar business.

When people ask me if I loved my product line – a line that consisted of colorful nylon wallets, nylon watchbands, and nylon shoe pockets that attached to the laces of a running shoe and held a key, money, and ID card – I answer, 'No. I was not in love with the product line. But I did enjoy the challenge of building the business.'

I mention this point specifically because so many people today say to me such things as:

1.   'I have a great idea for a new product.'

2.   'You have to feel passionate about your product.'
3.   'I'm looking for the right product before I begin my business.'

To these people, I generally say, 'The world is filled with great ideas for new products. The world is also filled with great products. But the world is short of great businesspeople. The primary reason in starting a business part-time is not so much to make a product great. The real reason for start a part-time business is to make you a great businessperson. Great products are a dime a dozen. But great businesspeople are rare and rich.'

If you look at Bill Gates, founder of Microsoft, he did not even invent his software product. He bought it from a group of computer programmers and then went on to build one of the most powerful and influential companies in world history. Gates did not build a great product, but he did build a great business that helped him become the richest man in the world. The message is, therefore, do not bother trying to make a great product. Focus more on starting a business so you can learn to become a great business owner.

Michael Dell of Dell Computers started his part-time business in his dormitory of the University of Texas. He had to quit school because his part-time business was making him far richer than any job he was studying for could.

Amazon.com was also started in a garage on a part-time basis. That young man is a billionaire today.

### The Lesson in Hindsight

Many people dream of starting their own business but never do because they're afraid of failing. Many other people dream of becoming rich but don't become so because they lack the skills and experience. The business skill and experience is where money really comes from.

Rich dad said to me, 'The education you receive in school is important, but the education you receive on the street is even better.'

Starting a business at home, part-time, allows you to learn priceless business skills and subjects such as:

1. Communication skills
2. Leadership skills
3. Team-building skills
4. Tax law
5. Corporate law
6. Securities law

These skills or subjects cannot be learned in a weekend course or in a single book. I continue to study them today, and the more I study them, the more my businesses improve.

One reason people learn so much by starting a part-time business is that they start as insiders, insiders in their own business. If someone can learn to build businesses, a whole new world with virtually unlimited financial opportunity becomes available. One of the problems with being in the E quadrant or the S quadrant, however, is that the opportunities are often limited by how hard one person can work and how many hours there are in a day.

## Chapter 29

# The Entrepreneurial Spirit

People invest for two basic reasons:

1. To save for retirement
2. To make a lot of money

While most of us invest for both reasons – and both are important – it seems that the majority of people lean more toward the first reason. They put money away as savers do and hope it will increase in value over time. They invest but they are more concerned about losing than winning. I have met many people whose fear of losing prevents them from acting. People need to be true to their emotional senses when investing. If the pain and the fear of losing are too great, it is best for that investor to invest very conservatively.

Yet, if you look at the great wealth of this world, that wealth has not come from cautious investors. The great changes in this world have come from investors backing what my rich dad called the entrepreneurial spirit.

One of my favorite stories is that of Christopher Columbus, a brave explorer who believed the world was round and who had a bold plan to find a faster route to the riches of Asia. However, the popular belief of his day was that the world was flat. Everyone thought that Columbus would sail off the edge of the earth if he attempted his plan. In order to test his theory that the world was round, Columbus, an Italian, had to go to the royalty of Spain and convince them to invest in his business venture. King Ferdinand and Queen Isabella put up what is called the 'front money' and invested in his business venture.

My history teacher in school tried to tell me that the money was raised to further knowledge via exploration. My rich dad told me that it was purely a business venture that needed capital. The king and queen knew that if this entrepreneur named Columbus succeeded in sailing West to reach the East, they would earn a high return on their investment. Columbus and the king and queen who backed him all had the true spirit of the entrepreneur. The king and queen did not invest to lose money. They invested because they wanted to make more money. it was the spirit of venturing or risk with the possibility of great reward. They invested in that spirit.

### Why Start a Business

As I began to formulate my plans to start my part-time business, rich dad was adamant about the spirit with which I undertook this new adventure, the adventure of building a worldwide business. He said, 'You build a business because of the challenge. You build a business because it is exciting, it's challenging, and it will require all of you to make it successful.'

Rich dad wanted me to start a business in order to find my entrepreneurial spirit. He often said, 'The world is filled with people with great ideas but only a few people with great fortunes from their ideas.' So he encouraged me to start a business, any business. He did not care about what the product was or how much I liked the product. He was not concerned about me failing. He just wanted me to start. Today I see so many people with great ideas who are afraid to start, or they start, fail and quit. That is why rich dad often quoted Einstein's saying of, 'Great spirits have often encountered violent opposition from mediocre minds.' He wanted me to simply start any business just so that I could challenge my own mediocre mind and, in the process, develop my entrepreneurial spirit. Rich dad would also say, 'The main reason so many people buy assets rather than create them is because they have not called upon their own entrepreneurial spirit to take their ideas and turn those ideas into great fortunes.'

## Don't Do It for Only $200,000

In coming back to the definition of the accredited investor, rich dad said, 'All a person needs to do to be an accredited investor is have a salary of $200,000. That is a lot of money to some people, but it is not enough of a reason to start building a business. If all you dream of is a salary of $200,000, then stay in the E or S quadrants. The risks are too great in the B and I quadrants for such a small sum. If you decide to build a business, don't do it for a mere $200,000. The risks are too high for a payoff so low. Do it for a much bigger payday. Do it for millions, maybe billions, or don't do it at all. But if you decide to pursue building a business, you must call on your entrepreneurial spirit.'

Rich dad also said, 'There is no such thing as a successful poor entrepreneur or business owner. You can be a successful and poor doctor, or a successful and poor accountant. But you cannot be a successful and poor business owner. There is only one kind of successful business owner, and that is a rich one.'"

## Lessons in Hindsight

I am often asked, 'How much is too much?' or 'How much is enough?' The person who asks that question is often someone who has never built a successful business that made a lot of money. I have also noticed that many of the people who ask that question are on the E and S side of the Quadrant. Another big difference between people on the left side of the Quadrant and people who operate on the right side is:

The people on the left side generally have only one financial state-

ment because they often have only one source of income. Those on the right side have multiple financial statements and multiple sources of income. My wife and I are employees of several corporations in which we also have ownership interests. Therefore, wc have financial statements as individuals and financial statements from our businesses. As our businesses become successful and generate cash flow for us, we need less income as employees. Many people on the left side do not know what it feels like to have more and more money coming in that requires less and less work.

While the money is important, it is not the primary motivating factor for building a business. I think the question can best be answered by asking the same question in another way. The question asked is similar to asking a golfer, 'Why do you keep playing golf?' The answer is found in the spirit of the game.

Although it took me many years of occasional pain and misery, the challenge and the spirit were always the propelling factors for me wanting to build a business. Today, I have friends who have sold their businesses for millions of dollars. Many of them take a few months off, and then they are right back in the game. It is the excitement, the challenge, the spirit, and the potential for a big payoff at the end that keeps the entrepreneur going. Before I built my nylon and Velcro wallet business, my rich dad wanted me to make sure I was doing it with that spirit.

The entrepreneurial spirit is a valuable asset in building a successful B business. Many successful capitalists today are still entrepreneurs in their hearts.

*Phase Three*

# *How Do You Build a Strong Business?*

## Chapter 30

# *Why Build a Business?*

Rich dad said, 'There are three reasons for building a business more than to simply create an asset':

1.  'To provide you with excessive cash flow.' In his book *How to Be Rich*, J. Paul Getty states that his first rule is that you must be in business for yourself. He goes on to imply that you will never get rich working for someone else.

    One of the primary reasons rich dad started so many businesses was that he had excessive cash flow from his other businesses. He also had the time because his businesses required minimal effort on his part. This allowed him the free time and extra money to keep investing in more and more assets tax-free. That is why he became rich so quickly and why he said to 'Mind your own business.'

2.  'To sell it.' Rich dad went on to explain that the problem with having a job is that you cannot sell the job, regardless of how hard you work. The problem with building a business in the S quadrant is that there is usually a limited market that would want to buy it. For example, if a dentist builds a practice, generally the only other person who may want to buy it is

another dentist. To rich dad, that was too narrow a market. He said, 'For something to be valuable, there must be many more people than you who want it. The problem with an S quadrant business is that you are often the only person who wants it.'

Rich dad said, 'An asset is something that puts money in your pocket, or it can be sold to someone else for more than you have paid for or invested in it. If you can build a successful business, you will always have a lot of money. If you learn to build a successful business, you will have developed a profession that few people ever achieve.'

In 1975, while I was learning to sell Xerox machines, I came across a young man who owned four quick-copy print shops in Honolulu. The reason he was in the business of making copies was interesting. While in school, he had run the university's copy shop and learned the business side of the operation. When he came out of school, there were no jobs, so he opened up a copy shop in downtown Honolulu doing what he knew best. Soon, he had four of these copy centers in four of the bigger downtown office buildings, all on long-term leases. A major copy shop chain came to town and made him an offer he could not refuse. He took their $750,000, a giant sum in those days, bought a boat, gave $500,000 to a professional money manager, and sailed around the world. When he returned a year and half later, the manager had grown his investment to nearly $900,000, so the young man just sailed off again, back to the islands of the South Pacific.

I was the guy who sold him the copy machines, and all I got was my small commission. He was the guy who built a business, sold it, and sailed away. I never saw him again after 1978, but I have heard that he pulls back into town every so often, checks his portfolio, and sails off again.

As my rich dad said, 'As a business owner, you don't have to be right 51% of the time. You need to be right only once.' He also said, 'Building a business is the riskiest road for most people. But if you can survive and keep improving your skills, your potential for wealth is unlimited. If you avoid risk and play it safe on the E and S side, you may be safer, but you'll also limit what you can truly earn.'

3.  'To build a business and take it public.' This was rich dad's idea of becoming what he called the ultimate investor. It was building a business and taking it public that made Bill Gates, Henry Ford, Warren Buffet, Ted Turner, and Anita Roddick very, very wealthy. They were the selling shareholders, while we were all the buying shareholders. They were insiders, while we were outsiders trying to look in.

## *You're Never Too Old and You're Never Too Young*

If anyone tells you that you can't build a business that others want to buy, use that small-minded thought to inspire you. It is true that Gates was very young when he started Microsoft but Colonel Sanders was 66 when he started Kentucky Fried Chicken.

In the next few chapters, I will be describing what rich dad called the B-I Triangle. I use this triangle as a guide to building a business. It outlines the primary technical skills that are required. Rich dad also felt certain personal traits were required to be a successful entrepreneur:

1.  **Vision:** the ability to see what others could not see.
2.  **Courage:** the ability to act despite tremendous doubt.
3.  **Creativity:** the ability to think outside the box.
4.  **The ability to withstand criticism:** There is not one successful person who has not been criticized.

5. **The ability to delay gratification:** It can be very difficult to learn to deny short-term immediate self-gratification in favor of a greater long-term reward.

## Chapter 31

# The B-I Triangle

### The Key to Great Wealth

The following is a diagram rich dad called the B-I Triangle, the key to great wealth.

The B-I Triangle was very important to rich dad because it gave structure to his ideas. As he often said, 'There are many people with great ideas but few people with great fortunes. The B-I Triangle has the power to turn ordinary ideas into great fortunes. The B-I Triangle is the guide to taking an idea and creating an asset.' It represents the knowledge required to be successful on the B and I side of the CASH-FLOW Quadrant. I have modified it a little over the years.

I was about 16 years old when I first saw this diagram. Rich dad drew it for me when I started asking him the following questions:

1.  'How is it that you have so many businesses and other people can barely handle one?'
2.  'Why do your businesses grow while other people's stay small?'
3.  'How do you have free time when other business owners work constantly?'
4.  'Why do so many businesses start and then fail so quickly?'

I did not ask him all these questions at the same time, yet they were questions that came to mind as I studied his businesses. Rich dad was about 40 years old, and I was amazed at how he could run several different companies all in different industries. For example, he had a restaurant business, a fast food business, a convenience store chain, a trucking company, a real estate construction business, and a property management business. I knew he was following his plan to have his businesses buy his true investments, which for him was real estate, but it was amazing how many businesses he could run all at the same time. When I asked him how he could start, own, and manage so many businesses, his response was to draw the B-I Triangle.

Today, I own interests in several different companies in completely different businesses because I use the B-I Triangle as a guide. I do not own as many companies as rich dad did, but by following the same formula outlined in the B-I Triangle, I could own more if I wanted.

## Explaining the B-I Triangle

Obviously, the amount of material that could be written — and needs to be written — to cover the information represented by the B-I Triangle is more than this book could cover. However, we will review the basics.

## *The Mission*

Rich dad said, 'A business needs both a spiritual and a business mission to be successful, especially at the beginning.' When he explained this diagram to his son and me, he always began with the mission since he thought it to be the most important aspect of the triangle and why it was at the base. 'If the mission is clear and strong, the business will weather the trials every business goes through during its first ten years. When a business gets big and it forgets its mission, or the mission it was created for is no longer needed, the business begins to die.'

Rich dad chose the words 'spiritual' and 'business.' He said, 'Many people start a business only to make money. Just to make money is not a strong enough mission. Money alone does not provide enough fire, drive, or desire. The mission of a business should fill a need that the customers want, and if it fills that need, and fills it well, the business will begin to make money.'

When it came to a spiritual mission, rich dad said, 'Henry Ford was a man driven by a spiritual mission first and a business mission second. He wanted to make the automobile available to the masses, not just the rich. That is why his mission statement was "Democratize the automobile." Rich dad went on to say, 'When the spiritual mission and business mission are both strong and in line, the combined power builds huge businesses.'

Rich dad's spiritual mission and business mission were closely in line. His spiritual mission was to provide jobs and opportunities for many of the poor people to whom he served food in his restaurants. Rich dad thought the mission of a business was very important although it was hard to see and to measure. He said, 'Without a strong mission, a business is not likely to survive its first five to ten years.' He also said, 'At the start of a business, the mission and the entrepreneur's spirit are essential for the business to survive. The spirit and mission must be preserved long after the entrepreneur is gone, or the business dies.' Rich dad would say, 'The mission of a business is a reflection of the spirit of the entrepreneur. General Electric was a company founded from the brilliance of Thomas Edison, and it has grown by preserving the spirit of the great inventor by continuing to invent new and innovative products. Ford Motor Company has survived by continuing in the tradition of Ford.'

Today, I believe that Bill Gates's spirit continues to drive Microsoft to dominate the world of software. By contrast, when Steven Jobs was pushed out of Apple and a management team from the traditional corporate world replaced him, the company went downhill rapidly. As soon as Jobs was brought back into Apple, the spirit of the company returned, new products came forth, profitability increased, and the share price went up.

Although the mission of a business is hard to measure, impossible to see, and for all practical purposes an intangible, most of us have experienced it. We can identify the mission of someone who is trying to sell us something for a commission as contrasted to someone trying to help answer our needs. As the world becomes crowded with more and more products, the businesses that survive and do well financially will be businesses that focus on serving and fulfilling the company's mission and their customers' needs, rather than just increasing the company's revenues.

CASHFLOW Technologies, Inc. – the company that Kim, Sharon, and I created to bring you this book as well as our other financial-education products – has the following mission: 'To elevate the financial well-being of humanity.' By being clear and true to the spiritual and business mission of this company, we have enjoyed success that goes beyond luck. By being clear on our mission, we attract individuals and other groups aligned with a similar mission. Some people call it luck . . . I call it being true to our mission. Over the years, I have come to believe that rich dad was right about the importance of having the spiritual mission and business mission be strong and in line.

In all truthfulness, not all of my businesses have as strong a dual mission as CASHFLOW Technologies, Inc. does. Other businesses in which I own interests have stronger business missions than spiritual missions.

I now realize that my nylon and Velcro wallet business had a very different mission than I first thought. The mission for building that business was to give me a fast education about building a worldwide business. That business fulfilled that mission rather painfully. In other words, I got what I wanted. The business grew very quickly, success was fast and furious, and so was the crash. Yet, as painful as the experience was, I realized that I had achieved my mission. After I dug myself out from under the rubble and rebuilt the business, I learned what I set out to learn. As rich dad said, 'Many entrepreneurs don't really become businesspeople until after they lose their first business.' In other words, I learned more by losing the business and rebuilding it than I did by being successful. As rich dad said, 'School is important, but the street is a better teacher.' So, my first big business venture after leaving the Marine Corps was expensive and painful, but the lessons I learned were priceless. And the business had fulfilled its mission.

### Sharon's Note

A company's mission helps it maintain focus. In the early stages of development, many factors can cause distraction. The best way to get back on track is to revisit your mission. Does the distraction affect the achievement of your mission? If so, you must deal with the distraction as quickly as possible so that you can re-focus your efforts on the overall mission.

Today, I notice many people becoming instant millionaires, even billionaires, just by taking a company public through an IPO. I often wonder if the company's mission was just to make money for owners or investors or was the company really formed to fulfill a mission or some kind of service? I am afraid that many of these new IPOs will ultimately fail because their only mission was to make money quickly. Besides, it is in the mission of the company where the entrepreneur's spirit is found.

### The Team

Rich dad always said, 'Business is a team sport.' He went on to say, 'Investing is a team sport.' He would also say, 'The problem with being in the E and S quadrant is that you play the game as an individual, playing against a team.'

Rich dad would draw the CASHFLOW Quadrant to illustrate his point:

One of rich dad's strongest criticisms of the educational system was: 'In school, they train students to take tests on their own. If a child attempts to cooperate at test time, it is called "cheating."' Rich dad would also say, 'In the real world of business, business owners cooperate at test time, and in the world of business, every day is test time.'

### A Very Important Lesson

For people considering building a powerful and successful business, I think this lesson on teamwork is crucial. It is one of the primary keys to my financial success. Business and investing are team sports, and remember that every day in business is test time. To be successful in school, you had to take tests alone. In business, success comes from taking tests as a team, not as an individual.

People in the E and S quadrant often make less money than they could or would like to because they attempt to do things on their own. If they work as a group, especially those in the E quadrant, they form a union instead of a team. And that is what is happening to medical doctors in America today. They are forming a professional union to combat the power of a team, the business team known as the health maintenance organizations (HMOs).

Many investors today are trying to invest as individuals. I see and read about thousands of people who are doing online day trading. This is a perfect example of an individual trying to trade against well-organized teams. That is why so few of them succeed as well as why many lose their money. I was taught that when it comes to investing, you should invest as a member of a team. Rich dad would say, 'If people want to become sophisticated investors and above, they must invest as a team.' On rich dad's team were his accountants, his attorneys, his brokers, his financial advisors, his insurance agents, and his bankers. I use the plurals here because he always had more than one advisor. When he made a decision, it was with input of the team. Today, I do the same.

### Not a Big Boat . . . A Big Team

On television today, I see commercials of a rich couple, sailing their yacht in some warm tropical waters. The ad seems to draw in all the individuals who are trying to get rich on their own. Whenever I see that commercial, I often think of rich dad saying to me, 'Most small-business people dream of someday owning a boat or a plane. That is why they will never own that boat or plane. When I was first starting out, I dreamed of having my own team of accountants and attorneys, not a boat.'

Rich dad wanted me to aim to have a team of accountants and attorneys working only on my business – before I dreamed of a boat. To drive his point home, he had me go to an accountant in town with my meager little tax return. As I sat across the table from Ron, the CPA, the first thing I noticed was a stack of manila folders sitting on his desk. Immediately, I got rich dad's lesson. This CPA was minding about 30 other businesses on that day alone. How could he pay full attention to my business?

Returning to rich dad's office that afternoon, I saw something I had never noticed before. As I sat in the reception area waiting for rich dad's personal secretary to let me in, I could see a team of people working only on rich dad's business. In the working area of his office was a row of bookkeepers, about fourteen of them. There were also five full-time accountants, and a chief financial officer (CFO). He also had two full-time attorneys working in his main office. When I sat down in front of rich dad, all I said was, 'They're all minding your businesses and no one else's.'

Rich dad nodded. 'As I said, most people work hard and dream of getting away on their own boat. I first dreamed of having a team of full-time accountants and attorneys. That is why I can now have the big boat and the free time. It is a matter of priorities.'

## *How Do You Afford the Team?*

In my seminars, I am often asked, 'How can you afford to pay for this team?' That question usually comes from someone in the E or S quadrant. Again, the difference goes back to the different laws and rules for the different quadrants. For example, when a person in the E quadrant pays for professional services, the transaction looks like this:

```
┌─────────────────────────┐
│ Income                  │
│                         │
│                         │
│                         │
├─────────────────────────┤
│ Expense                 │
│    Taxes                │
│                         │
│    Professional Services│
│                         │
└─────────────────────────┘
```

For people in the B and S quadrants, the transaction looks like this:

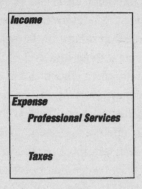

There is also a difference between the B quadrant business owner and the S quadrant business owner. The B quadrant business owner does not hesitate to pay for these services because the business system, the entire B-I Triangle, is paying for the services. S quadrant business owners are often paying for the services out of their own sweat and blood, so most of them cannot afford to hire a full-time staff because they often do not earn enough to cover their own financial needs.

## The Best Education

My answer is the same when I am asked questions such as:

1.  'How did you learn so much about investing and business?'
2.  'How do you get such high returns with such low risk?'
3.  'What gives you the confidence to invest in what others see as risky?'
4.  'How do you find the best deals?'

I answer, 'My team.' My team consists of my accountants, attorneys, bankers, brokers, etc.

When people say, 'Building a business is risky,' they often speak from a point of view of doing it alone, a habit they learned from school. In my opinion, not building a business is risky. By not building a business, you are failing to gain priceless real-world experience, and you are failing to get the best education in the world, the education that comes from your team of advisors. As rich dad would say, 'People who play it safe lose out on the best education in the world and they waste a lot of precious time.' He would also say, 'Time is our most valuable asset, especially as you get older.'

Tolstoy said it a little differently. He is quoted as saying, 'The most unexpected thing that happens to us is old age.'

## *Tetrahedrons and Teams*

I am often asked, 'What is the difference between a B quadrant business and an S quadrant business?' My reply is 'The team.'

Most S quadrant businesses are either structured as sole proprietorships or partnerships. They could be teams, but not the kind of team I think of. Just as people in the E quadrant often bind together as a union, people in the S quadrant often organize as a partnership. When I think of a team, I think of different types of people with different skills coming together to work together. In a union or partnership (e.g., the teachers' union or a law partnership), the same kinds of people and professions often come together.

One of my greatest teachers was Dr R. Buckminster Fuller. Dr Fuller set out years ago to find what he called 'the building blocks of the universe.' In his search, he found out that squares and cubes do not exist in nature. He would say, 'Tetrahedrons are the basic building blocks of nature.'

When I look at the great pyramids of Egypt, I understand a little more about what Dr Fuller was talking about. While tall skyscrapers come and go, those pyramids have withstood the test of tens of centuries. While a skyscraper can come down with a few well-placed sticks of dynamite, the pyramids would not budge with the same blast.

Dr Fuller was looking for a stable structure in the universe, and he found it in the tetrahedron.

### The Different Models

The following are graphic portrayals of different business structures.

1. This is a sole proprietorship: •

2. This is a partnership: •——•

3. This is a B quadrant business:

The prefix 'tetra' means four. In other words, it has four points. After studying with Dr Fuller, I began to see the importance of having structures be in a minimum of fours. For example, when you look at the CASHFLOW Quadrant, it has four parts. Therefore, a stable business structure would look like the following diagram:

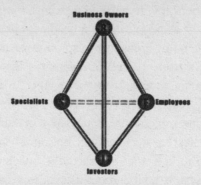

A well-managed business will have excellent employees. In this instance, I say the E stands for both 'excellent' and 'essential' because the employees are responsible for the day-to-day activities of the business. The E also stands for 'extension' because the employees are the extension of the business owner and represent the business to the customer.

The specialists are typically from the S quadrant. The S stands for 'specialized' because each specialist will guide you based on his or her trained area of expertise. While specialists may not participate daily, their guidance is invaluable to keep your business moving in the right direction.

The structure has a better chance of being stable and enduring if the four points are working in alignment. While the investors provide the funding, the business owners must work with the specialists and employees to develop the business and make it grow so there will be a return on the investors' original investment.

Another interesting tetra-relationship I came across is the four fundamental elements that make up this world we live in, which the ancients believed to be earth, air, fire, and rain (water). In a sole proprietorship as well as in a partnership, in order to be successful, the individual needs to be all four, which is difficult.

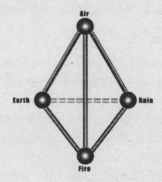

While most of us have all four elements in us, we each tend to be weighted predominantly to one of the elements. For example, I am fire, born under the sign of Aries and the planet Mars. That means I am good at starting things but not completing them. By having a tetra-hedron, I am better able to be successful than if I were on my own. My wife, Kim, on the other hand, is earth. She and I have a good marriage because she has a grounding effect on me as well as on the people I upset around me. She often says, 'Speaking to you is like speaking to a blowtorch.' Without her, I would have nothing but angry and upset people around the company. Sharon, on the other hand, fulfills the role of air in this company. She feeds the fire, moves the company in the right direction, and keeps all systems running smoothly. As CEO of our company, Sharon ensures that all four of us stay in alignment and work toward our mission. When Mary, our operations manager, joined us, the company suddenly took off. Mary completed the company by making sure that we delivered what we promised. It's important to note that it took two years for this team to come together. People came and went until the right tetra-team finally locked in place. Once this model stabilized, the company began to radiate out, growing rapidly and with stability.

I am not saying this is a hard and fast rule for a successful business. However, all one needs to do is look at the pyramids of Egypt and a sense of strength, stability, and longevity comes to mind.

### Only Two Elements

I often jokingly say that if you put only two elements together, as in a partnership, you get some strange phenomena. For example:

1. Air and Water = Spray
2. Air and Earth = Dust
3. Water and Earth = Mud
4. Earth and Fire = Lava or ashes
5. Fire and Water = Steam
6. Fire and Air = Flame

### A Team Is Made Up of Different Levels

One of the first things I look at as an investor is the team behind the business. If the team is weak or lacks experience and a track record, I rarely invest. I meet many people who are running around trying to raise money for their new product or business. The biggest problems most of them have are that they personally lack experience and they have no team behind them, a team that inspires confidence.

Many people want me to invest in their business plan. One of the things most of them say is, 'Once this company is up and running, we're going to take it public.' That statement always intrigues me, so I ask what all of you should ask: 'Who on your team has experience taking a company public, and how many companies has that person taken public?' If the answer to that question is weak, I know I am listening to a sales pitch more than to a business plan.

Another line I look at in the numbers of a business plan is the line item called 'salaries.' If the salaries are high, I know I am looking at people who are raising money in order to pay themselves fat salaries. I ask them if they are willing to work for free or to cut the salaries in half. If the answer is weak or a definite 'No,' I know the true mission of their business. The mission of the business is probably to provide them a job with a nice salary.

Investors invest in management. They look at the team within the proposed business and want to see experience, passion, and commitment. It is hard for me to believe there is a high level of commitment from people who are trying to raise money to pay their own salaries.

## A Word on Our CASHFLOW Games

Many people have asked why we did not create our educational board games as electronic board games. One of the primary reasons is because we want to encourage cooperative learning. In the real world, being able to cooperate with as many people as possible and helping people without crippling them are very important human skills.

While we may release an electronic game of *CASHFLOW* in the future, for the moment, we are happy to encourage people to learn cooperatively – to teach each other – because the more we teach, the more we learn. Too much of our children's lives is already spent in isolation. They spend hours alone in front of a computer, alone watching TV, and alone taking tests. We then wonder why so many children are anti-social. To be successful, we all need to learn to get along with many different types of people. For this reason, *CASHFLOW* is still a board game that requires you play with other human beings. We need to learn to operate as individuals as well as members of a team – and we can always improve those skills.

## Sharon's Notes

Robert has often mentioned that 'money follows management' in the world of business capital. To succeed, a business must have the proper expertise in key areas.

When you do not have the money up front to hire the talent you need, consider attracting the talent as members of an advisory board with the understanding that once sufficient capital is raised, your team will come on board. Your chance of success is much stronger if your management team has a track record of success in the business or industry of your proposed business.

Your team also includes your outside advisors. Proper guidance from your accountants, tax advisors, financial advisors, and legal counsel is imperative for building a strong successful business. If your business is real estate, your real estate brokers become an important part of your team. Although these advisors can be 'expensive,' their advice can provide you with an incredible return on your investment by helping you structure a strong business while avoiding pitfalls along the way.

And that leads to the next part of the B-I Triangle: leadership, because every team needs a leader.

## Leadership

One reason I attended a federal military academy rather than a normal university was that rich dad knew I needed to develop leadership skills if I wanted to become an entrepreneur. After graduation, I went into the U.S. Marine Corps and became a pilot to test my skills in the real world, in a place called Vietnam. As rich dad said, 'School is important, but the street is a better teacher.'

I still remember the commanding officer of my squadron saying, 'Gentlemen, your most important job is to ask your troops to risk their lives for you, your team, and your country.' He went on to say, 'If you don't inspire them to do that, they will probably shoot you in the back. Troops do not follow a leader who does not lead.' The same thing goes on in business today and every day. More businesses fail from the inside than from the outside.

In Vietnam, I learned that one of the most important qualities of a leader is trust. As a helicopter pilot with a crew of four, I had to trust my life to my team, and they had to entrust their lives to me. If that trust was ever broken, I knew that we would probably not come back alive. Rich dad would say, 'A leader's job is to bring out the best in people, not to be the best person.' He would also say, 'If you are the smartest person on your business team, your business is in trouble.'

When people ask how they can gain leadership skills, I always say the same thing: 'Volunteer more.' In most organizations, it is hard to find people who actually want to lead. Most people just hide in the corner hoping no one will call on them. I tell them, 'At your church, volunteer to take on projects. At work, volunteer to lead projects.' Now, volunteering alone will not necessarily make you a great leader, but if you accept the feedback and correct yourself well, you can grow into a great leader.

Through volunteering, you can get feedback on your real-life leadership skills. If you volunteer to lead and no one follows, you have some real-life learning and correcting to do. If you volunteer to lead and no one follows, ask for feedback and corrective support. Doing so is one of the greatest traits of a leader. I see many businesses that struggle or fail because the leader will not accept feedback from peers or the workers in the company. My squadron's commanding officer in the Marine Corps would often say, 'True leaders are not born leaders. True leaders want to be leaders and are willing to be trained to be leaders, and training means being big enough to take corrective feedback.'

A true leader also knows when to listen to others. I have said before I am not a good businessman or investor, I am average. I rely on the advice of my advisors and team members to help me be a better leader.

### Sharon's Notes

A leader's roles are a combination of visionary, cheerleader, and pit boss.

As a visionary, the leader must keep his or her focus on the corporate mission. As a cheerleader, he or she must inspire the team as it works together towards that mission as well as herald the successes along the way. As the pit boss, he or she must be able to make the tough calls regarding issues that distract the team from achieving the mission. The unique ability to take decisive action while maintaining focus on the ultimate mission is what defines a true leader.

With the right mission, team, and leader you are well on your way to building a strong B business. As I said earlier, money follows management. It is at this point that you can start attracting money from outside investors. Five building blocks are essential to developing a strong business. Each will be discussed separately.

*Chapter 32*

# *Cash Flow Management*

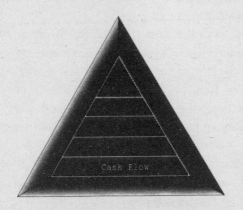

Rich dad would say, 'Cash flow management is a fundamental and essential skill if a person truly wants to be successful in the B and I quadrants.' That is why he insisted that Mike and I read financial statements of other companies so we could better understand cash flow management. In fact, he spent most of his time teaching us to be financially literate. He would say, 'Financial literacy allows you to read the numbers, and the numbers tell you the story of the business, based on facts.'

If you ask most bankers, accountants, or loan officers, they will tell you that many people are weak financially simply because they are not financially literate. I have a friend who is a respected accountant in Australia. He once said to me, 'It is shocking to see a perfectly good business go down just because the owners are not financially literate.' He went on to say, 'Many small-business owners fail because they do not know the difference between profit and cash flow. As a result, many very profitable businesses go broke. They fail to realize that profit and cash flow are not the same things.'

Rich dad would drum into my head the importance of cash flow management. He would say, 'Business owners need to see the two types of cash flow if they want to be successful. There is actual cash flow and phantom cash flow. It is the awareness of these two cash flows that makes you rich or poor.'

One of the skills the game *CASHFLOW, Investing 101* teaches is how to recognize the differences between these two types of cash flow. Repeatedly playing the game helps many people begin to sense the differences. That is why the positioning statement of the game is 'The more you play this game, the richer you become.' You become richer because your mind begins to sense the often-invisible phantom cash flow.

Rich dad also said, 'The ability to run a company from financial statements is one of the primary differences between a small-business owner and a big-business owner.'

## *Sharon's Notes*

Cash flow is to a business what blood is to the human body. Nothing can impact a business more dramatically than not being able to make payroll one Friday. Proper cash flow management starts on the first day you begin your business. When Robert, Kim, and I started CASH-FLOW Technologies, Inc., we agreed that no purchase would be made if it were not justified by an increase in sales. In fact, we often chuckle about our strategy for increasing book sales early in 1998 so we could buy a $300 copy machine. Our strategy worked, and by

December 1998 we were able to replace that $300 well-worn copy machine with a new $3,000 one. It is this attention to detail in the early stages of your business that will set the tone for your success. A good cash flow manager reviews his or her cash position daily, looking at cash sources and needs for the next week, month, and quarter. This allows him or her to plan for any large cash need before it becomes a cash crisis. This type of review is imperative for a company that is growing quickly.

I have listed some cash flow tips that may help you in structuring your business. Each step applies to your business whether it is an international business, a single rental unit, or a hot dog stand.

**Initial Corporate Startup Phase:**

- Delay taking a salary until your business is generating cash flow from sales. In some cases, this may not be possible due to an extended development period. However, your investors will be much more supportive if they see that you are sharing in the development process by 'investing your time.' In fact, we advise keeping your full-time job and starting your business part-time. By delaying taking a salary, you can re-invest sales to help grow your business.

**Sales and Accounts Receivable:**

- Invoice your customers quickly upon shipment of goods or when services are provided.

- Require payment up front until credit has been established. Require that credit applications be completed before granting credit, and always check references. Standard credit forms are available at business supply stores.

- Establish a minimum dollar amount for orders before granting credit.

- Establish late-payment penalties as part of your terms and conditions – and enforce them.

- As your business grows, to speed up the receipt of cash, you may want to have your customers pay their bills directly to lockboxes or directly to your bank.

**Expenses and Accounts Payable:**

- Many businesses forget that a crucial part of cash flow is managing their own bill paying. Make sure you pay your bills promptly. Ask for extended payment terms up front. After you have paid timely for two to three months, ask for additional extensions on your payable terms. A supplier will usually extend credit for 30 to 90 days to a good customer.

- Keep your overhead to a minimum. Before purchasing something new, set a goal for increasing sales to justify the expense. Preserve your investors' funds for costs directly related to business operations, not overhead, if at all possible. As your sales increase, you can purchase the overhead-related items from the cash flow – but only if you have set and achieved new higher sales goals.

**General Cash Management:**

- Have an investment plan for your cash on hand to maximize its earning potential.

- Establish a line of credit with your bank before you need it.

- To make sure you can move quickly to borrow if needed, keep an eye on your current ratio (assets over liabilities – at least 2:1 is good) and quick ratios (liquid assets divided by current liabilities – should be over 1:1).

- Establish good internal controls over the handling of cash.

  - The people who record the cash receipts on the bank deposits are different from those who post it to the accounts receivable and general ledger.

  - Checks should be endorsed immediately 'For Deposit Only.'

  - The people authorized to sign checks should not prepare the vouchers or record the disbursements and post to the accounts payable and general ledger.

  - The person who reconciles the bank statement should have no regularly assigned functions related to cash receipts or cash disbursements. (Our outside accountant does this.)

While this may sound very complicated, each step of cash management is important. Call on your accountant, banker, and personal financial advisor for advice in structuring your cash management system. Once you establish a system for how to manage your cash, ongoing supervision is still essential. Review your cash position and funding needs daily, and prepare early for additional funding that may be required for your expanding business. Many people lose sight of cash management when their businesses become successful. This is a major cause of business failures. Proper cash management (and therefore expense management) is crucial to the on-going success of any business.

For those of you considering purchasing a franchise or joining a network marketing organization, you may find much of the cash management system will be provided for you. With a franchise, you will still need to implement the system and oversee it. Network marketing organizations often handle the cash management on your behalf. In these cases, the corporate headquarters performs the accounting functions for your organization and sends you a report of your earnings periodically with payment. In either case, it is still important to have your own advisors to help you structure your personal cash management.

## Chapter 33

# *Communications Management*

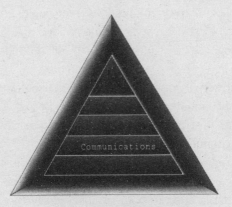

Rich dad would say, 'The better at communicating you are, and the more people you communicate to, the better your cash flow will be.' This is why communications management is the next level up on the B-I Triangle.

He would also say, 'To be good at communications, you first need to be good at human psychology. You never know what motivates people. Just because something makes you excited does not mean it makes others excited. To be good at communications, you need to know what buttons to push. Different people have different buttons.' He also said, 'Many people are talking, but only a few are listening.' He also said, 'The world is filled with fabulous products, but the money goes to the best communicators.'

I am always amazed at how little time businesspeople put into improving their overall communication skills. When I first balked in 1974 at the idea of learning to sell Xerox machines door to door, all rich dad said was, 'Poor people are poor communicators.' I repeat this negative statement with the intent of inspiring further study and practice of this vast subject.

Rich dad also said, 'Cash flowing into your business is in direct proportion to communication flowing out.' Whenever I find a business that is struggling, it is often a reflection of poor communications going out, not enough communications going out, or both. In general, I find a six week cycle between communication and cash flow. Stop communicating today and in six weeks you will see an impact on your cash flow.

However, external communications are not the only communications. Internal communications are also vital. By looking at the financial statements of a company, you can easily see which areas of a business are communicating and which are not.

A public company has increased communications problems. It is like two companies in one: one for the public and one for the shareholders. Communication to both groups is vitally important. When I hear people say, 'I wish I had not taken my company public,' it usually means that they are having shareholder communication problems.

As a general policy, rich dad attended one communications seminar a year. I continue in that tradition. I have always noticed that soon after I attend the seminar, my income increases. Over the years, I have attended courses on:

1. Sales
2. Marketing systems

3.  Advertising, headlines, and copy writing
4.  Negotiations
5.  Public speaking
6.  Direct-mail advertising
7.  Running a seminar
8.  Raising capital

Of all of these topics, raising capital interests budding entrepreneurs the most. When people ask me how to learn to raise capital, I refer them to numbers 1 through 7 above, explaining that raising capital requires each of them in one way or the other. Most businesses do not get off the ground because the entrepreneur does not know how to raise capital, and as rich dad said, 'Raising capital is the entrepreneur's most important job.' He did not mean that the entrepreneur was constantly asking for money from investors. What he meant was that an entrepreneur was always ensuring that capital was flowing in, through sales, direct marketing, private sales, institutional sales, investors, etc. Rich dad would say, 'Until the business system is built, the entrepreneur is the system to keep the money flowing in. At the start of any business, keeping the cash flowing in is the entrepreneur's most important job.'

The other day, a young man came to me and asked, 'I want to start my own business. What would you recommend I do before I start?' I answered with my usual response: 'Get a job with a company that will train you in sales.' He replied, 'I hate sales. I don't like selling and I don't like salespeople. I just want to be the president and hire salespeople.' Once he said that, I simply shook his hand and wished him luck. A priceless lesson that rich dad taught me was, 'Don't argue with people who ask for advice but don't want the advice you're giving them. End the discussion immediately and go on minding your own business.'

Being able to communicate effectively with as many people as possible is a very important life skill. It is a skill worthy of annual updating, which I do by attending seminars. As rich dad had already told me, 'If you want to be a B quadrant person, your first skill is being able to communicate and speak the language of the other three quadrants. People in the other three quadrants can get away with speaking the language of only their quadrant, but those in the B quadrant cannot. Simply put, the primary – and possibly only – job of those in the B quadrant is to communicate with people in the other quadrants.'

I have recommended that people join a network marketing company to gain sales experience. Some network marketing organizations have excellent communications and sales training programs. I have seen shy introverted individuals come out as powerful and effective communicators who are no longer afraid of rejection or ridicule. That thick-skin mind-set is vital for anyone in the B quadrant, especially when your personal communication skills are not yet polished.

### *My First Sales Call*

I still remember my first sales call on the street along Waikiki Beach. After spending about an hour working up the nerve to knock on the door, I finally got in to see the owner of a small tourist trinket store. He was an older gentleman who had seen new salespeople like me for years. After stammering and sweating through my memorized sales pitch on the benefits of a Xerox copier, all he did was laugh. After he was through laughing, he said, 'Son, you're the worst I have ever seen. But keep going because if you can get over your fears, your world will be very bright. If you quit, you may wind up like me, sitting behind this counter fourteen hours a day, seven days a week, three hundred and sixty-five days a year, waiting for tourists to come in. I wait here because I am too afraid to go out and do what you're doing. Get through your fears and the world will open up. Give in to your fears and your world will get smaller every year.' To this day, I give thanks to that wise, older man.

After I began to overcome my fear of selling, rich dad had me join the Toastmasters organization to learn to overcome my fear of speaking in front of large groups. When I complained to rich dad, he would say, 'All great leaders are great public speakers. Leaders of great businesses need to be great speakers. If you want to be a leader, you must be a speaker.' Today, I can speak comfortably to tens of thousands of people in convention halls because of my training in sales and my early training from the Toastmasters organization.

If you are thinking about starting your own B quadrant business, I recommend those same two skills. First, develop the skill to overcome your fears, to overcome rejection, and to communicate the value of your product or service. Second, develop the skill of speaking to large groups of people and keeping them interested in what you have to say. As rich dad said to me, 'There are speakers that no one listens to, there are salespeople that cannot sell, there are advertisers that no one watches, there are entrepreneurs that cannot raise capital, and there are business leaders that no one follows. If you want to be successful in the "B" quadrant, don't be any of those people.'

My first book in the Rich Dad series, *Rich Dad Poor Dad*, has been on the prestigious *Sydney Morning Herald* (Australia) best-selling booklist for well over two years. In the United States, it has been on the *Wall Street Journal*'s bestseller list for nearly nine months, and it made *The New York Times* bestseller list in September 1999. When other authors ask me what my secret to getting on those lists is, I simply repeat a sentence from *Rich Dad Poor Dad*: 'I am not a best-writing author. I am a best-selling author.' I add that I flunked out of high school twice because I could not write and that I never even kissed a girl in high school because I was too shy. I end by saying the same thing my rich dad said to me: 'Unsuccessful people find their strengths and spend their lives making their strengths stronger, often ignoring their weaknesses, until one day their weaknesses cannot be ignored any more. Successful people find their weaknesses and make them strengths.'

A person's physical appearance often communicates far more than their words. Often, people who come to me with a business plan or to ask for money look like mice that have been chewed on by a cat. No matter how good their plan, their physical appearance is a limiting factor. In public speaking, it is said that body language accounts for approximately 55% of communication, voice tone 35%, and words 10%. If you remember President Kennedy, JFK, he had 100% working for him and it made him a very powerful communicator. While not all of us can be as physically attractive as he was, we can all do our best to dress and groom appropriately to make our points stronger.

An investigative TV program recently sent in very attractive job applicants and unattractive job applicants with exactly the same qualifications on their résumés to interview for the same jobs. It was interesting to note that the attractive applicants got more job offers than the unattractive ones.

A friend of mine sits on the board of a bank and shared with me that the president they had just hired was brought on board because of his appearance; he looks like a president. When I asked about his qualifications, all he said was, 'His appearance was his qualification. He looks like a bank president should look and speaks in the way a bank president should speak. The board will run the business. We just want him to attract new customers.' I use this example for anyone who says, 'Oh, my appearance does not matter.' In the world of business, appearance is a powerful communicator. Repeating an old cliché, 'You have only one chance to make a first impression.'

## The Difference between Sales and Marketing

While still on the subject of communications, rich dad insisted that Mike and I know the difference between sales and marketing. He would say, 'The big mistake that most people make when it comes to communication is that they say "sales and marketing." That is why they suffer with low sales or poor communications with staff and investors.' Rich dad would go on to explain that the real statement looked like this:

SALES

MARKETING

He would add, 'The real trick to communication is knowing that it is really "sales over marketing," not "sales and marketing."' He added, 'If a business has strong and convincing marketing, the sales will come easily. If the business has weak marketing, the company must spend a lot of time and money and work very hard at gathering sales.'

He also said to Mike and me, 'Once you learn to sell, you need to learn how to market. An S quadrant business owner is often good at sales, but to be a successful B quadrant business owner, you must be good at marketing as well as sales.'

He then drew the following diagram:

He said, 'Sales is what you do in person, one on one. Marketing is sales done via a system.' Most S quadrant businesspeople are very good at one-on-one sales. For them to make the transition to the B quadrant, they need to learn how to sell through a system, which is called marketing.

In conclusion, communications is a subject worthy of lifelong study because there is more to communication than just speaking, writing, dressing, or demonstrating. As rich dad said to me, 'Just because you're speaking doesn't mean anyone is listening.' When people ask where to start to build a strong communications foundation, I encourage them to begin with the two basic skills of selling one-on-one and public speaking to a group. I also advise them to carefully watch their results and listen for feedback. As you go through the process of transforming from a poor communicator to an excellent communicator with these two skills, you will find your fundamental everyday communication skills will also improve. When all three improve, you will see your cash flow increase as a result.

## *Sharon's Notes*

Good first impressions are vital. Your marketing and sales efforts will often be the first impression your business makes on your potential customer. Whenever you are speaking, both your passion for your business and your appearance will have a lasting impact on your audience. Any published or printed material you produce or distribute is also important. It is a public representation of your business.

As Robert mentions, marketing is selling through a system. Always make sure you know your audience and that your marketing tool has been designed for that audience. In every marketing or sales effort, include these three key ingredients: identify a need, provide a solution, and answer your customers' question 'What's in it for me?' with a special offer. It also helps if you can create a sense of urgency for your customers to respond to.

Most communication is directed towards external communication, but a business's internal communication is also vitally important.

Some examples of each are:

### External Communication

> Sales
> Marketing
> Customer service
> To investors
> Public relations

### Internal Communication

> Sharing of wins and successes with your entire team
> Regular meetings with employees
> Regular communication with advisors
> Human Resource policies

One of the most powerful forms of communication that affects a business is one over which you have little control: the communication from your existing customers to your potential customers. At CASHFLOW Technologies, Inc., we attribute a large part of our success to our customers telling other people about us. The power of this word-of-mouth advertising is immeasurable. This form of advertising can drive a company to success or failure very quickly. For this reason, customer service is a very vital communications function for any company.

When you buy a franchise or join a network marketing company, the communication systems are often provided for you. In addition, their communication materials have already been proven successful by other franchisees or members of your organization. You therefore have a tremendous head start over people trying to develop their own materials. These people won't know if their materials are successful until they use them and measure the results.

As Robert mentions, the ability to speak is vital to building a successful business. The personal development and mentoring programs offered by select franchises and network marketing organizations provide wonderful opportunities for personal growth.

## Chapter 34

# *Systems Management*

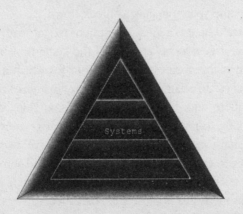

The human body is a system of systems. So is a business. The human body is made up of a blood system, oxygen system, food system, waste system, etc. If one of those systems stops, there is a good chance the body will be crippled or die. The same is true with a business. A business is a complex system of inter-operating systems. In fact, each item listed on the B-I Triangle is a separate system that is inter-linked into the overall business the triangle represents. It is difficult to separate the systems because they are interdependent. It is also difficult to say that one is more important than another.

For any business to grow, individuals must be accountable for each of the systems and a general overall director must be in charge of making sure all the systems operate to their highest capacity. When reading a financial statement, I am like a pilot sitting in the cockpit of the plane reading the gauges from all the operating systems. If one of the systems begins to malfunction, emergency procedures must be implemented. So many small startup businesses or S quadrant businesses fail because the operator of the system has too many systems to monitor and take care of. When one system fails, such as when cash flow dries up, all the other systems begin to fail almost simultaneously. It is like when a person gets a cold and fails to take care of him- or herself. Pneumonia soon sets in and if it's not treated, the person's immune system begins to break down.

I believe real estate is a great investment to start with because the average investor gets to tinker with all the systems. A building on a piece of land is the business – the system for which a tenant pays you rent. Real estate is fairly stable and inert, so it gives the new businessperson more time to correct things if something begins to go wrong. Learning to manage property for a year or two teaches you excellent business management skills. When people ask me where to find the best real estate investments, I say, 'Just find someone who is a poor business manager and you will find a real estate bargain.' But never buy a property just because it is a bargain because some bargains are cleverly disguised nightmares.

Banks like to lend money on real estate because it is generally a stable system that retains its value. Other businesses are often hard to finance because they may not be considered stable systems. I have often heard the following: 'The only time a bank will loan you money is when you don't need it.' I see it differently. I have always found that the bank will loan you money when you have a stable system that has value and when you can demonstrate that the money will be paid back.

A good businessperson can manage multiple systems effectively without becoming part of the system. A true business system is much like a car. The car does not depend upon only one person to drive it. Anyone who knows how to drive it can do so. The same is true for a B quadrant business but not necessarily for an S quadrant business. In most cases, the person in the S quadrant is the system.

One day, I was considering starting a small coin shop that specialized in rare collectable coins, and rich dad said to me, 'Always remember that the B quadrant gets more money from investors because investors invest in good systems and people who can build good systems. Investors do not like to invest in businesses where the system goes home at night.'

## Sharon's Notes

Every business, whether large or small, needs to have systems in place to enable it to conduct its day-to-day activities. Even a sole proprietor has to wear different hats to conduct his or her business. In essence, the sole proprietor is all systems in one.

The better the system, the less dependent you become on others. Robert described McDonald's in this way: 'It's the same everywhere in the world – and is run by teenagers.' This is possible because of the excellent systems in place. McDonald's depends on systems, not people.

### The Role of a CEO

A CEO's job is to supervise all systems and identify weaknesses before the weaknesses turn into system failures. This can happen in many different ways, but it is exceptionally disconcerting when your company is growing rapidly. Your sales are increasing, your product or service is getting attention from the media, and suddenly you can't deliver. Why? Usually, it's because your systems imploded from the increased demand. You didn't have enough phone lines, or operators answering the phones; you didn't have enough production capacity or enough hours in the week to meet the demand; or you didn't have the money to build the product or hire additional help. Whatever the reason, you missed the opportunity to move your business to the next level of success due to a failure of one of your systems.

At each new level of growth, the CEO must start planning the systems needed to support the next level of growth, from phone lines to lines of credit for production needs. Systems drive both cash flow management and communication. As your systems get better, you or your employees will have to exert less and less effort. Without well-designed and successful operating systems, your business will be labor intensive. Once you have well-designed and successful operating systems, you will have a saleable business asset.

## Typical Systems

In the next section is a list of typical systems that successful businesses must have. In some instances, the system required might be defined differently from the way it is listed, but it is still necessary to the business operations. (For instance, 'Product Development Systems' might be 'Procedures for Providing Services' in a service organization. While the specifics may differ, the basic elements are the same. Both of these require the business to develop the product [or service] that it will ultimately offer to its customers.)

In the case of franchises and network marketing organizations, many of these systems are automatically provided. For the cost of the franchise or membership fee of the network marketing organization, you will be given an operations manual that describes the systems provided for your business. This is what makes these 'ready-made' businesses so attractive to many people.

If you want to build your own business, review the list of systems. Although you are already performing many of these functions, you may not have defined them as separate systems. The more you can formalize your operations, the more efficient your business will become.

## Systems Required by Every Business for Optimal Efficiency

**Daily Office Operations Systems:**
- Answering the telephone and 800 line system
- Receiving and opening the mail
- Purchasing and maintaining office supplies and equipment
- Faxing and e-mailing
- Dealing with incoming/outgoing delivery needs
- Backing up and archiving data

**Product Development Systems:**
- Developing product and protecting it legally
- Developing packaging and collateral material (e.g., catalogs, etc.)
- Developing manufacturing method and process
- Developing manufacturing costing and bidding process

**Manufacturing and Inventory Systems:**
- Selecting vendors
- Determining product or service warranties offered
- Establishing product or service pricing (retail and wholesale)
- Establishing reorder process for inventory production
- Receiving and storing product as inventory
- Reconciling physical inventory with accounting records

**Order Processing Systems:**
- Taking orders and recording the orders – by mail, fax, phone, or online
- Fulfilling and packaging the orders

- Sending the orders

**Billing and Accounts Receivable Systems:**
- Billing customers for the orders
- Receiving payments for the orders and crediting customers for payment (whether cash, check, or credit card)
- Starting the collection process for delinquent receivables

**Customer Service Systems:**
- Returns procedure for inventory receiving and customer payment return
- Responding to customer complaints
- Replacing defective product or performing other warranty service

**Accounts Payable Systems:**
- Purchasing procedures and approvals required
- Payment process for supplies and inventory
- Petty cash

**Marketing Systems:**
- Creating an overall marketing plan
- Designing and producing promotional materials
- Developing general leads and prospects
- Creating an advertising plan
- Creating a public relations plan
- Creating a direct mail plan
- Developing and maintaining a database
- Developing and maintaining a website
- Analyzing and tracking sales statistics

**Human Resources Systems:**
- Hiring procedures and employee agreements
- Training employees
- Payroll process and benefit plans

**General Accounting Systems:**
- Managing the accounting process with daily, weekly, monthly, quarterly, and annual reports
- Managing cash with future borrowing needs secured and available
- Budgeting and forecasting
- Reporting payroll taxes and withholding payments

**General Corporate Systems:**
- Negotiating, drafting, and executing contracts
- Developing and protecting intellectual property
- Managing insurance needs and coverage
- Reporting and paying federal and state or other jurisdictional taxes
- Planning for federal and state or other jurisdictional taxes
- Managing and storing records
- Maintaining investor/shareholder relations
- Ensuring legal security
- Planning and managing growth

**Physical Space Management Systems:**
- Maintaining and designing telephone and electrical systems
- Planning permits and fees
- Licensing
- Ensuring physical security

You may want to record your operations in a policies and procedures manual. Such a manual can become an invaluable reference to your staff. In creating the manual, you will find ways to streamline your operations and improve your profitability. You will also be a step closer to owning a B quadrant business.

## Chapter 35

# *Legal Management*

This level of the B-I Triangle, legal management, was one of the most painful lessons I ever had to learn. My rich dad identified a serious flaw in my business: I had failed to secure the legal rights to the nylon and Velcro products I had designed before I started producing them. More specifically, I failed to patent some of my products (I failed to do so because I believed the $10,000 in patent attorney fees was too expensive and not important enough to spend that much money on). Another company quickly came along and copied my idea, and I could do nothing about it.

Today, I am now an evangelist for the other side. Today, especially in the Information Age, your intellectual property attorney and your contract attorney are some of your most important advisors because they help create your most important assets. These attorneys, if they are good, will protect your ideas and your agreements from intellectual bandits, people who steal your ideas and therefore your profits.

The world of business is filled with stories of smart entrepreneurs with great ideas who begin selling their products or ideas before protecting them. In the world of intellectual property, once your idea is exposed, it is almost impossible to protect. Not too long ago, a company came out with a spreadsheet program for small businesses. I bought this brilliant product for my company. A few years later, the company was out of business. Why? Because it had failed to patent its idea and another company, which I will not mention, came along, took its idea, and put it out of business. Today, the company that took the idea is a prominent leader in the software business.

It is said that Bill Gates became the richest man in the world with only an idea. In other words, he did not get rich by investing in real estate or factories. He simply took information, protected the information, and became the richest man in the world while still in his thirties. The irony of it all is that he didn't even create the Microsoft operating system. He bought it from other programmers, sold it to IBM, and the rest is history.

Aristotle Onassis became a shipping giant with a simple legal document. It was a contract from a large manufacturing company guaranteeing him the exclusive rights to transport its cargo all over the world. All he had was this document. He owned no ships. Yet with this legal document, he was able to convince the banks to lend him the money to buy the ships. Where did he get the ships? He got them from the U.S. government after W.W. II. The U.S. government had a surplus of Liberty and Victory class ships used to haul war materials from America to Europe. There was one catch. In order to buy the ships, the person needed to be a U.S. citizen and Onassis was a Greek citizen. Did that stop him? Of course it didn't. By understanding the laws of the B quadrant, Onassis purchased the ships using a U.S. corporation he controlled. This is another example of the laws being different for different quadrants.

## Protect Your Ideas

My intellectual property attorney is Michael Lechter, one of the leading IP attorneys today. He is responsible for securing worldwide patents and trademarks for CASHFLOW Technologies, Inc. He is also the husband of my business partner and co-author, Sharon Lechter. Although he is married to Sharon, we still pay the same hourly rate as any other of Michael's clients. No matter what we pay him, the value he returns to our company is priceless. He has made us so much money and protected our rights to continue making money by protecting what we do and guiding us through some delicate negotiations. Michael has written a book, *The Intellectual Property Handbook*, which is a wonderful explanation of the various protection mechanisms available. He discusses each individually (patents, trademarks, copyrights, and mask works) as well as how they can be used in combinations to give you the broadest protection. It is available through our website.

## In Summary

Many a business has been started and has survived by a simple piece of paper. One legal document can be the seed of a worldwide business.

## Sharon's Notes

Some of the most valuable assets you can own are the intangible assets called patents, trademarks, and copyrights. These legal documents grant you specific protection and ownership to your intellectual property. As Robert found out with his Velcro wallet business, without this type of protection, you risk losing everything. Once you have protected your rights, not only can you keep others from using your property, but you can also sell or license those rights and receive royalty income when doing so. Licensing your rights to a third party is a perfect example of your assets working for you!

However, legal issues can also surface in almost every facet of a business. Obtaining competent legal counsel is very important not only as you are forming your business but as an ongoing part of your advisory team. Legal fees may seem expensive at first. However, when you compare them to the cost of legal fees from lost rights or subsequent litigation, it is much less expensive to set out your agreements properly in the beginning. In addition to the monetary expense, you must also factor in the cost of lost time. Instead of focusing on your business, you may be forced to focus on legal matters.

This is another area where franchising and network marketing can help you jumpstart your business. Typically, when you purchase a franchise or join a network marketing organization, most of the necessary legal documents to start and grow your business will be provided for your use. This saves you not only a lot of money but also a tremendous amount of time, and it allows you to focus your efforts on the business development. It is still advisable to have your own counsel review the documents on your behalf.

Some specific areas where proper legal counsel can help you avoid potential problems in legal aspects of a business are:

**General Corporate:**
- Choice of business entity
- Buy-sell agreements
- Business licenses
- Regulatory compliance
- Office lease or purchase contracts

**Consumer Laws:**
- Terms and conditions of sales
- Direct mail
- Product liability laws
- Truth in advertising laws
- Environmental laws

**Contracts:**
- With suppliers
- With wholesale customers
- With employees
- Uniform commercial code
- Warranties
- Jurisdiction

**Intellectual Property:**
- Work-for-hire agreements
- Nondisclosure agreements
- Copyrights
- Mask works
- Patents
- Trademarks
- Licensing of intellectual property

**Labor Laws:**
- Human Resource issues
- Employee agreements
- Employee disputes
- OSHA
- Workers' compensation

**Security and Debt Instruments:**
- Equipment leasing or purchase
- Loan documents
- Private placements
- IPOs

**Shareholder Issues:**
- Corporate bylaws
- Board authority
- Stock issuance
- Mergers and acquisitions
- Spin-offs

## Chapter 36

# *Product Management*

The company's product, which the customer ultimately buys from the business, is the last important aspect of the B-I Triangle. It could be a tangible item such as a hamburger or an intangible item such as consulting services. It is interesting to note that when evaluating a business, many average investors focus on the product rather than the rest of the business. Rich dad thought that the product was the least important piece to inspect when evaluating a business.

Many people come to me with ideas for new innovative products. My response is that the world is full of great products. People also say to me that their new idea or product is better than an existing product. Thinking that a better product or better service is most important is usually the domain of the E and S quadrant, where being the best or highest quality is important for success. In the B and I quadrants, however, the most important part of a new business is the system behind the product or idea, or the rest of the B-I Triangle. I then point out that most of us can cook a better hamburger than McDonald's but few of us can build a better business system than McDonald's.

## Rich Dad's Guidance

In 1974, I decided I was going to learn to build a business following the model of the B-I Triangle. Rich dad warned me by saying, 'Learning to build a business according to this model is high risk. Many people attempt it, and few accomplish it. However, although there is high risk at the start, if you learn how to build businesses, your earning potential is unlimited. For the people who are not willing to take the risk, those who don't wish to undertake such a steep learning curve, their risk may be lower but so will their lifetime returns.'

I still recall experiencing the highest of highs and lowest of lows as I learned to build a solid business. I remember some of the advertising copy I wrote that never sold anything. I remember some of the brochures I wrote where no one could understand what I was trying to say. And I remember the struggle of learning to raise capital and learning to spend the investors' money wisely in the hopes of building a powerful business. I also remember going back to my investors and telling them that I had lost their money. I am forever grateful for the investors who understood and told me to come back when I had another venture for them to invest in. However, through it all, each mistake was a priceless learning experience as well as character-building experience. As rich dad said, the risk at the start was very high, yet if I could stick it out and continue to learn, the rewards were unlimited.

In 1974, I was very weak at every level of the B-I Triangle. I think I was weakest in cash flow management and communications management. Today, although I am still not great on any one sector of the triangle, I would say I am the strongest in cash flow management and communications management. Because I can create synergies among all the levels, my companies are successful. The point I make here is that even though I was not strong at the start, and am still not great at this stage of my development, I continue with my learning process. For anyone who wants to acquire great wealth in this manner, I offer encouragement to start, to practice, make mistakes, correct, learn, and improve.

When I look at the 10% of people who control 90% of all the shares in America and 73% of the wealth, I understand exactly where their wealth was derived. Many acquired that wealth in much the same way as Henry Ford and Thomas Edison (who was worth far more than Bill Gates at his day and age). The list includes Bill Gates, Michael Dell, Warren Buffet, Rupert Murdoch, Anita Roddick, Richard Branson, and others who all acquired their wealth the same way. They found their spirit and their mission; built a business; and allowed others to share in the dreams, the risks, as well as the rewards. You can do the same thing if you want. Just follow the same diagram rich dad guided me with: the B-I Triangle.

Helen Keller said, 'True happiness is not attained through self-gratification but through fidelity to a worthy purpose.'

## Sharon's Notes

The product is at the top of the B-I Triangle because it is the expression of the business's mission. It is what you are offering to your customer. The rest of the B-I Triangle lays the foundation for long-term success of your business. If your communication to the marketplace is strong, your systems are set up to facilitate production, ordering, and fulfillment. If your cash is managed properly, you will be able to sell your product successfully and support a strong growth curve for your business.

## The B-I Triangle and Your Ideas

Rich dad said, 'It is the B-I Triangle that gives shape to your ideas. It is knowledge of the B-I Triangle that allows a person to create an asset that buys other assets.' Rich dad guided me in learning how to create and build many B-I Triangles. Many of these businesses failed because I was not able to put all the pieces together harmoniously. When people ask me what caused some of my businesses to fail, it was very often the failure of one or more of the sectors of the B-I Triangle. Rather than become permanently discouraged as many people who fail become, rich dad encouraged me to keep practicing, building these triangles. Instead of calling me a failure when my first big venture failed, rich dad encouraged me to continue on and learn how to build new triangles. He said, 'The more you practice building these B-I Triangles, the easier it will be for you to create assets that buy other assets. If you diligently practice, it will become easier and easier for you to make more and more money. Once you are good at taking ideas, building a B-I triangle around the idea, people will come to you and invest money with you and then it will be true for you that it does not take money to make money. People will be giving you their money to make more money for yourself and for them. Instead of spending your life working for money, you will be getting better at creating assets that make more and more money.'

### *The B-I Triangle and the 90/10 Rule Go Hand in Hand*

One day while rich dad was teaching me more about the B-I Triangle, he made a comment I found interesting. He said, 'There is a B-I Triangle inside each of us.' Not understanding what he meant, I inquired further. Even though his explanation was a good one, it took me awhile to realize how true his statement was. Today whenever I find a person, a family, a business, a city, or a country that is having financial difficulties, to me that means one or more segments of the B-I Triangle are missing or out of synchronicity with the other parts. When one or more parts of the B-I Triangle are not functioning, the chances are the individual, or family, or country, will be in the 90% that are sharing in 10% of the money available. So if you, your family or your business is struggling today, look at the model of the B-I Triangle and do an analysis of what can be changed or improved.

## *Solving the B-I Triangle Riddle*

Rich dad gave me another reason to begin mastering the B-I Triangle that I thought was unique. He said, 'Your dad believes in hard work as the means of making money. Once you master the art of building B-I Triangles, you will find that the less you work the more money you will make and the more valuable what you are building becomes.' At first I did not understand what rich dad was saying, but after a number of years of practice, I understand more fully. Today I meet people who work hard building a career, working their way up the corporate ladder, or building a practice based upon their reputation. These people generally come from the E and S quadrants. In order for me to become rich, I needed to learn to build and put together systems that could work without me. After my first B-I Triangle was built and I sold it, I realized what rich dad meant by the less I work the more money I will make. He called that thinking 'solving the B-I Triangle riddle.' If you are a person who is addicted to hard work, or what rich dad calls 'staying busy in your busyness and not building anything,' then I would suggest sitting down with other people who are busy in busyness and discuss how working less can make you more money. I have found that the difference between people in the E and S quadrants and the people in the B and I quadrants is that the E and S side are often too 'hands-on.' Rich dad used to say, 'The key to success is laziness. The more hands-on you are, the less money you can make.' One of the reasons so many people do not join the 90/10 club is because they are too 'hands on,' when they should be seeking new ways of doing more with less and less. If you are going to become the kind of person who creates assets that buy other assets, you will need to find ways of doing less and less so you can make more and more. As rich dad said, 'They key to success is laziness.' That is why he could create so many assets that bought other assets. He could not have done it if he were like my real dad who was a very hard working man.

## A *Summary of the B-I Triangle*

The B-I Triangle as a whole represents a strong system of systems — supported by a team with a leader — all working toward a common mission. If one member of the team is weak, or falters, the overall success of the business can be jeopardized. I would like to highlight three important points in summarizing the B-I Triangle:

1.  Money always follows management. If any of the management functions of the five individual levels are weak, the company will be weak. If you are personally having financial difficulty, or not having the excessive cash flow that you desire, you can often find the weak spot(s) by analyzing each level. Once you identify your weakness, you may then want to consider turning it into your strength, or hiring someone with that strength.

2.  Some of the best investments and businesses are the ones you walk away from. If any of the five levels are weak and the management is not prepared to strengthen them, it is best to walk away from the investment. Too many times, I have discussed the five levels of the B-I Triangle with a management team with which I am considering investing and I hear arguments instead of discussion. When business owners or business teams are weak in any of the five levels, they will become defensive rather than receptive to questioning. If they do become defensive rather than excited to identify and correct a weakness, I usually walk away from the investment. I have on a wall in my house a photo of a pig I took on Fiji. Under it is printed: 'Don't teach pigs to sing. It wastes your time and it annoys the pigs.' There are too many excellent investments out there to waste your time trying to teach pigs to sing.

3.  The personal computer and the Internet make the B-I Triangle more available, affordable, and manageable for everyone. In my talks, I say that it has never been easier to access great

wealth. In the Industrial Age, you needed millions of dollars to build a car factory. Today, with a $1,000 used computer, some brainpower, a telephone line, and a little education in each of the five aspects of the B-I Triangle, the world can be yours.

If you still desire to build a business on your own, there has never been greater opportunity for success. I recently met a young man who sold his small Internet company to a major computer software company for $28 million. All he said to me was, 'I made $28 million at the age of 28. How much will I make when I am 48?'

## Sharon's Notes

If you want to be an entrepreneur who builds successful businesses or invests in businesses, the entire B-I Triangle must be strong and interdependent. If it is, the business will grow and flourish. The good news is that if you are a team player, you don't have to be an expert at every level of the B-I Triangle. Just become part of a team with a clear vision, a strong mission, and an iron stomach.

**B-I Triangle**

## From B-I Triangle to Business Tetrahedron

A business with a defined mission, a determined leader, and a qualified and unified team begins to take shape as the sections of the

B-I Triangle come together. This is when the B-I Triangle becomes three-dimensional and turns into a tetrahedron.

The point of completion is the introduction of integrity. The definition of integrity is wholeness, entirety, as well as perfect condition and soundness. The more common definition of integrity is honesty or sincerity. While the definitions may sound different, they are in fact the same.

A business run with honesty and sincerity when built on the principles of the B-I Triangle will become complete, whole, and sound.

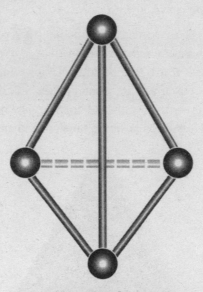

**Your Business**

*Phase Four*

# *Who Is a Sophisticated Investor?*

## Chapter 37

# *How a Sophisticated Investor Thinks*

'Now that you understand the B-I Triangle, are you ready to build a business?' rich dad asked me.

'Yes, absolutely. Even though it is a little intimidating,' I replied. 'There is so much to remember.'

'That's the point, Robert. Once you build a successful business, you will have the skills to build as many as you want. You will also have the skills to analyze other businesses from the outside before you invest in them.'

'It still seems like an impossible mission,' I replied.

'Maybe it is because you're thinking of building huge businesses,' rich dad continued.

'Of course I am. I am going to be rich,' I answered vehemently.

'To learn the skills needed for the B-I Triangle, you need to start small. Even a hot dog cart or a small rental home needs its own B-I Triangle. Every component of the B-I Triangle applies to even the smallest business. You will make mistakes. If you learn from those mistakes, you can build bigger and bigger businesses. In the process, you will become a sophisticated investor.'

'So learning to build a business will make me a sophisticated investor?' I asked. 'Is that all it takes?'

'If you learn the lessons along the way and build a successful business, you can become a sophisticated investor,' rich dad continued, as he brought out his infamous yellow pad. 'It's making the first million dollars that's difficult. After you've made the first million, the next ten million are easy. Let's discuss what makes a successful businessperson and investor a sophisticated investor.'

## Who Is a Sophisticated Investor?

'A sophisticated investor is an investor who understands each of the ten investor controls. The sophisticated investor understands and benefits from the advantages of the right side of the Quadrant. Let's go through each investor control so you get a better understanding of how a sophisticated investor thinks,' rich dad explained.

### The Ten Investor Controls

1. The control over yourself
2. The control over income/expense and asset/liability ratios
3. The control over the management of the investment
4. The control over taxes
5. The control over when you buy and when you sell
6. The control over brokerage transactions
7. The control over the E-T-C (entity, timing, characteristics)
8. The control over the terms and conditions of the agreements
9. The control over access to information
10. The control over giving it back, philanthropy, redistribution of wealth

'It is important to understand that a sophisticated investor may choose not to become an inside investor or ultimate investor; rather, he or she understands the benefits of each control,' rich dad continued. 'The more controls these investors possess, the less risk they have in the investment.'

### *Investor Control #1:*

#### *The Control over Yourself*

'The most important control you must have as an investor is control over yourself.' It can determine your success as an investor and is why the entire first phase of the book is dedicated to getting control over yourself. Rich dad often also said, 'It isn't the investment that is risky, it is the investor who is risky!'

Most of us were taught in school to become employees. There was only one right answer, and making mistakes was horrible. We were not taught financial literacy in school. It takes a lot of work and time to change your thinking and to become financially literate.

A sophisticated investor knows that there are multiple right answers, that the best learning comes through making mistakes, and that financial literacy is essential to be successful. They know their own financial statement, and they understand how each financial decision they make will ultimately impact their financial statement.

To become rich, you must teach yourself to think like a rich person.

### *Investor Control #2:*

#### *The Control over Income/Expense and Asset/Liability Ratios*

This control is developed through financial literacy. My rich dad taught me the three cash flow patterns of the poor, middle class, and the rich. I decided at an early age that I wanted to have the cash flow pattern of a rich person.

The cash flow pattern of the poor:

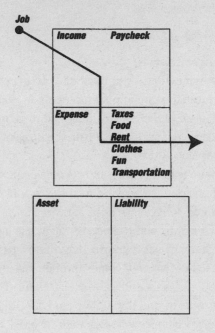

The poor spend every penny they make – they have no assets and no debt.

The cash flow pattern of the middle class:

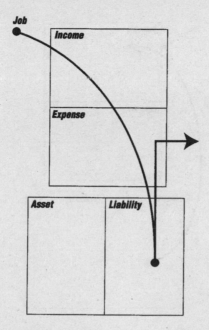

Individuals in the middle class accumulate more debt as they become more successful. A pay raise qualifies them to borrow more money from the bank so they can buy personal items like bigger cars, vacation homes, boats, and motor homes. Their wage income comes in and is spent on current expenses and then on paying off this personal debt.

As their income increases, so does their personal debt. This is what we call the 'Rat Race.'

The cash flow pattern of the rich:

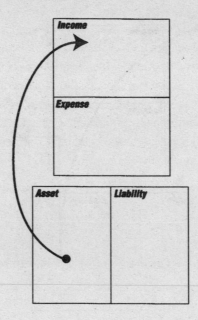

The rich have their assets work for them. They have gained control over their expenses and focus on acquiring or building assets. Their businesses pay most of their expenses, and they have few, if any, personal liabilities.

You may have a cash flow pattern that is a combination of these three types. What story does your financial statement tell? Are you in control of your expenses?

## Buy Assets Not Liabilities

Sophisticated investors buy assets that put money in their pockets. It is just that simple.

## *Turning Personal Expenses into Business Expenses*

Sophisticated investors understand that businesses are allowed to deduct all the ordinary and necessary expenses paid or incurred for the business. They analyze their expenses and convert non-deductible personal expenses into deductible business expenses whenever possible. Not every expense will be an allowable deduction.

Review your business and personal expenses with your financial and tax advisors so that you can maximize the deductions available to you through your business. Some examples of personal expenses that could be legitimate business expenses are:

| Personal Expense | Business Expense | Justification |
| --- | --- | --- |
| Computer | Business equipment | Business use |
| Cellular phone | Business equipment | Use your phone to call clients |
| Meals out | Business meals | Note business purpose and with whom |
| Medical expense | Medical reimbursement | Adopt medical reimbursement plan |
| Tuition | Education | Authorize and document applicability for business |
| Home costs | Home office | Follow guidelines – track all home expenses and reimburse based on square footage |

These are just a few examples of the types of business expenses that are deductible expenses for business owners. The same expenses are not usually deductible for employees. Your expenses must be properly documented and have a legitimate business purpose. Can you think of expenses you are paying personally today that could be deductible business expenses if you owned a business?

### *Investor Control #3:*
### *The Control over the Management of the Investment*

An inside investor who owns enough of an interest in the investment whereby he or she can control the management decisions has this investor control. It can be as a sole owner or where the investor owns enough of an interest that he or she is involved in the decision-making process.

The skills learned through building a successful business using the B-I Triangle are essential to this investor.

Once the investor possesses these skills, he or she is better able to analyze the effectiveness of the management of other potential investments. If the management appears competent and successful, the investor is more comfortable investing funds.

## Investor Control #4:

### The Control over Taxes

The sophisticated investor has learned about the tax laws, either through formal study or by asking questions and listening to good

advisors. The right side of the CASHFLOW Quadrant provides certain tax advantages, which the sophisticated investor uses thoughtfully to minimize his or her taxes paid as well as to increase tax deferrals wherever possible.

In the United States, those on the right side of the Quadrant enjoy many tax advantages that are not available to those on the left side. Three specific advantages are:

1. 'Social insurance' taxes (Social Security in the United States, Medicare tax, unemployment tax, and disability income, to name just a few) do NOT apply to passive and portfolio income (right side of the Cashflow Quadrant) but do apply to earned income (left side of the Cashflow Quadrant).

2. It may be possible to defer payment of taxes, perhaps indefinitely, by using the laws available to you related to real estate and owning a company (an example would be a profit-sharing plan sponsored by your business corporation).

3.  C-Corporations may pay for a number of expenditures with pre-tax dollars that E income recipients must pay for with after-tax dollars. Some examples are included under Investor Control #2.

Sophisticated investors recognize that each country, state, and province has difference tax laws, and they are prepared to move their business affairs to the place best suited for what they are doing.

Recognizing that taxes are the largest expense in the E and S quadrants, sophisticated investors may well seek to reduce their income in order to reduce income taxes while increasing funds for investment simultaneously. See the example under Investor Control #7.

## Investor Control #5:

### The Control over When You Buy and When You Sell

The sophisticated investor knows how to make money in an up market as well as in a down market.

In building a business, the sophisticated investor has great patience. I sometimes refer to this patience as 'delayed gratification.' A sophisticated investor understands that the true financial reward is after the investment, or business, becomes profitable and can be sold or taken public.

## Investor Control #6:

### The Control over Brokerage Transactions

The sophisticated investor operating as an inside investor can direct how the investment is sold or expanded.

As an outside investor in other companies, the sophisticated investor carefully tracks the performance of his or her investments and directs his or her broker to buy or sell.

Many investors today rely on their brokers to know when to buy and sell. These investors are not sophisticated.

## *Investor Control #7:*

### *The Control over the E-T-C (Entity, Timing, Characteristics)*

'Next to control over yourself, the control over the E-T-C is the most important control,' rich dad would repeat often. To have control over the entity, timing, and characteristics of your income, you need to understand corporate, security, and tax law.

Rich dad truly understood the benefits offered through choosing the right entity, with the right year-end, and converting as much earned income into passive and portfolio income as possible. This, combined with the ability to read financial statements and 'think in terms of financial statements,' helped rich dad build his financial empire more quickly.

To illustrate what proper E-T-C planning can do, let's review the following case studies about James and Cathy.

CASE #1

James and Cathy are the absentee owners of a restaurant.

The restaurant is operated as a sole proprietorship.

They have two children.

Their net income from the restaurant is $60,000.

James and Cathy have one financial statement.

## James and Cathy's Financial Statement

**Income**

| | |
|---|---|
| Business net income | $60,000 |
| (after restaurant mortgage payments and depreciation of $120,000) | |

**Expense**

| | | |
|---|---|---|
| Social Insurance Taxes | $9,200 | |
| Income Taxes | $5,000 | |
| Total Taxes | | $14,200 |
| Home Mortgage | $10,200 | |
| Living Expenses: | | |
|    Utilities | $3,000 | |
|    Auto | $3,000 | |
|    Food | $12,000 | |
|    Health Insurance | $8,000 | |
|    Legal & Accounting | $2,000 | |
|    Education | $1,000 | |
|    Charity | $1,000 | |
| Total Living Expenses | | $40,200 |

| | |
|---|---|
| Net Cash Flow | $5,600 |

| Assets | Liabilities |
|---|---|
| Restaurant Building | Home Mortgage |
| Restaurant Fixtures | Restaurant Mortgage |

## CASE #2

James and Cathy met with their financial and tax advisors to structure their businesses to maximize their cash flow and minimize the amount they must pay in taxes.

James and Cathy own two corporations; one owns the restaurant, and the other owns the building where the restaurant is located.

James is the general manager for both corporations.

James and Cathy have two children.

James and Cathy have three sets of financial statements that impact their financial position.

### How Did James and Cathy Benefit from the Advice of Their Financial and Tax Advisors?

By setting up this two-corporation structure:

1. James and Cathy can convert certain personal expenses into legitimate business expenses (health insurance, legal and accounting expenses, education expenses, and a home office and auto deduction).
2. They were able to reduce the total amount paid in taxes by $7,885.
3. They were able to put $12,000 into a retirement fund.
4. Both #2 and #3 were made possible although they reduced their personal income to zero.
5. They have protected their personal assets by putting their business operations into corporations, one owned 100% by James and the other owned 100% by Cathy.

Let's see how they were able to accomplish all of this:

## James and Cathy's Financial Statement

### Income

| General Manager Salary | | |
|---|---|---|
| Restaurant | $20,000 | |
| Real Estate Company | $10,000 | |
| Office Reimbursement | $ 1,000 | |
| Auto travel Reimbursement | $ 1,000 | |
| | | |
| Total Income | | $32,000 |

### Expense

| Social Insurance Taxes | $ 2,300 | |
|---|---|---|
| Income Taxes | $ 1,500 | |
| Total Taxes | | $ 3,800* |
| Home Mortgage | $10,200 | |
| Living Expenses | | |
| Utilities | $ 3,000 | |
| Auto | $ 3,000 | |
| Food | $12,000 | |
| Total Living Expenses | | $28,200 |
| | | |
| Net Cash Flow | | $    0 |

| Assets | Liabilities |
|---|---|
| Restaurant Company | Home Mortgage |
| Real Estate Company | |

### Restaurant's Financial Statement

#### Income

| Food Service | $180,000 |
|---|---|

#### Expense

| General Manager | $20,000 |
|---|---|
| Social Ins Taxes | $1,500* |
| Rent Expense | $155,000 |
| Reimbursement | $1,000 |
| Legal & Acct | $1,000 |
| | |
| Income Taxes | $225* |
| Net Income | $1,275 |

| Assets | Liabilities |
|---|---|
| | |

### Real Estate Co's Financial Statement

#### Income

| Rental Income | $155,000 |
|---|---|

#### Expense

| General Manager | $10,000 |
|---|---|
| Social Ins Taxes | $750* |
| Mortgage + Depreciation | $120,000 |
| Reimbursement | $1,000 |
| Legal & Acct | $1,000 |
| Retirement Plan | $12,000 |
| Health Plan | $8,000 |
| Education Reim | $1,000 |
| Charity | $1,000 |
| Income Taxes | $40* |
| Net Income | $210 |

| Assets | Liabilities |
|---|---|
| Building | Building Mortgage |
| Fixtures | |

* Total Taxes = $6,315

Now let's compare CASE #1 to CASE #2

|  | CASE #1<br>Sole Proprietorship | CASE #2<br>Individual +<br>Two Corporations | Difference |
|---|---|---|---|
| Taxes Paid | ($ 14,200) | ($ 6,315) | $ 7,885 |
| Income: | | | |
| Retirement funds | 0 | $ 12,000 | |
| Profit | | | |
|   Personal | $ 5,600 | $ 0 | |
|   Corp #1 | | $ 1,275 | |
|   Corp #2 | | $ 210 | |
| Total Cash Flow | $ 5,600 | $ 13,485 | $ 7,885 |

The end result of this financial plan for James and Cathy is that they have added $7,885 to their personal wealth by saving $7,885 in taxes. More importantly, however, they have protected their personal assets by moving their businesses into corporations. By having validly established corporations, their personal assets should be safe even if a judgment is awarded against one of the corporations. For instance, if a customer becomes ill in the restaurant, he or she can sue the corporation that owns the restaurant. Any judgment against the restaurant corporation would be paid out of the assets of that corporation. The corporation that owns the building, and the personal assets of James and Cathy, should be protected.

James and Cathy's example is very simplified and provided for illustration purposes only. It is extremely important that you seek professional legal and tax advice before structuring your own financial plan. You must consider many complex issues to ensure you comply with all laws.

All of these numbers look very complicated to me so I have also included the simple diagram rich dad showed me when he described his restaurant and real estate corporations. I learn better with pictures than numbers, so maybe it will help you too.

### More Control, Not Less

Rich dad would say, 'Once you can think automatically in financial statements, you can then operate multiple businesses as well as evaluate other investments quickly. However, most importantly, once you can think in financial statements, you will gain even greater control over your financial life and make even more money, money that the average person doesn't realize can be made.'

He then drew the following diagram:

## My Personal

| Income |
| --- |
| |

| Expense |
| --- |
| |

| Assets | Liabilities |
| --- | --- |
| My Wife's Restaurant Company | |
| My Real Estate Company | |

## My Wife's Restaurant    My Real Estate Company

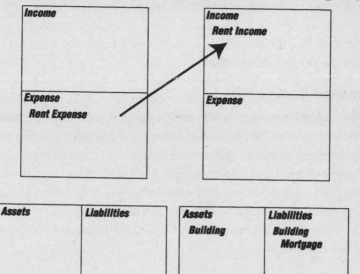

I looked at the diagram and said, 'Your expenses go to what you have control of. In this case, your restaurant business pays its rent to your real estate investment company.'

Rich dad nodded, saying, 'And technically, what am I doing?'

'You are taking earned income from your restaurant business and converting it into passive income for your real estate company. In other words, you are paying yourself.'

'And that is just the beginning,' said rich dad. 'Yet, I want to caution you that from here on in, you will need the best accounting and legal advice possible. This is where unsophisticated investors begin to get into trouble. They get into trouble because the diagram I showed you can be done legally and it can be done illegally. There must always be a business purpose for the transactions between the corporations, and certain control group ownership issues must be considered when you own stock in multiple corporations. It is too easy to make money legally, so hire the best advisors, and you will learn even more about how the rich get richer, legally.'

## Investor Control #8:

### The Control over the Terms and Conditions of the Agreements

The sophisticated investor is in control over the terms and conditions of agreements when he or she is on the inside of the investment. For instance, when I rolled over the sale of several of my small houses into a small apartment building, I used a Section 1031 exchange (U.S. law), which allowed me to roll over the gain. I did not have to pay any taxes on the sale because I controlled the terms and conditions of the agreements.

## Investor Control #9:

### The Control over Access to Information

As an inside investor, the sophisticated investor again has control over access to information. This is where the investor needs to understand the legal requirements of insiders imposed by the SEC in the United States (other countries have similar oversight organizations).

## Investor Control #10:

### The Control over Giving It Back, Philanthropy, Redistribution of Wealth

The sophisticated investor recognizes the social responsibility that comes with wealth and gives back to society. This may be through charitable giving, philanthropy. Some of it will be through capitalism, by creating jobs and expanding the economy.

## Chapter 38

# *Analyzing Investments*

'The numbers tell a story,' my rich dad would say. 'If you can learn to read financial statements you can see what is happening within any company or investment.'

My rich dad taught me how he used financial ratios to manage his businesses. Whether it is an investment in the stock of a company or purchase of real estate I always analyze the financial statements. I can determine how profitable a business is, or how highly leveraged a business is, just by looking at its financial statements and calculating financial ratios.

For a real estate investment, I calculate what the cash on cash return will be based on the amount of cash I need to spend for the down payment.

But the bottom line always came back to financial literacy. This chapter will cover some of the important thought processes every sophisticated investor goes through in choosing investments for their financial plan:

Financial Ratios of a Company

Financial Ratios of Real Estate

Natural Resources

Is It Good Debt or Bad Debt?

Saving Is Not Investing

## Financial Ratios of a Company

$$\text{Gross Margin Percentage} = \frac{\text{Sales - Cost of Goods Sold}}{\text{Sales}}$$

The Gross Margin Percentage is the Gross Margin divided by Sales, which tells you what percentage of sales is left after deducting the cost of goods sold. Sales minus the cost of the things sold {"Cost of Goods Sold"} is called the Gross Margin. I remember rich dad saying, 'if the gross isn't there, there'll be no net (income).'

How high the Gross Margin Percentage needs to be depends on how a business is organized and the other costs it has to support. After calculating the gross margin percentage, rich dad's convenience stores still had to rent the building, pay the clerks, the utilities, the taxes and government permit fees, pay for wasted or damaged goods, and a long list of other expenses, plus have enough left over to give rich dad a good return on his original investment.

For Internet e-commerce sites today, these additional costs are usually much lower, so these businesses can afford to sell and make a profit with a lower Gross Margin Percentage.

The higher the gross margin the better.

$$\text{Net Operating Margin Percentage} = \frac{\text{EBIT}}{\text{Sales}}$$

The Net Operating Margin Percentage tells you the net profitability of the operations of the business before you factor in your taxes and cost of money. EBIT stands for Earnings Before Interest and Taxes, or Sales minus all costs of being in that business, not including capital costs (Interest, Taxes, Dividends).

The ratio of EBIT to Sales is called the Net Operating Margin

Percentage. Businesses with high Net Operating Margin Percentages are typically stronger than those with low percentages.

The higher the net operating margin the better.

$$\text{Operating Leverage} = \frac{\text{Contribution}}{\text{Fixed Costs}}$$

Contribution is the name for Gross Margin (Sales less Cost of Goods Sold) minus Variable Costs (all costs that are not Fixed Costs are Variable and will fluctuate with sales). Fixed costs include all sales, general, and administrative costs that are fixed and do not fluctuate based on sales volume. For instance, the labor costs related to full-time employees, and most costs related to your facilities, are generally considered fixed costs. Some people refer to this as 'overhead.'

A business that has an operating leverage of 1 means that the business is generating just enough revenue to pay for its fixed costs. This would mean that there is no return for the owners.

The higher the operating leverage the better.

$$\text{Financial Leverage} = \frac{\text{Total Capital Employed (Debt \& Equity)}}{\text{Shareholders' Equity}}$$

Total Capital Employed is the book or accounting value of all interest-bearing debt (leave out payables for goods to be resold and liabilities due to wages, expenses and taxes owed but not yet paid), plus all owners' equity. So if you have $50,000 of debt and $50,000 of shareholders' equity, your financial leverage would be 2 (or $100,000 divided by $50,000).

$$\text{Total Leverage} = \text{Operating} \times \text{Financial Leverages}$$

The total risk that a company carries in its present business is the multiple of its Operating Leverage and its Financial Leverage. Total Leverage tells you what total effect a given change in the business should have on the equity owners (common shares or General

Partner). If you are the business owner, and therefore on the inside, your company's Total Leverage is at least partly under your control.

If you are looking at the stock market, Total Leverage will help you decide whether you want to invest. Well run, conservatively managed (publicly traded) American companies usually keep the Total Leverage figure under 5.

$$\text{Debt to Equity Ratio} = \frac{\text{Total Liabilities}}{\text{Total Equity}}$$

The Debt to Equity Ratio measures just that, the portion of the whole enterprise [Total Liabilities] financed by outsiders in proportion to the part financed by insiders [Total Equity]. Most businesses try to stay at a ratio of one-to-one or below. Generally speaking, the lower the debt-to-equity ratio the more conservative the financial structure of the company.

$$\text{Quick Ratio} = \frac{\text{Liquid Assets}}{\text{Current Liabilities}}$$

$$\text{Current Ratio} = \frac{\text{Current Assets}}{\text{Current Liabilities}}$$

The significance of the quick and current ratios is that they tell you whether or not the company has enough liquid assets to pay its liabilities for the coming year. If a company doesn't have enough current assets to cover its current liabilities, it is usually a sign of impending trouble. On the other hand a current ratio and quick ratio of 2 to 1 is more than appropriate.

$$\text{Return on Equity} = \frac{\text{Net Income}}{\text{Average Shareholders' Equity}}$$

The Return on Equity is often considered one of the most important ratios. It allows you to compare the return this company is making on its shareholders' investment compared to alternative investments.

## *What Do the Ratios Tell Me?*

My rich dad taught me to always consider at least three years of these figures. The direction and trend of Margin Percentages, Contribution Margin, Leverages and Returns on Equity tell me a lot about a company and its management and even its competitors.

Many published company reports do not include these ratios and indicators. A sophisticated investor learns to calculate these ratios (or hires someone knowledgeable to do so) when they aren't provided.

A sophisticated investor understands the terminology of the ratios and can use the ratios in evaluating the investment. However, the ratios cannot be used in a vacuum. They are indicators of a company's performance. They must be considered in conjunction with analysis of the overall business and industry. By comparing the ratios over at least a three-year period as well as with other companies in the same industry, you can quickly determine the relative strength of the company.

For example, a company with excellent ratios over the last three years and strong profits could appear to be a sound investment. However, after reviewing the industry you find out that the company's main product has just been rendered obsolete by a new product introduced by the company's main competitor. In this instance, a company with a history of strong performance may not be a wise investment due to its potential loss in market share.

While the ratios may appear complicated at first, you will be amazed at how quickly you can learn to analyze a company. Remember these ratios are the language of a sophisticated investor. Through educating yourself on financial literacy, you too can learn to 'speak in ratios.'

While the ratios may appear complicated at first, you will be amazed at how quickly you learn to analyze a company.

## Investing in Real Estate: Financial Ratios for a Piece of Real Estate

When it came to real estate, rich dad had two questions.

1. Does the property generate a positive cash flow?
2. If yes, have you done your due diligence?

The most important financial ratio of a piece of real estate to rich dad was his cash on cash return.

$$\text{Cash on Cash Return} = \frac{\text{Positive Net Cash Flow}}{\text{Down Payment}}$$

Let's say you buy an apartment building for $500,000. You put $100,000 down and secure a mortgage for the $400,000 balance. You have a monthly cash flow of $2,000 after all expenses and mortgage payment are paid. Your cash on cash return is 24% or $24,000 ($2,000 x 12 months) divided by $100,000.

Before buying the apartment building, you must decide how you will purchase it. Will you buy it through a C-Corporation, an LLC Corporation, or a limited partnership? Consult with your legal and tax advisors to make sure that you choose the entity that will provide the most legal protection and tax advantages to you.

## Due Diligence

In my opinion, the words due diligence are some of the most important words in the world of fiancial literacy. It is through the process of due diligence that a sophisticated investor sees the other side of the coin. When people ask me how I find good investments I simply reply, 'I find them through the process of due diligence.' Rich dad said, 'The faster you are able to do your due diligence on any investment, regardless if it is a business, real estate, a stock, mutual fund or bond, the better able you will be to find the safest investments with the greatest possibility for cash flow or capital gains.'

In the audio cassette learning program entitled *Financial Literacy: How Sophisticated Investors Find the Investments That Average Investors Miss* is a workbook filled with very sophisticated due diligence forms that can be adapted to evaluate many investments quickly. If you would like to find out more about this audio educational program and workbook, please refer to our website, www.richdad.com. Not only will you listen to very sophisticated investors share their investment secrets, you will learn how to use these due diligence forms. These rarely publicized due diligence forms have the power to not only make you a more sophisticated investor, the forms can save you a lot of time analyzing investments, and they may also help you find the high yielding investments you have been looking for.

For example, once you have determined that a piece of real estate will generate a positive cash flow for you, you still need to perform due diligence on the property.

Rich dad had a checklist that he always used. I use a due diligence checklist created by Cindy Shopoff. It is very thorough and includes items that did nto exist 30 years ago (e.g. Phase I Environmental Audit). I have included Cindy's checklist as a reference for you.

If I have questions about the property, I often bring in the experts and have my attorneys and accountants review the deal.

### Due Diligence Checklist

_____  1.  Current rent roster with paid to dates

_____  2.  List of security deposits

_____  3.  Mortgage payment information

_____  4.  Personal property list

_____  5.  Floor plans

_____  6.  Insurance policy, agent

_____  7.  Maintenance, service agreement

_____  8.  Tenant information: leases, ledger cards, applications, smoke detector forms

_____ 9. List of vendors and utility companies, including account number

_____ 10. A statement of structural alterations made to the premises

_____ 11. Surveys and engineering documents

_____ 12. Commission agreements

_____ 13. Rental or listing agreements

_____ 14. Easement agreements

_____ 15. Development plans, including plans and specifications and as-built architectural, structural, mechanical, electrical and civil drawings

_____ 16. Governmental permits or zoning restrictions affecting development of the property

_____ 17. Management contracts

_____ 18. Tax bills and property tax statements

_____ 19. Utility bills

_____ 20. Cash receipts and disbursements journals pertaining to the property

_____ 21. Capital expenditure disbursement records pertaining to the property for the past five years

_____ 22. Income and expense statements pertaining to the property for two years prior to the submission date

_____ 23. Financial statements and state and federal tax returns for the property

_____ 24. A termite inspection in form and content reasonably satisfactory to the buyer

_____ 25. All other records and documents in Seller's possession or under Seller's control which would be necessary or helpful to the ownership, operation or maintenance of the property

_____ 26. Market surveys or studies of the area

_____ 27. Construction budget or actuals

_____ 28. Tenant profiles or surveys

_____ 29. Work-order files

_____ 30. Bank statements for two years showing operating account
for property

_____ 31. Certificates of occupancy

_____ 32. Title abstract

_____ 33. Copies of all surviving guarantees and warranties

_____ 34. Phase I Environmental Audit (if exists) for every
investment

## Natural Resources

Many sophisticated investors include investments in the earth's natural resources as part of their portfolio. They invest in oil, gas, coal and precious metals, just to name a few.

My rich dad strongly believed in the power of gold. As a natural resource, gold has a limited supply. As rich dad told me, people throughout the centuries have cherished gold. Rich dad also believed that owning gold attracted other wealth to you.

To read more about my rich dad's lesson about investing in gold, please visit www.richdadgold.com.

## Is It Good Debt or Bad Debt?

A sophisticated investor recognizes good debt, good expenses and good liabilities. I remember rich dad asking me, 'How many rental houses can you afford to own where you lose $100 per month?' I, of course answered, 'Not too many.' Then he asked me, 'How many rental houses can you afford to own where you earn $100 per month?' The answer to that question is, 'As many as I can find!'

Analyze each of your expenses, liabilities and debts. Does each particular expense, liability or debt apply to a corresponding income or an asset? If so, is the resulting cash flow in from the income and/or asset greater than the cash flow out for the expense/liability/debt?

For example, a friend of mine, Jim, has a mortgage on an apartment building for $600,000, for which he pays out $5,500 each month in mortgage and interest payments. He receives rental income from his tenants of $8,000 each month. After all other expenses he has a net positive cash flow of $1,500 each month from that apartment building. I would consider Jim's mortgage a GOOD DEBT.

## *Saving Is Not Investing*

A sophisticated investor understands the difference between saving and investing. Let's look at the case of two friends, John and Terry, both of whom believe themselves to be sophisticated investors.

John is a highly paid professional and invests the maximum in his 401(k) retirement plan at work. John is 42 and has $250,000 in his 401(k) plan already because he has been adding to it for 11 years. There is no return, or cash flow, from it until he retires and then it will be fully taxable at his regular earned income rates.

John's details:   Earning $100,000 salary

Taxes – assume average rate of 25% (low)

Investment – Pension Plan – 401(k)

Maximum 15% contribution or $15,000

Pension Plan – earns 8% per year

Current Cash Flow from investments – none

Terry is the same age as John and makes a similar salary. She has invested in a series of real estate deals over the past 11 years and just put $250,000 down on a $1,000,000 property. Terry is earning a cash on cash return of 10% and expects a conservative appreciation of her property of 4% per year. When she retires, Terry expects to 1031 Exchange into another property to take advantage of the high equity and cash flow. Terry has never contributed to the 401(k) plan and the income from her property is taxed currently.

Terry's details: Earning $100,000 salary
Taxes — assume average rate of 25% (low)
Investment — Buy Real Estate at $1,000,000
with 25% or $250,000 down
Property — earns 10% cash on cash return
Appreciates 4% per year
Current Cash Flow — $25,000 per year from Real
Estate investment

The following chart shows the asset accumulation, annual after-taxes cash flow available for spending, and the annual retirement cash flow (also after taxes) for both John and Terry. I thank my tax advisor, Diane Kennedy, CPA, for preparing this analysis so I could share it with you.

| | Beginning | | yrs 1–19 | | At 20 years | | Annual Retired |
| | Assets | Cash Flow | Invests | Cash Flow | Assets | Cash Flow | Cash Flow |
|---|---|---|---|---|---|---|---|
| John | $250,000 | $63,750 | $15,000 | $63,750 | $1,968,000 | $63,750 | $118,100 |
| Terry | $250,000 | $73,560 | 0 | $73,560 | $2,223,000 | $73,560 | $342,700 |

As you see, Terry's family will be able to spend almost $10,000 more per year than John's family, each and every year for the next 20 years. After which, they both retire at age 62, having worked 31 years.

At retirement, John begins drawing out 8% of his accumulated 401(k) plan, receiving $118,100 per year ($157,400 before taxes). He plans to withdraw none of the principal amount. He succeeded, after 31 total years of investing $15,000 in his plan each year, in replacing 150% of his work income.

Even though Terry had only put $250,000 down on the property, she benefited from the 4% appreciation on the total $1,000,000 value of the property. During the 20 years, the rental income from the property paid off the mortgage of $750,000, so when Terry retires she can roll over the complete equity of $1,000,000 into a much larger property (worth $8,892,000 according to these calculations). This new property will generate a cash flow of $342,700 per year for Terry.

While John's retirement will be comfortable, Terry's will be rich.

If, for some reason, John needs more income in retirement, he must start drawing out the principal from his retirement plan. Terry would only need to do another tax-free exchange into other buildings to capture the mortgage principal paid down by her tenants, leveraging that into higher income.

John's example will have taught his children to go to school, get good grades, get a good job, work hard, 'invest' in the retirement plan regularly; and as a result, be comfortable in retirement.

Terry's example will have taught her children that if they learn how to invest by starting small, to mind their own business, and to keep their money working hard for them, they'll be rich.

It is easy to see that investing in a building generated much more cash flow and income for Terry than saving in his 401(k) did for John. I would categorize Terry as an investor and John as a saver.

A sophisticated investor understands the difference between investing and saving and generally has both as part of his or her financial plan.

# Chapter 39

# *The Ultimate Investor*

So the question remains, how does a person like Bill Gates become the richest businessperson in the world in his thirties? Or how does Warren Buffet become the richest investor in America? Both men came from middle-class families so they were not handed the keys to the family vault. Yet, without great family wealth behind them, they rocketed to the apex of wealth within a span of a few years. How? They did it how many of the ultra-rich have done so in the past and will be doing so in the future. They became ultimate investors by creating an asset that is worth billions of dollars.

The September 27, 1999, issue of *Fortune* ran a cover story titled 'Young and Rich, the 40 wealthiest Americans under 40.' Some of these young billionaires are:

| Position | Name | Age | Wealth | Business |
|----------|------|-----|--------|----------|
| #1 | Michael Dell | 34 | $21.5 billion | Dell Computer |
| #2 | Jeff Bezos | 35 | $5.7 billion | Amazon.com |
| #3 | Ted Waitt | 36 | $5.4 billion | Gateway Computer |
| #4 | Pierre Omidyar | 32 | $3.7 billion | eBay |
| #5 | David Filo | 33 | $3.1 billion | Yahoo! |
| #6 | David Yang | 30 | $3.0 billion | Yahoo! |

| #7   | Henry Nicholas  | 39 | $2.4 billion  | Broadcom    |
| #8   | Rob Glaser      | 37 | $2.3 billion  | RealNetworks |
| #9   | Scott Blum      | 35 | $1.7 billion  | Buy.com     |
| #10  | Jeff Skoll      | 33 | $1.4 billion  | eBay        |

You may notice that the top 10 of the top 40 young rich are from computer or Internet companies. Yet there were other types of businesses listed as well:

| #26  | John Schattner  | 37 | $403 million | Papa John's Pizza |
| #28  | Master P        | 29 | $361 million | Recording star    |
| #29  | Michael Jordan  | 36 | $357 million | Sports star       |

I find it interesting to note that the non-Internet-related rich people came from businesses such as a pizza company, the rap music business, and sports. Everyone else was in computers or the Internet.

Bill Gates and Warren Buffet did not make the list because they were over 40. In 1999, Bill Gates was 43 and worth $85 billion. Warren Buffet was 69 and worth $31 billion, according to *Forbes*.

## *They Made It the Old-Fashioned Way*

So how did most of these people join the ranks of the ultra-rich so early in life? They made it the old-fashioned way: the same way that Rockefeller, Carnegie, and Ford became yesterday's ultra-rich and the same way that tomorrow's ultra-rich will do it. They built companies and sold shares in their company to the public. They worked hard to become selling shareholders rather than buying shareholders. In other words, it could be said that by being selling shareholders, they printed their own money – legally. They created a valuable business and then sold shares of ownership in the business to others, buying shareholders.

In *Rich Dad Poor Dad*, I wrote about how at the age of 9, I began making my own money by melting down lead toothpaste tubes and forging lead coins in plaster of Paris molds. My poor dad told me what the word 'counterfeiting' meant. My first business opened and closed on the same day.

My rich dad, on the other hand, told me that I was very close to the ultimate formula for wealth: to print or invent your own money – legally. And that is what the ultimate investor does. In other words, why work hard for money when you can print your own? In *Rich Dad Poor Dad*, rich dad's lesson #5 is 'the rich invent their own money.' Rich dad taught me to invent my own money with real estate or with small companies. That technical skill is the domain of the inside and ultimate investors.

### How 10% Own 90% of the Shares

One reason the wealthiest 10% own 90% of all the shares, as reported in *The Wall Street Journal*, is that the wealthiest 10% include the ultimate investors, the people who created the shares. Another reason is that only this 10% are eligible (per SEC rules) to invest in a company at the early stages before it becomes available to the public through an IPO. In this elite group are founders of companies (a.k.a. founding shareholders), friends of the founders, or a select list of investors. These are the people who become richer and richer, while the rest of the population often struggles to make ends meet, investing the few dollars they may have left over as buying shareholders, if they have any dollars left at all.

### The Difference between Selling and Buying

In other words, the ultimate investor is someone who builds a company and sells shares in his or her company. When you read an IPO prospectus, ultimate investors are the ones listed as the selling shareholders; they are not buying shareholders. And as you can tell by the net worth of these individuals, there seems to be a tremendous difference in wealth between those who sell and those who buy shares.

## The Last Leg

By 1994, I felt I had successfully completed much of the plan rich dad and I had created back in 1974. I felt relatively comfortable with my abilities to manage most of the components of the B-I Triangle. I understood corporate law well enough to talk to an attorney and/or accountant. I knew the differences among the entity types (S-Corporation, an LLC, an LLP, and a C-Corporation, a limited partnership), and when to use one versus the other. I felt fairly comfortable with my ability to successfully buy and manage real estate investments. By 1994, our expenses were under control with as much as possible becoming pre-tax business expenses. We paid little in regular income tax simply because we did not have jobs in the normal sense. Most of our income was in the form of passive income with a little from portfolio income, primarily from mutual funds. We had some income from investments in other people's businesses.

But one day, while I was evaluating my tetrahedron, it was glaringly obvious that one leg of my tetrahedron was really weak: the leg dedicated to paper assets.

My tetrahedron looked like this:

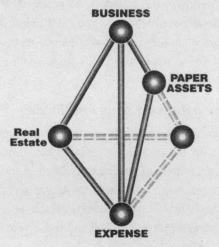

In 1994, I felt good about my success. Kim and I were financially free and could afford not to work for the rest of our lives, barring financial disaster. However, it was obvious that one leg of my tetrahedron was weaker. My financial empire looked out of balance.

I took a year off in the mountains between 1994 and 1995 and spent a lot of time contemplating the idea of strengthening the last leg, paper assets. I had to decide if I really wanted to do all the work needed to strengthen it. I was doing OK financially, and in my mind, I really did not need much more in the way of paper assets to be financially secure. I was fine exactly the way I was, and I could have gotten richer and richer without paper assets.

After a year of mental turmoil and vacillation, I decided that the paper asset leg of my portfolio needed to be strengthened. If I did not do so, I would be quitting on myself. That was a disturbing thought.

I also had to decide if I wanted to invest from the outside, as most people did when it came to buying stocks in companies. In other words, I needed to decide if I wanted to be a buying shareholder and invest from the outside or learn to invest from the inside. Either would be a learning experience, almost like starting over.

It is relatively easy to get into the inside of a real estate deal or the acquisition of a small business. That is why I recommend to individuals who are serious about gaining experience of the ten investor controls to start with small deals in those types of investments. However, to get to the inside of a company before it went public, through a pre-IPO, was another story. Generally, to be invited to invest in a company before it goes public is reserved for a very elite group of people, and I did not belong to that elite group. I was not rich enough, and my money was too new for me to belong to the elite group. In addition, I do not come from the right family or university. My blood is red, not blue; my skin is not white; and Harvard has no record of me applying to its prestigious institution. I had to learn how to become part of the elite group that is invited to invest in the best companies before they go public.

I felt sorry for myself for a few moments, enjoying a brief moment of self-discrimination, a lack of self-confidence, and a strong dose of self-pity. Rich dad had already passed on, and I had no one to turn to for advice. After my few moments of misery were over, I realized that this is a free country. If Bill Gates can drop out of college, build a company, and take it public, why can't I? Isn't this why we want to live in a free country? Can't we be as rich or poor as we want? Isn't this why the barons in 1215 forced King John to sign the Magna Carta? In late 1994, I decided that since no one was going to ask me to join the insiders' club, I might have to find one and ask to be invited to join — or start my own club. The problem was that I did not know where to start, especially in Phoenix, Arizona, two thousand miles from Wall Street.

On New Year's Day 1995, my best friend Larry Clark and I hiked up to a mountaintop near our home. We went through our annual New Year's Day ritual of discussing our past year, planning for the next year, and writing down our goals for the coming year. We spent about three hours up on the rocky peak discussing our lives; the past year; and our hopes, dreams, and goals for the future. Larry and I have been best friends for over 25 years (we started at Xerox together in Honolulu in 1974). He had become my new best friend because he and I had more in common than Mike and I did at that stage of my life. Mike was already very, very rich, and Larry and I were just starting out with virtually nothing but a strong desire to become very, very rich.

Larry and I spent years together as partners, starting several businesses. Many of those businesses failed even before they got off the drawing board. When he and I reflect back on some of those businesses, we laugh at how naive we were back then. Yet, some of those businesses did very well. We were partners in starting the nylon and

Velcro wallet business in 1977 and developing it into a worldwide business. We became best friends through starting businesses together
and have remained best friends ever since. After the nylon and Velcro
wallet business began to fail in 1979, Larry moved back to Arizona
and began to build his fame and fortune as a real estate developer.
In 1995, *Inc.* magazine named him America's fastest-growing home-
builder and he joined its prestigious list of fast-growing entrepreneurs.
In 1991, Kim and I moved to Phoenix for the weather and golf, but
more importantly for the millions of dollars of real estate the federal
government was giving away for pennies on the dollar. Today, Kim
and I are neighbors of Larry and his wife Lisa.

On that bright New Year's Day in 1995, I showed Larry the diagram
of my tetrahedron and my need to increase my paper assets leg. I
shared my desire to either invest in a company before it went public,
or maybe even build a company and take it public. At the end of my
explanation, all Larry said was 'Good luck.' We ended that day by
writing our goals on a 3x5 card and shaking hands. We wrote down
our goals because rich dad had always said, 'Goals have to be clear,
simple, and in writing. If they are not in writing and reviewed daily,
they are not really goals. They are wishes.' Sitting on the chilly mountain peak, we then went over Larry's goal of selling his business and
retiring. At the end of his explanation, I shook his hand and said,
'Good luck' and we hiked back down the mountain.

Periodically, I would review what I had written on that 3x5 card.
My goal was simple. It was stated as, 'To invest in a company before
it goes public and acquire 100,000 shares or more for less than $1.00
a share.' At the end of 1995, nothing had happened. I had not achieved
my goal.

On New Year's Day 1996, Larry and I sat on the same mountain
peak and discussed our results for the year. Larry's company was on
the verge of being sold, but it had not yet happened. So we had not
accomplished our goals for 1995. Larry was close to achieving his goal,

but I seemed far away from achieving mine. Larry asked if I wanted to drop the goal or choose something new. As we discussed the goal, I began to realize that although I had written the goal, I did not believe that it was possible for me. In my soul, I did not really believe that I was smart enough, qualified enough, or that anyone wanted me to belong to that elite group. The more we talked about my goal, the angrier I got at myself for doubting myself and putting myself down so much. 'After all,' Larry said, 'you have paid your dues. You know how to build and run a profitable private company. Why shouldn't you be a valuable asset to a team that takes a company public?' After rewriting our goals and shaking hands, I walked down the mountain with a lot of nervousness and self-doubt because I now wanted my goal more than ever. I also walked down with more determination to have my goal become reality.

Nothing happened for about six months. I would read my goal in the morning and then go about my daily activities, which at that time was to produce my board game *CASHFLOW*. One day, my neighbor Mary knocked on my door and said, 'I have a friend I think you should meet.' I asked her why. All she said was, 'I don't know. I just think the two of you would get along. He's an investor like you.' I trusted Mary so I agreed to meet her friend for lunch.

A week or two later, I met her friend Peter for lunch at a golf club in Scottsdale, Arizona. Peter is a tall, distinguished man who is well spoken and about the same age my own dad would have been if he were still alive. As lunch went on, I found out that Peter had spent much of his adult life on Wall Street, owning his own brokerage firm, occasionally forming companies and taking them public. He has had his own companies listed on the American Exchange, the Canadian exchanges, NASDAQ, and on the big board of the New York Stock Exchange. Not only was he a person who created assets, he was a person who invested from the other side of the coin of the public stock markets. I knew he could guide me into a world very few investors ever see. He could guide me through the looking glass, get me behind the scenes and increase my understanding of the greatest capital markets of the world.

After retiring, he had moved to Arizona with his wife and lives in relative seclusion on his own desert estate, far away from the hustle and bustle of the growing city of Scottsdale. When Peter told me that he had been involved in taking nearly 100 companies public during his career, I knew why I was having lunch with him.

Not wanting to appear too excited or overly aggressive, I did my best to control myself. Peter is a very private individual and grants time to very few people. (That is why I use the name Peter instead of his real name. He continues to prefer his anonymity.) Lunch ended pleasantly without me discussing what I wanted to discuss. As I said, I did not want to appear too eager and naive.

For the next two months, I called asking for another meeting. Always the gentleman, Peter would politely say 'No,' or avoid setting a time to get together. Finally, he said 'Yes,' and gave me directions to his home way out in the desert. We set a date, and I began rehearsing what I wanted to say.

After a week of waiting, I found myself driving up to his home. The first thing that greeted me was a 'Beware of dog' sign. My heart raced as I drove up his long driveway and when I saw this large black lump lying in the middle of the road. It was the dog I was supposed to be wary of, and it was a very big dog. I parked the car just in front of the dog because the dog would not move out of the way. About twenty feet separated my truck and the front door of the house, and this big dog was in between. I opened the door of my truck slowly until I realized the dog was sound asleep. I slowly stepped down from the cab of the truck, but as soon as my foot hit the gravel, the dog suddenly came to life. This big black dog stood to full height, it looked at me, and I looked at it. My heart raced as I prepared to jump back into the cab of the truck. Suddenly, the dog began wagging its stubby tail as well as its whole back end and walked forward to greet me. I spent five minutes petting and being licked to death by this large black guard dog.

My wife Kim and I have a personality rule when it comes to business: 'Never do business with pets you don't trust.' Over the years, we have discovered that people and their pets are very similar. Once, we did a real estate transaction with a husband and wife who had many pets. He loved small dogs known as 'pugs,' and she loved colorful exotic birds. When Kim and I went to their house, their small cute dogs and birds appeared friendly, but once you got close to them, they were vicious. As soon as we approached them, they would snap at us and start to bark or squawk loudly and aggressively. A week after the deal was closed, Kim and I found out that the owners were just like their pets – cute on the outside but vicious on the inside. In the fine print of the contract, we had been bitten badly. Even our attorney at the time had missed the subtle bite. The investment came out all right, but since then, Kim and I have developed this new policy: If we are having any doubts about whom we are doing business with and they have pets, find a way to check out their pets. Humans are able to put forth a pleasant front and say things they really don't mean with a smile, but their pets don't lie. Over the years, we have found this simple guideline to be fairly accurate. We have found that a person's insides are reflected on his or her pet's outside. My meeting with Peter was therefore off to a good start. Besides, his big black dog's name was 'Candy.'

The meeting with Peter did not go so well at first. I asked Peter if I could apprentice with him and be an inside investor with him. I told him that I would work for free if he would teach me what he knew about the process of taking a company public. I explained to him that I was financially free and that I did not need money to work with him. Peter was skeptical for about an hour. He and I went back and forth discussing the value of his time and questioning my ability to learn quickly and willingness to stick with the process. He was afraid that I would quit once I found out how hard it was, since my background was weak when it came to finance and the capital markets such as Wall Street. He also said, 'I've never had anyone offer to work for free just so they could learn from me. The only times people have ever asked me for anything is when they wanted to borrow money or they wanted a job.' I reassured him that all I wanted was the opportunity to work with him and to learn. I told him about my rich dad guiding me for years and my working for free much of the time. Finally, he asked, 'How badly do you want to learn this business?' I looked him squarely in the eye and said, 'I want to learn it very badly.'

'Good,' he said. 'I am currently looking at a bankrupt gold mine located in the Andes Mountains of Peru. If you really want to learn from me, then fly to Lima this Thursday, inspect the mine with my team, meet with the bank, find out what it wants for it, return, and give me a report on your findings. And by the way, this entire trip is at your own expense.'

I sat there with a stunned look on my face. 'Fly to Peru this Thursday?' I restated.

Peter smiled, 'Still want to join my team and learn the business of taking a company public?' My stomach turned into a knot and I broke out in a mild cold sweat. I knew my sincerity was being tested. This was a Tuesday and I had appointments already scheduled for Thursday. Peter sat patiently as I thought over my options. Finally, he asked quietly with a very pleasant tone and smile, 'Well, still want to learn my business?'

I knew I was at a defining moment. I knew it was time to put up or shut up. I was now testing myself. My choice had nothing to do with Peter. It had everything to do with the next evolution of my personal development. At times like this, I recall the wisdom of the great philosopher Johann Wolfgang Von Goethe:

*'Until one is committed there is hesitancy,*
*a chance to draw back, always ineffectiveness.*
*Concerning all acts of initiative and creation,*
*There is one elementary truth,*
*the ignorance of which*
*kills countless dreams and splendid plans.*
*That the moment one definitely commits oneself,*
*then Providence moves too.'*

It is the line 'then Providence moves too' that has kept me from taking a step forward when the rest of me wanted to step backwards over the years. Webster defines 'providence' as 'Divine guidance or care. God conceived as the power sustaining and guiding human destiny.' Now I am not intending to preach or say that God is on my side. All I am saying is that whenever I come to the edge of my world, or when I am about to take a step into the unknown, all I have at that moment is my trust in a power much larger than myself. It is at such moments – moments when I know I must step over the edge – that I take a deep breath and take the step. It can be called a leap of faith. I call it a test of my trust in a power much bigger than I am. In my opinion, it is those first steps that have made all the difference in my life. The initial results have not always been as I would have liked them to be, but my life has always changed for the better in the long run.

I have learned a deep respect for one of Goethe's couplets:
*'Whatever you can do or dream you can, begin it.*
*Boldness has genius, power, and magic in it.'*

As the words of the poem faded, I looked up and said, 'I'll be in Peru this weekend.'

Peter smiled a wide quiet smile. 'Here is a list of people you are to meet and where to meet them. Call me when you get back.'

## *This Is Not a Recommendation*

This is definitely not the path I would recommend for anyone wanting to learn to take a company public. There are smarter and easier paths. Yet this was the path that was laid forth for me. Therefore, I faithfully describe to you the process via which I came to achieve my goal. In my opinion, everyone must be true to his or her own mental and emotional strengths and weaknesses. I am simply relating the process I went through once I knew the next direction in my life. It was not mentally hard but emotionally challenging, as most significant changes in life tend to be.

Rich dad often said, 'An individual's reality is the boundary between faith and self-confidence.' He would draw a diagram that looked like this:

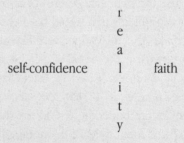

He would then say, 'The boundaries of a person's reality often do not change until that person forsakes what he or she feels confident in and then goes blindly with faith. So many people do not become rich because they are limited by their self-confidence rather than the limitlessness of faith.'

On that Thursday, in the summer of 1996, I was on my way to the Andes Mountains to inspect a gold mine that was once mined by the Incas and then the Spaniards. I was taking a bold step of faith into a world I knew nothing about. Yet, because of that step, a whole new world of investing opened to me. My life has not been the same since I decided to take that step. My reality on what is possible financially has not been the same. My reality on how rich a person can become has expanded. The more I continue working with Peter and his team, the further those limits to wealth expand.

Today, I continue to expand my limits, and I can hear my rich dad say, 'A person is limited only to his or her reality of what is possible financially. Nothing changes until that person's reality changes. And a person's financial reality will not change until he or she is willing to go beyond the fears and doubts of his or her own self-imposed limits.'

## Peter Kept His Word

Upon returning from the trip, I reported back to Peter. The mine was a great mine with strong and proven veins of gold, but it had financial problems as well as many operational challenges. I recommended against acquiring it because the mine had severe social problems and had severe environmental problems that would have cost millions to clean up. In order to make the mine operate efficiently, any new owners would have to downsize the workforce by at least 40%. It would destroy the town's economy. I said to Peter, 'For centuries, these people have lived there at 16,000 feet above sea level. Generations of their families are buried here. I do not think it is wise for us to be the ones to force them to leave the home of their ancestors to seek work in the cities at the base of the mountain. I think we would have more problems than we want to deal with.'

Peter agreed with my findings and — more importantly — agreed to teach me. We were soon looking at mines and oil fields in other parts of the world, and a new chapter in my educational process began.

From the summer of 1996 to the fall of 1997, I worked as an apprentice to Peter. He was busy working on developing his company, EZ Energy Corporation (not the real name), which was just about to go public on the Alberta Stock Exchange when I joined him. Since I was late joining his team, I was not able to acquire any of the pre-IPO shares at the insider's price. It would not have been appropriate for me to invest with the founders since I was still new and untested. Yet, I was able to acquire a sizeable block of stock at the IPO price of $0.50 (Canadian) a share.

After striking oil in Colombia, and possibly finding what appears to be a large oil and gas field in Portugal, EZ Energy's stock is trading at around $2.00 to $2.35 (Canadian) a share. If the find in Portugal is proven to be as big as the tests indicate, the price per share of the stock may be as high as $5.00 (Canadian) a share sometime in 2000. If, and that is a qualified if, the field in Portugal proves to be as big as we hope it is, the price per share of EZ Energy could climb from $15.00 (Canadian) to $25.00 (Canadian) in the next two to three years. That is the upside. There is also a downside with these micro-cap stocks. The shares could also go to $.00 a share in the next two to three years. A lot of things are possible when companies are at this stage of development.

Although EZ Energy is a very small company, the increase in value for what Peter calls the 'front money investors' is pretty good to date. If things go as hoped, these investors will make a lot of money. The front money investors (pre-IPO accredited investors) put up $25,000 (U.S.) for 100,000 shares of stock, or 25 cents per share. They invested this money on the reputation of Peter, the strength of the board of directors, and the business expertise of the oil-exploration team. At the time of the private offering, and even the public offering, there were no guarantees or certain value to invest in. In other words, in the beginning, this investment was all 'P' (price) and no 'E' (earnings). It was initially offered only to Peter's friends and his circle of investors.

At this stage of the investment cycle, investors invest in the people on the team. The people – much more than the product, be it oil, gold, an Internet product, or widgets – are far more important than any other part of the equation. The golden rule of 'Money follows management' is extremely important at this stage of a company's development.

The management of EZ Energy has done extremely well. But rather than go into the hype, hopes, and dreams of this company, I think it best to quote you just the facts of this publicly traded company.

The founders of the company put up their time and expertise in exchange for shares in the company. In other words, most of the founders work for free, investing their time and expertise in return for blocks of shares of stock. The value of their stock when issued is very small, so they have very little, if any, earned income. They work without pay, intending to increase the value of their stock, which will generate portfolio income rather than earned income. A few of the founders are paid a small salary for their services. They work for the bigger payoff, which comes if they do a good job of growing the company and making it more valuable.

Since most of the directors are not drawing a salary, it is in their best interest to increase and keep increasing the company's value. Their personal interest is the same as the shareholders', which is an ever-increasing price per share. The same is true for many of the company's officers. They may draw a small salary but are really more interested in the price per share going up.

The founders are very, very important to the success of a startup because their reputation and expertise give credibility, confidence, momentum, and legitimacy to a project that often exists only on paper. Once the company is public and successful, some of the founders may resign, taking their stock with them. A new management team replaces them, and the founders move on to another startup, repeating the process.

### History of EZ Energy

The following is a sequence of events that occurred after the company was founded:

1. Front money investors put up $25,000 (U.S.) for 100,000 shares, or 25 cents per share. At this stage, the company had a tentative

plan but owned no exploration leases. There were no assets. Front money investors invested in management.

2. The shares currently trade in range between $2.00 and $2.35 (Canadian) per share.

3. Therefore, the front money investors' block of 100,000 shares is currently worth $200,000 to $235,000 (Canadian) — $160,000 to $170,000 (U.S.) The directors' job now is to keep increasing the value of the company and its share price by bringing to market the oil it has found, drilling more wells, and finding more oil reserves. On paper, the front money investors have made about $140,000 on their $25,000 investment. They have been in the deal for five years, so their annual rate of return would be 45% if they could sell their shares.

4. The problem for the investors is that the company is small and the shares are very thinly traded. An investor with 100,000 shares would be hard pressed to sell 100,000 shares all at once without seriously depressing the price of the stock. So, the valuation of the entire block of stock is in many ways a paper valuation at this time.

If things go as planned, the company will grow and more people will begin to follow the company and the stock. Buying and selling larger blocks of these shares should then become easier. It is safe to say that due to the good news of the discoveries, most large-block investors are holding on to their shares rather than selling.

## Why a Canadian Exchange?

When I first began working with Peter, I asked him why he used the Canadian exchanges rather than the more well-known NASDAQ or

Wall Street. In America, the Canadian exchanges are often treated as the Rodney Dangerfields of the North American Securities industry. Yet, Peter uses the Canadian exchanges because:

1. The Canadian exchanges are the world leaders for financing small natural-resource companies. Peter uses them because he primarily develops these types of companies. Peter is like Warren Buffet, who tends to stay with businesses he understands. 'I understand oil and gas, silver and gold,' Peter says. 'I understand natural resources and precious metals.' If Peter were to develop a technology company, he would probably list it on an American exchange.

2. NASDAQ and Wall Street have gotten too big for a small company to gain any attention there. Peter said, 'When I started in this business in the 1950s, a small company could gain some attention from the brokers on the major exchanges. Today, Internet companies, many without any earnings, are commanding more money than many larger well-known Industrial Age companies. Hence, most larger brokerage houses are not very interested in small companies that need to raise only a few million dollars. Brokerage houses in America are interested primarily in offerings of $100 million or more.

3. The Canadian exchanges let the small entrepreneurs stay in the business. I think Peter uses Canadian exchanges mainly because he is retired. He often says, 'I don't need the money, so I don't need to build a big company to make a big score. I just enjoy the game; it keeps me active, and where else can my friends get into an IPO play for only $25,000 for 100,000 shares of stock? I do this because it's still fun, I love the challenges, and the money can be rewarding. I love starting companies, taking them public, and watching them grow. I also love having my friends and their families become rich.'

4. Peter offers a word of caution. 'Just because the Canadian exchanges are small does not mean that anyone can play their game. Some of the Canadian exchanges have gained a shaky reputation due to past transactions. To work with these exchanges, a person should be very familiar with the ins and outs of taking a company public.'

The good news is that the Canadian system of stock exchanges appears to be tightening up on regulations, which are being enforced more closely. In a few years, I think the Canadian exchanges will grow as more and more small companies from all over the world look to the smaller exchanges to raise the capital they need.

Beware of the stock promoter: In the few years I have been actively involved in this business, I have come across three individuals who had the right credentials as well as the right alphabets after their name, told a great story, raised tens of millions of dollars, and had absolutely no idea how to start a business and build one from scratch. For several years, such people fly around in first class or on private jets, stay at the best hotels, put on lavish dinner parties, drink the best wines, and live high on the hog on their investors' money. The company soon dies because there is no actual development. The cash flow has all been going out. These people then go on to start another company and do it all over again. How do you spot a sincere entrepreneur from a big-spending dreamer? That I do not know. Two of the three sure had me fooled until their companies folded. The best advice I can give is to ask for a past track record, check references, and let your sixth sense or intuition be your guide.

5. If a small company grows and prospers, it can later move from a small exchange to a bigger exchange such as NASDAQ or

NYSE due to its success. Companies that make the move from a Canadian exchange to an American exchange average a substantial increase in the valuation of the company (sometimes over 200%).

Most of today's big name companies started out as small companies that were unknown. In 1989, Microsoft was a small company whose stock sold for $6 a share. That same stock has since split eight times. In 1991, Cisco stock was just $3 a share, which was eight splits ago. These companies used their investors' money wisely and grew into major powerhouses in the world economy.

## Sharon's Notes

The entry requirements of the major stock markets in the United States have made the IPO a difficult process for most businesses. As described in the *Ernst & Young Guide to Taking Your Company Public*, the New York Stock Exchange requires a company to have net tangible assets of $18 million and pre-tax income of $2,500,000. The American Stock Exchange requires a stockholders' equity of $4 million and a market value of the IPO to be a minimum of $3 million. And the NASDAQ National Market requires net tangible assets of at least $4 million and a market value of the IPO to be a minimum of $3 million.

In addition, it has been estimated that the IPO process can cost $400,000 to $500,000 for one of these major exchanges. These costs include the registration fees as well as the fees paid to legal counsel, accountants and underwriters.

Many small to medium companies that cannot meet these qualifications look for 'reverse merger' opportunities, which allow them to merge with an existing public company. Through that process, the company can become a publicly traded company by taking control of the newly combined public company.

Companies may also look to other foreign exchanges, like the Canadian exchange, where the entry requirements are not as severe.

## Who Buys Canadian?

During one of my talks on investing in Australia two years ago, a member of the audience questioned my sanity at investing in precious metals and oil. He asked, 'If everyone else is in high-tech and Internet stocks, why are you working on the dogs of the economy?'

I explained that it is always less expensive to be a contrarian investor, which is an investor who seeks out-of-favor or out-of-cycle stocks. 'A few years ago,' I said, 'when everyone was into gold, silver, and oil, the prices of the exploration leases that make up these startups were very high. It was very difficult to find a deal at a good price. Now that the prices of oil, gold, and silver are down, finding good properties is easy and people are more willing to negotiate because these commodities are out of favor.'

The price of oil has begun to rise, making the shares in our oil company much more valuable. Also, during this period, Buffet announced that he was taking a sizeable position in silver. In February 1998, the billionaire investor disclosed that he had acquired 130 million ounces of silver and stored it in a warehouse in London. On September 30, 1999, *Canadian Business* ran an article indicating that the world's richest man, Gates, had made a buy in silver, acquiring a 10.3% stake for $12 million (U.S.) of a Canadian silver company listed on the Vancouver Stock Exchange. Gates had been quietly acquiring shares in the company since February 1999. When this announcement went out to our investors, the news was welcome relief for their years of trust and confidence.

## You Don't Always Hit Home Runs

Not all startup companies do as well as EZ Energy. Some never get off the ground even after going public, and the investors lose most if not all of their front money. Investors therefore need to be accredited, and they are warned about the 'all or nothing' type of investments we bring to market.

As one of Peter's partners, I now speak to potential investors about becoming front money investors in new companies. I explain the risks to potential investors before I discuss the business, the people involved, or the rewards. I often start my presentation by saying, 'The investment I am about to talk about is a very high-risk speculative investment, offered primarily to individuals who meet the requirements of an accredited investor.' If a person does not know the requirements for being an accredited investor, I explain the guidelines as laid out by the SEC. I also stress the possibility that they can lose all of their invested money, repeating that statement several times. If they are still interested, I go on to explain that any money placed with us should never be more than 10% of their total investment capital. Then and only then, if they are still interested, do I go on to explain the investment, the risks, the team, and the possible rewards.

At the end of my presentation, I ask for questions. After all the questions have been answered, I again reiterate the risks. I end by saying, 'If your money is lost, all I can offer you is the first opportunity to invest in our next business.' By this time, most people are fully aware of the risks, and I would say that 90% decide not to invest with us. We give the 10% that are still interested more information as well as more time to think things over and to back out if they desire.

I suspect that many of today's high-flying Internet IPOs will come crashing down in the next few years and investors will lose millions, if not billions, of dollars. Although the Internet does provide a tremendous new frontier, the forces of economics allow only a few of the pioneering companies to be winners. So regardless of if the company going public is a gold-mining company, a plumbing-supply company, or an Internet company, the forces of the public market still have much of the control.

## A *Great Education*

Deciding to fly to Peru has turned out to be a great decision for me. I have learned as much from being Peter's student and partner as I did from my rich dad. After I put in about a year and a half as an apprentice to Peter and his team, he offered me a partnership in his private venture-capital company.

Since 1996, I have gained the experience of a lifetime watching EZ Energy Company go public and develop into a viable company that someday may become a major oil company. I have not only become a wiser businessperson because of my association, but I have also learned much about how stock markets work. One of my policies is to invest five years in the learning process – and so far I have spent four in this phase. At this time, I have still not made any real money – at least not money I can put in my pocket. My gains have been all paper gains, yet the business and investment education has been priceless. Maybe someday in the future I will build a company to take public on an American exchange.

## *Future IPOs*

Currently, Peter and his private venture-capital team in which I am a partner are developing three other companies to bring to the public market: a precious-metals company that secures leases in China, an oil company that secures oil and gas leases in Argentina, and a silver company that acquires leases in Argentina.

The company that has taken the longest to develop is the Chinese precious-metals company. We were doing fine with our negotiations with the Chinese government, and then suddenly, in 1999, a U.S. warplane bombed the Chinese Embassy in Kosovo. They say the maps were not updated. Whatever the reason for the bombing, the incident set our relations back two years. Yet we continue to make steady but slow progress.

When people ask why we take such great risks working in China, we reply, 'It will soon be the largest economy in the world. Although the risks are huge, the potential payoff could be staggering.'

Investing in China today is like the English investing in America in the 1800s. We are investing in contacts and goodwill. We are well aware of the political differences and the human-rights issues. As a company, we do our best to develop strong relationships and open communications with our contacts in China in the hope that we can be part of the transformation of the American/Chinese relationship. The educational experience has been priceless for me. It is like being a part of history. Sometimes, it almost feels like being on the same boat with Columbus as he set sail for the New World.

It usually takes three to five years to bring a company to the public market. If things go well, we may bring two of the three companies to the public market within the next year. When that happens, I will have achieved my goal of becoming an ultimate investor. It will be my first public company but Peter's number ninety-something. So although I have not yet qualified as an ultimate investor, I am closing in on that goal, a goal I set for myself in 1995.

Given the risk involved, every one of these projects I am currently working on could fail and never go public. And if that happens, the pieces will be picked up and new projects will be started. Our investors know the risks involved and also know that their investment plan is to put a little money in several of these smaller ventures. They also know that they will be called and asked to invest in any new start up we have. All it takes is one project to hit a home run. In investments such as these it is definitely not wise to put all your eggs in one basket. It is because of such risks that the SEC has the minimum requirements for investors in such speculative investments.

The next chapter briefly outlines the basic steps of starting with an idea, building a company, and perhaps eventually taking that company public. Although it has not been an easy process for me, it has been a very exciting one.

## *The Right of Passage*

Taking a company public is the rite of passage for any entrepreneur. It would be like a college sports star being selected to play for a professional team. According to the September 27, 1999 issue of *Fortune*, 'If you're acquired, a company validates you. If you go public, the market – the world – validates you.'

That is why rich dad called a person who could build a company from scratch, and take it public, an ultimate investor. That title eluded him. Although he invested in several businesses that ultimately did go public, none of the companies he actually started ever did go public. His son Mike took over his business and continued to grow it, but he has never built a company to take public. So to become an ultimate investor will mean that I will have completed rich dad's training process.

## Chapter 40

# *Are You the Next Billionaire?*

The 1999 edition of *Forbes*' richest 400 people states on the cover, 'The Billionaire Next Door.' That issue has an article titled 'A Century of Wealth' and a subtitle that reads, 'Where does great wealth come from?' Years ago, oil and steel were the foundations of many American fortunes. Today, it's more a matter of how many eyeballs you command.

According to the article: 'If you want to talk about super-rich, you have to set your sights higher: to billionaires, who are being minted faster than ever, using ever more ephemeral products to make their money. It took Rockefeller 25 years of finding, drilling and distributing oil to make his first billion. Last year, Garry Winnick joined the billionaires' club just 18 months after putting his money into Global Crossing, a company that intends to, but has yet to, develop a global fiber optic telecommunications network.'

So how long does it take to become super-rich these days? The answer is 'not long.' That reality becomes even more apparent for someone like me, a member of the Baby Boomer generation, when I look at the ages of the new billionaires. For example, billionaire Jerry

Yang was born in 1968 – a year before I finished college – and David Filo, his partner, was born in 1966 – a year after I entered college. Together, they founded Yahoo! and are now worth over $3 billion each and climbing. At the same time these young people are super-rich, I meet individuals who are wondering if they will have enough money in their retirement plans when they retire in ten years. Talk about a gap between the haves and future have nots.

### *I'm Taking My Company Public*

In 1999, all I hear and read about are IPOs. There is definitely a mania. As someone who is often asked to invest in other people's businesses, I often hear sales pitches like this: 'Invest in my company, and in two years we'll be going public.' The other day, a budding future billionaire CEO called me and asked for an opportunity to show me his business plan and offer me the opportunity to invest in his future Internet company. After the presentation, he nodded slowly with a sly cockiness as he said, 'And of course you know what will happen to the price of your shares after the IPO.' I felt like I was talking to a new car salesman who had just informed me that the car I wanted was the last one of its kind and he was doing me a special favor by letting me have it for the list price.

The IPO mania, also called the 'new issues' mania, is back on. Just a little while ago, even Martha Stewart took her company public and became a billionaire. She became a billionaire because she teaches civilized and common-sense social graces to the masses, people who feel the need to be more civilized and more gracious. I think her service is valuable, but I wonder about the billion dollars of value. Yet if you follow the *Forbes* 400 definition (wealth is dictated by how many eyeballs you command), Martha Stewart qualifies to be a billionaire. She definitely commands many eyeballs.

My concern about all these new tech stock IPOs and Internet IPOs is that the 90/10 rule of money is still in control. Too many of these new start ups are started by individuals with very little business experience. I predict that when we look back upon this time in history, we will find that 90% of the new IPOs will have failed and only 10% have survived. Statistics for small business show that in 5 years, 9 out of 10 small businesses have failed. If this statistic holds true for these new IPOs, this mania could put us into the next recession and possible depression. Why? Because millions of average investors will be depressed. Not only will millions lose their investment money, the ripple effect could spread to them not being able to afford their new homes, cars, boats, and planes. This could take down the rest of the economy. There was a joke going around Wall Street after the 1987 crash that went like this. 'What is the difference between a seagull and a stock broker?' Answer: 'The seagull can still leave a deposit on a BMW.'

## The Flavor of the Month

I first began working on an IPO back in 1978 in Hawaii. Rich dad wanted me to learn the process of building a company to sell to the public while I was building my nylon and Velcro wallet company. He said, 'I've never taken a company public, but I have invested in several businesses that have gone public. I'd like you to learn the process from the gentleman I invest with.' The person he introduced me to was Mark, a man similar to my partner Peter. The difference was that Mark was a venture capitalist, or VC, as they say in the trade. I am a Vietnam veteran, so the letters have a different initial meaning to me.

Small businesses came to Mark when they needed venture capital, or money to expand their businesses. Since I needed lots of money to expand, rich dad encouraged me to meet with him and learn from his point of view. It was not a pleasant meeting. Mark was far tougher than my rich dad. He looked at my business plan and my actual financial statements, and listened for about 23 seconds to my glorious plans for the future. Then he began to tear me apart. He told me why I was an idiot, a fool, and completely out of my league. He told me that I should never have quit my daytime job and that I was lucky my rich dad was his client. Otherwise, he would never have wasted any time on someone as incompetent as me. He then told me how much he thought my business was worth, how much money he could raise for it, his terms and conditions for the money, and that he would become my new partner with a controlling interest in the company. As I said, the term VC had a very familiar ring to it.

In the business of IPOs, investment bankers, and VCs, there is a sheet of paper known as the 'term sheet.' It is similar to the sheet of paper that real estate agents call the listing agreement. Simply, a term sheet states the terms and conditions of the sale of your business, just as a listing agreement states the terms and conditions for the sale of your house.

Just as in listing agreements with real estate, a term sheet is different for different people. In real estate, if you're selling just one little house in a bad neighborhood and you want a high price, the terms on the listing agreement will be tough and inflexible. However, if you are a real estate developer with thousands of homes to sell, and the houses are nice, easy to sell, and priced low, the real estate agent is more likely to soften his or her terms in order to get your business. The same is true in the world of the VC. The more successful you are, the better terms you get and vice-versa.

Well, after looking at Mark's term sheet, I felt his terms were too severe. I definitely did not want to give him 52% of my company to end up working for him in the company I started. Those were his terms. I am not blaming Mark and, in retrospect, maybe I should have taken those terms. Given what I know today, and how little I knew back then, if I had been in Mark's position, I would have offered the same terms. I think the only reason he offered me anything was out of respect for my rich dad. I was a new businessperson, and I was successfully incompetent. I say successfully incompetent because I had a growing company but I was not able to manage its growth.

Although Mark was tough, I liked him and he seemed to like me. We agreed to meet regularly, and he agreed to give me free advice as I grew. His advice might have been free but it was always tough. He eventually began to trust me more as my knowledge and understanding of business grew. I even worked with him briefly on an oil company he was bringing to the public market. It was similar to the oil company I am working on today. Working with him on that oil company in 1978, I got my first taste of the excitement that comes from working on an IPO.

During one of my lunches with him, he said something about the IPO business that I never forgot. He said, 'The new issues and IPO market is just like any other business. The market is always looking for the flavor of the month.'

Mark was saying that, at certain times, the stock market favors certain businesses more than others. He went on to say, 'If you want to become very rich, part of your strategy as a business owner is to be building the company the market wants, before the market wants it.'

Mark went on to explain that history makes famous the pioneer who has the business that is the flavor of the month. He said that inventions such as television created new millionaires just as oil and cars made billionaires at the start of this century. Mark's concept of the progression of wealth is in line with that seen in this abbreviated list from *Forbes* magazine:

1.  1900 – Andrew Carnegie made his fortunes in steel – $475 million
2.  1910 – John D. Rockefeller became a billionaire in oil – $1.4 billion
3.  1920 – Henry Ford became a billionaire in the auto industry – $1 billion

4. 1930 – John Dorrance became a millionaire condensing soup into a can (Campbell's Soup) – $115 million
5. 1940 – Howard Hughes became a billionaire with military aircraft contracts, tools, and movies – $1.5 billion
6. 1950 – Arthur Davis became a millionaire in aluminum – $400 million
7. 1960 – H. Ross Perot founded EDS (1962) – $3.8 billion
8. 1970 – Sam Walton took retailing giant Wal-Mart public (1970) – $22 billion
9. 1980 – Ron Perelman made his fortune as a Wall Street deal maker – $3.8 billion
10. 1990 – Jerry Yang co-founded Yahoo! – $3.7 billion

## Obsolete at 35

I did not work with Mark after 1978. As he predicted, my business success had begun to sour and I had massive internal problems in my company. I therefore had to put all my attention into my business rather than spend time trying to take someone else's business public. However, I never forgot his lesson on businesses being the flavor of the month. As I plod along continuing to gain my fundamental business experience, I often wonder what the next business flavor of the month will be.

In 1985, I stopped by the Marine Base at Camp Pendelton, California, where I had been stationed in 1971 just before going to Vietnam. My friend and fellow pilot James Treadwell was now the commanding officer of the squadron on the base. Kim and I were shown around the squadron where Jim and I had been new pilots 14 years earlier. Walking on to the flight line, Jim showed Kim an aircraft that looked like the ones he and I flew in Vietnam. Opening up the cockpit, he said, 'You and I are now obsolete. We are not able to fly these aircraft.'

He said that because the instruments and controls were now fully electronic and video oriented. Jim continued, saying, 'These new pilots grew up in video arcades. You and I grew up on pinball machines and pool tables. Our brains are not the same as theirs. That is why they fly and I sit behind a desk. I am obsolete as a pilot.'

I remember that day clearly because I too felt obsolete then. I felt old and out of date at age 37. I remember thinking that my own dad was obsolete by age 50 and here I was obsolete by age 37. On that day, I fully realized how fast things were changing. I also realized that if I did not change myself as rapidly, I would be left further and further behind.

Today, I work with Peter, continuing my education in the IPO and VC business. I am making paper money because I am acquiring paper assets. However, the most important thing I am gaining is experience in capital markets. Even though I work on oil, gas, and precious-metal companies – industries that were the flavor of the month 20 to 30 years ago – my mind continues to race ahead and wonder what the next frontier in business will become. I wonder what the next flavor of the month will be and if I will be part of that next explosion of wealth. Who knows? I am 52 today; Colonel Sanders was 66 when he started. My goal is still to become a billionaire in my lifetime. Maybe I'll get there and maybe I won't, but I am working every day towards that goal. Becoming a billionaire is quite possible today – if you have the right plan. So I'm not giving up, and I have no plans on becoming poor or becoming more obsolete. As rich dad said, 'It's the first million that was the hardest.' If that is the case, then the first billion could be the second hardest task I take on.

## *Are You the Next Billionaire?*

For those of you who may have similar ambitions and aspirations, I offer the following guidelines on taking your company public. The information comes generously from my partner Peter, a person who has taken almost a hundred companies public.

Although there is a tremendous amount to learn, these guidelines will help you get started.

## Why Take a Company Public?

**Peter lists six primary reasons to do so:**

1.  You need more money. This is one of the main reasons you take a company public. In this case, you might have an established profitable company and need capital to grow. You have already been to your banker and have raised some funds through private placements and your VC, but now you need really big money from an investment banker.

2.  Your company – an Internet company, for example – is new, and you need massive amounts of money to gain market share. The market gives you the money, although your company is unprofitable today because the market is investing in your future earnings.

3.  Many times, a company will use its own company stock to acquire other companies. It is what rich dad called 'printing your own money.' In the corporate world, it is called 'mergers and acquisitions.'

4.  You want to sell your company without giving up control. In a private company, the owner all too often gives up control or gains a new partner who wants to tell him how to run the business when raising capital. By getting the money from the public market, the owner gains cash by selling yet maintains control of the business. Most shareholders have very little power to influence the operations of the company they are invested in.

5.  Estate reasons. Ford Motor Company went public because the family had many heirs but no liquidity. By selling a part of the company to the public, it raised the cash the family needed

for the heirs. It is interesting how often a private company will use this strategy.

6.  To get rich and have cash to invest elsewhere. Building a business is much like building an apartment house and selling it. When you are building a business for sale through a public offering, however, only a part of the asset is broken off; it is broken into millions of pieces and sold to millions of people. The builder may therefore still own most of the asset, may still maintain control, and may generate a lot of cash by selling it to millions of buyers (instead of just one buyer). Talk about good things coming in small packages.

### Sharon's Note

There are restrictions that apply to the major shareholders and officers in a company issuing an IPO. While their holdings in the company may increase dramatically in value as a result of the IPO they are severely regulated when selling any of their shares. Their stock is usually called 'restricted' which means they have agreed not to sell it for a pre-determined amount of time.

A shareholder wanting to 'cash out' might be better served selling the company, or merging into another company with free-trading shares as opposed to using an IPO.

### Additional Points to Consider

**Peter offers these additional considerations to keep in mind before you go public:**

1.  Who on the team has run a business? There is a big difference between running a business and dreaming of a new product or a new business. Has the person handled payroll, employees, tax issues, legal issues, contracts, negotiations, product development, cash flow management, raising capital, etc.?

You may notice that much of what Peter thinks is important is found on rich dad's B-I Triangle. Therefore, the core of the question is: Are you (or someone on the team) successful at managing the entire B-I Triangle?

2.  How much of the company do you want to sell? This is where term sheets come in.

Another point I brought up with Peter is that in my three years of working with him, I noticed that he always knows his goal for a company before he starts the company. He knows before he starts that his goal is to sell the company on the public market. He may not know how he is going to achieve his goal, but the goal is set. I mention this because so many business owners start a business without a concrete goal in mind for the end of the business. Many business owners start a business because they think the business is a good idea, but they have no plan on how to get out of the business. Fundamental to any good investor is an exit strategy. The same is true for an entrepreneur who is considering building a business. Before you build it, have a solid plan on how you're going to get out of it.

Before you build a business, you might want to consider some of these issues:

a.  Are you going to sell it, keep it, or pass it on to heirs?
b.  If you are going to sell it, are you going to sell it privately or publicly?
    i.  Selling a company privately can be as difficult as selling it publicly.
    ii.  Finding a qualified buyer can be difficult.
    iii. Financing for the business may be difficult to come by.
    iv. You may get it back if the new owner cannot pay you or mismanages it.

3. Does the prospective public company have a well-written and well-thought-through business plan? This plan should include descriptions of:

    a. The team and team's experience
    b. Financial statements
       i. The standard is three years of audited financials.
    c. Cash flow projections
       i. I recommend three years of very conservative cash flow projections.

Peter states that investment bankers dislike CEOs and entrepreneurs who puff up their projections for future earnings. Peter also states that Bill Gates of Microsoft often understates its earning projections. That is an excellent strategy for keeping the price of the stock strong. When CEOs exaggerate and earnings expectations are not met, the price of their stock often falls and investors lose confidence in the company.

4. Who is the market, how big is the market, and how much growth is possible for the company's products into the market?

While there is a market for your products, there is another market for the shares in your business. At different times, certain types of companies are more attractive to stock buyers than other companies. As I write, technology and Internet companies are the flavors of the month.

When a person has a public company, it is often said that it is like having two companies instead of one. One company is for your regular customers, and one is for your investors.

5. Who is on your board of directors or advisory board? The market runs on confidence. If the company has a strong and respected board of directors or advisors, the market has more confidence in the future success of the business.

Peter advises, 'If someone comes to you and says, "I'm going to take my company public," ask that person, "Who on your team has taken a company public and how many companies has he or she taken public?" If that person cannot answer that question, ask him or her to come back with the answer. Most never come back.'

6. Does the company own something proprietary? A business should own or control something that another company does not. It could be a patent on a new product or drug, a lease of ground in an oil field, or a trademark such as Starbucks or McDonald's. Even people who are owners and respected experts in their field can be considered assets. Examples of people being assets are Martha Stewart, Steven Jobs when he started his new company (Apple Computer), and Steven Spielberg when he formed his new production company. People invested in these people because of their past success and future potential.

7. Does the company have a great story to tell? I am sure Christopher Columbus must have told a great story to his underwriters, the king and queen of Spain, before they raised the capital for him to sail off to the ends of the earth. A great story must interest, excite, and cause people to look into the future and dream a little. There should also be integrity behind the story, because our jails are filled with great storytellers who have no integrity.

8. Do those involved with the company have passion? This is the most important thing that Peter looks for. He says that the first and last thing he looks for in any business is the passion of the owner, the leaders, and the team. Peter says, 'Without passion, the best business, the best plan, and the best people will not become successful.'

Here is an excerpt from *Fortune* magazine's article on the 40 richest people under 40:

> The MBAs don't fit into the (Silicon) Valley scene. MBAs are traditionally risk-averse. The reason most people go to business school is to ensure getting a six-figure job after graduation. Valley veterans look at B-school people and don't see the fire in the belly they themselves had when they were romantic renegades. MBAs look at Silicon Valley and see something far different from what they were taught in business school. Michael Levine joined eBay after graduating from Berkeley's Haas School. The former investment banker does not speak with the same passion displayed by hardcore entrepreneurs. He also works shorter hours than most – 60 per week instead of the customary 80. 'I'd love it if in ten to 15 years I had $10 million to $15 million, well invested,' he told me. 'But I'd like to have a life. I don't know. Maybe I'm not there yet.'

Rich dad would say that he was definitely not there yet. Rich dad often cautioned me to be aware of the difference between successful corporate people and successful entrepreneurs. He would say, 'There is a difference between a person who climbs the corporate ladder and someone who is building his own corporate ladder. The difference is in the view when you look up the ladder. One sees the big blue sky and the other sees – well, you know that saying: "If you're not the lead dog, the view is always the same."'

## How Do You Raise Money?

**Peter discusses four sources of money:**

1. **Friends and family.** These people love you and will often give you money blindly. He does not recommend this method

of raising money. Both Peter and my rich dad have often said, 'Don't give your children money. It keeps them weak and needy. Teach them how to raise money instead.'

Rich dad took the issue of money one step further. As you may recall, he did not pay his son and me a salary for working for him. He said, 'Paying people to do work is training them to think like employees.' Instead, he trained us to look for business opportunities and to create a business out of that opportunity. You may recall the comic book story in *Rich Dad Poor Dad*. I continue to do the same thing today. I look around for opportunities to build a business, while others look for high-paying jobs.

Rich dad did not make being an employee wrong. He loved his employees. He was just training his son and me to think differently and to be aware of the differences between a business owner and other positions. He wanted us to have more choices as we grew older rather than fewer.

We created the educational board game *CASHFLOW for Kids* for parents who want to give their kids more financial choices and keep them from being trapped in debt as soon as they leave home. In addition, it was created for parents who may suspect that their children could be the next Bill Gates of Microsoft or the next Anita Roddick of the Body Shop. The game provides an early financial education on cash flow management that every entrepreneur needs. Most small businesses fail because of poor cash flow management. *CASHFLOW for Kids* will teach your children the skill of cash flow management before they leave home.

2. **Angels.** Angels are rich individuals who have a passion to help new entrepreneurs. Most major cities have angel groups that support budding new entrepreneurs financially as well as provide advice on how to become rich, young entrepreneurs.

Angels realize that a city with growing young businesses is a growing city. Thriving entrepreneurial spirit in a city will keep the city thriving as well. These angels provide a vital service for any city of any size. It is now possible with computers and the Internet for even the most remote towns to bring the entrepreneur's spirit to life.

Many young people leave small towns to look for great job opportunities in a bigger city. I think that this loss of smart young talent is caused by our schools teaching young people to look for jobs. If our young people were taught to create businesses, many small towns could continue to thrive because they could electronically hook into the rest of the world. Groups of private citizens operating as angel groups could do wonders to revitalize small towns everywhere.

When you look at what Bill Gates did for Seattle; what Michael Dell did for Austin, Texas; and what Alan Bond did for Freemantle, Western Australia, you can see the power of entrepreneurial spirit. Entrepreneurs and angels both play important roles in the vitality of a city.

3. **Private investors.** People who invest in private companies are called private investors. These accredited investors are hopefully more sophisticated than the average investor. They stand to gain – as well as lose – the most. Therefore, it is recommended to get both financial education and business experience before investing large sums of money into private companies.

4. **Public investors.** People who invest through publicly traded shares of public companies are called public investors. This is the mass market for securities. Because these investments are marketed to the masses, they generally come under great scrutiny

from agencies such as the Securities and Exchange Commission (SEC). Securities traded here are generally less risky than investments done privately. Yet, when it comes to investing, there is always risk. This may seem to contradict what I said earlier about having more control, and therefore less risk, as an insider. Please remember, however, that a private investor is not always in control. The SEC requires strict compliance with reporting and disclosure requirements to reduce the risk to a public investor who is definitely not in control of the investment.

## Peter's Recommendations

As I was interviewing Peter on the main points of taking a company public, I asked him what he would recommend for a person who wanted to learn to raise substantial sums of capital. He said: 'I recommend that a person become familiar with the following sources of funding if they want to take a company public,' he said. They are:

1. **Private placement memorandums (PPMs).** These should be the start of your formal capital-raising activities. They are sort of a do-it-yourself way of raising money. A PPM is a way for you to dictate the terms you want, and hopefully the investor will be interested.

   Peter strongly recommends that you begin this process by hiring a corporate attorney who specializes in securities. This is where your formal education begins if you are serious about starting small and getting big. It begins with paying for advice from the attorney and hopefully following that advice. If you do not like the advice, it is best to find a new attorney.

   Most attorneys will give you a free consultation, or you can invite them to lunch. This type of professional advisor is vital to your team at the beginning and as you get bigger. I personally have learned the hard way by trying to do such things on my own to save a few dollars. Those few dollars saved have cost me fortunes in the long run.

2.  **Venture Capitalists (VCs).** They, like my friend Mark, are in the business of providing capital. People usually go to VCs after they have exhausted personal funds, the money of family and friends, and their banker's money. Peter says, 'VCs often cut a tough deal, yet if they are good, they will earn their money.'

    A VC will often become a partner and help you get your company into shape to move to the next level of financing. In other words, just as a person may go to a gym and hire a personal trainer to get his or her body into shape and become more attractive, a VC may act as a personal trainer who gets your business into financial shape so that it will be attractive to other investors.

3.  **Investment bankers.** They are generally where you go when you are ready to sell your company to the public market. Investment bankers often raise money for IPOs and for secondary offerings. A secondary offering is a public offering of shares of a company that has already raised capital through an initial offering to the public. When you look in financial papers such as *The Wall Street Journal*, many of the large ads are from investment bankers informing the market about offerings they have sponsored.

## Sharon's Notes

There is another type of funding called mezzanine financing, sometimes referred to as bridge funding. A company usually looks for this kind of funding when it is past its early stages of development but not quite ready for an IPO.

## An Important First Step

If you are ready to try your hand at raising capital for your business, you may want to start with a PPM. Peter recommends starting with this for these reasons:

1.  You begin to interview and talk to corporate lawyers who specialize in this area. Interview several of them. Your education and knowledge will increase with each interview. Ask them about some of their failures as well as their successes.

2.  You begin to learn about the different kinds of offerings you can make and how to structure them legally. In other words, not all offerings are equal. Different offerings are designed to fill different needs.

3.  You begin to place a value on your business and develop the terms you want when you sell the business.

4.  You begin formally talking to potential investors as well as get to practice the art and science of raising capital. First, you may need to overcome your fear of asking. Second, you may need to get over your fear of criticism. Third, you get to learn how to handle rejection or phone calls that are not returned.

Peter offers this advice: 'I have seen individuals give the best presentation on their investment but fail to pick up the check at the end. The one thing an entrepreneur needs to do is learn how to pick up the check. If you cannot do that, then take along a partner who can.'

Peter also says the same thing my rich dad said: 'If you want to be in this business, you must know how to sell. Selling is the most important skill you can learn and continue to improve. Raising capital is selling a different product to a different audience.'

People are not successful financially mainly because they cannot sell. They cannot sell because they lack self-confidence, they are afraid of rejection, and they cannot ask for the order. If you are serious about being an entrepreneur and need more sales and confidence development, I strongly recommend finding a network marketing company with a good training program, stick with it for at least five years, and learn to be a confident salesperson. A successful salesperson is not afraid of approaching people, not afraid of being criticized or rejected, and not afraid of asking for the check.

Even today, I continue to work on overcoming my fear of rejection, improving my ability to handle disappointment, and finding ways of improving my bouts of low self-esteem. I have noticed a direct correlation between my ability to handle those obstacles in my life and my wealth. In other words, if those obstacles appear overwhelming, my income goes down. If I overcome those obstacles, which is a constant process, my income goes up.

### *How to Find Someone Like Peter or Mark to Advise You*

After you have gained some fundamental business experience and have achieved a degree of success – and you think you are ready to bring your business to market – you will need specialized advice. The advice and guidance I received from Peter, an investment banker, and Mark, a VC, has been priceless. That advice has created worlds of possibilities that did not exist for me before.

When you are ready, get *Standard & Poor's Security Dealers*, published by McGraw Hill. You can find it in most bookstores or your local library. This book lists security dealers by state. Get the book and find a person who would be willing to listen to your ideas and your business. Not all are willing to give free advice, but some are. Most are busy and do not have time for hand holding if you are not ready. I therefore suggest getting some real-life business experience and having success under your belt before finding one who would be willing to be part of your team.

## So Are You the Next Billionaire?

Only one person can answer this question: you. With the right team, the right leader, and a bold and innovative new product, anything is possible. The technology is already in place, or about to be developed soon.

Right after I knew that achieving my goal of making my first $1 million was possible, I began thinking about setting the next goal. I knew I could go on to make $10 million doing things much the same way. However, $1 billion would require new skills and a whole new way of thinking. That is why I set the goal despite continuing to come up against much personal self-doubt. Once I had the nerve to set the goal, I began to learn how others had made it. If I had not set the goal, I would not have thought it a remote possibility, and I would not have come across books and articles about how so many people are achieving that goal.

Several years ago, when I was deeply in debt, I thought becoming a millionaire was impossible. Therefore, in retrospect, I do not think actually achieving the goal is as important as writing down the goal and then going for it. Once I committed to the goal, my mind seemed to find the ways my goal could be possible. If I had said the goal of becoming a millionaire was impossible, I believe it would have become a self-fulfilling prophecy.

After I set the goal to become a billionaire, I was plagued with self-doubt. However, my mind began to show me ways it was possible. As I focus on the goal, I continue to see how becoming a billionaire could be possible for me. I often repeat this saying to myself: 'If you think you can, you can; if you think you can't, you can't. Either way you're right.' I don't know who the author is, but I thank that person for thinking it.

## Why It Is Possible to Be a Billionaire?

Once I set my goal to become a billionaire, I began to find reasons you can become a billionaire today more easily than ever before.

They are:

1.  With just a telephone line, the Internet is making a world of customers available to most of us.

2.  The Internet is creating more business beyond the Internet. Just as Henry Ford created more business as a ripple effect of mass producing cars, the Internet will magnify its effect. The Internet makes it possible for 6 billion of us to each become a Henry Ford or Bill Gates.

3.  In the past, the rich and the powerful controlled the media. With technological changes yet to come, the Internet is almost like each of us having the power of owning our own radio and television stations.

4.  New inventions breed more new inventions. An explosion of new technology will make other areas of our lives better. Each new technological change will allow more people to develop more new and innovative products.

5.  As more people become more prosperous, they will want to invest more and more money into new start up businesses, not only to help the new business but also to share in the profits. Today, it is hard for most people to grasp the reality that there are literally tens of billions of dollars looking for new innovative companies to invest in every year.

6.  It does not have to be high tech to be a new product. Starbucks made a lot of people rich with just a cup of coffee, and McDonald's became the largest holder of real estate with just a hamburger and fries.

7.  The key word is 'ephemeral.' In my opinion, that word is one of the most important words for anyone who desires to become rich or super-rich. Webster's defines the word as meaning lasting only a day, or lasting only a short time.

One of my teachers, Dr R. Buckminster Fuller, often used the word 'ephemeralization.' I understood him to use the word in the context of 'the ability to do so much more with so much less.' A more common term is the word 'leverage,' or the ability to do a lot with just a little. Dr Fuller said that humans were able to provide more and more wealth for more and more people, while using less and less.

In other words, with all these new technological inventions – inventions that actually use very little raw material – each of us can now make a lot of money with very little time and effort.

On the flip side of ephemeral, the people who will make less and less in the future are those who use the most in raw materials and physically work the hardest in the process of earning their money. In other words, the financial future belongs to those who do the most with the least effort.

## So What Is My Plan to Become a Billionaire?

The answer is found in the word 'ephemeral.' To become a billionaire, I need to provide a lot for many, for very little. I need to find an area of business that today is fat, bloated, and inefficient, an area where people are dissatisfied with the current system and whose products need improving. The industry I have the most opportunity in is the biggest industry of all: education. If you take a moment and think about all the money that is spent on education and training, the dollar amount will stagger you. This goes beyond counting the money for public schools, colleges, etc. When you look at the amount of education that goes on in business, the military, homes, and professional seminars, the dollar amount is the biggest of all. Yet, education is the one industry that has remained the most mired in the past. Education as we know it is obsolete, expensive, and ready for change.

Earlier this year, a friend of mine, Dan Osborne, an international foreign exchange trader, sent me an article from *The Economist*'s website. The following are excerpts from that article:

Michael Milken, the junk-bond king who once earned $500 million in a single year, is now building one of the world's biggest education companies, Knowledge Universe. Kohlberg, Kravis and Roberts, a buyout firm that strikes fear into managers the world over, also owns an education company called Kindercare. In Wall Street firms, analysts have taken to issuing breathless reports making such assertions as the education industry is undergoing a paradigm shift toward privatization and rationalization.

Why is everyone suddenly so excited? Because of the parallels they see between education and healthcare. Twenty-five years ago, healthcare was mostly stuck in the public and voluntary sectors. Today it is a multi-billion-dollar, largely private industry. A lot of rich people, not just Mr Milken and Henry Kravis, but also Warren Buffett, Paul Allen, John Doerr, and Sam Zell, are all betting that education is moving in the same direction. Companies from a range of conventional industries are investing in the business, including Sun, Microsoft, Oracle, Apple, Sony, Harcourt General, and the Washington Post Group.

The U.S. government says that the country spends a total of $635 billion a year on education, more than it devotes to pensions or defense, and predicts that spending per pupil will rise by 40% over the next decade. Private companies currently have only 13% of the market, mostly in the area of training, and most of them are mom-and-pop companies, ripe for consolidation. International Data Corporation, a trends consultancy, reckons that this share will expand to 25% over the next two decades.

**The article continues by saying:**

America's public schools are increasingly frustrating parents and falling behind international standards. America spends more of its GDP on education than most countries, yet it gets mediocre results. Children in Asia and Europe often trounce their American counterparts in standardized scholastic tests. More than 40% of American ten-year-olds cannot pass a basic reading test; as many as 42 million adults are functionally illiterate. Part of the reason for this dismal performance is that close to half of the $6,500 spent on each child is eaten up by non-instructional services, mostly administration.

Now the barriers between public and private sectors are eroding, allowing entrepreneurs into the state system. The 1,128 (and growing) charter schools are free to experiment with private management without losing public money.

**The article also points out:**

Not surprisingly, there is plenty of opposition to creeping privatization. The teachers' unions have an impressive record of crushing the challenges to their power . . .

## *Don't Go Where You Are Not Wanted*

In 1996, my educational board game *CASHFLOW* was submitted to a group of instructors at a prominent university for their feedback. Their verbal reply was, 'We do not play games in school, and we are not interested in teaching young people about money. They have more important subjects to learn.'

So there is a rule of thumb in business: 'Don't go where you're not wanted.' In other words, it is easier to make money where you and your products are wanted.

The good news is that more and more schools have been using our games as teaching products in their classrooms. However, the best news was that the public likes our products. Our board games are selling well to private individuals who want to improve their business and financial education.

We knew we had come full circle when in January 2000, Thunderbird, the American Graduate School of International Management, utilized *Rich Dad Poor Dad*, *CASHFLOW Quadrant*, and the *CASHFLOW* games in its curriculum for the Entrepreneurship Program. This very prestigious university is internationally recognized for its educational programs.

## Back to the Plan

I see a great need in the area of money management, business, and investing – subjects that are not taught in school. I predict that in the next few years, there will be a major stock market crash, and the grim reality that many people will not have enough money to retire on and get old with will emerge. I suspect that there will be a tremendous outcry in about ten years for more relevant financial education. Recently, the federal government let the American people know that they should not count solely on Social Security or Medicare when they retire. Unfortunately, that word is too late for millions of people, especially since the school system has never taught them how to manage their money. Sharon, Kim, and I intend to provide that education – both with our current products as well as over the Internet – for a much lower cost than the current school system could deliver it.

Once we have those educational programs ready for delivery over the Internet, we will become a technology and Internet company rather than just the publishing company we are today. Once we can deliver our products in that ephemeral way, the value and multipliers on the value of our company will go up because we will be able to deliver a better product to our international market, more conveniently, and for much less money. In other words, we will be able to do more and more with less and less, which is the key to becoming very, very rich.

So will I ever become a billionaire? I don't know. I am continuing to go for the goal. How will I do it if I do it? I don't know that either. It has yet to be figured out. But I do know this: For years, I grumbled and complained that school never taught me anything about money, business, or becoming rich. I often wondered why they did not teach subjects I could use once I left school rather than teach subjects I knew I would never use. Then one day, someone said to me, 'Quit your complaining and do something about it.' And today I am. I figured that if I was unhappy about not learning much about money, business, and becoming rich, other people probably had the same complaint.

In closing, Kim, Sharon, and I do not want to compete with the school system. The current school system is designed to teach people to be employees or professionals. We can sell our ephemeral products to those who want what we offer, which is education for people who want to be entrepreneurs and own businesses or invest in business, rather than work in someone else's business. That is our target market, and we see the Internet as the perfect system to reach it without going through the antiquated school system. That is our plan; only time will tell if the three of us will reach our goal.

If you want to be financially free, a multi-millionaire, or maybe even the next billionaire, we want to be your financial-education company.

## Chapter 41

# *Why Do Rich People Go Bankrupt?*

I often hear people say, 'When I make a lot of money, my money problems will be over.' In reality, their new money problems are just beginning. One of the reasons so many newly rich people suddenly go broke is because they use their old money habits to handle new money problems.

In 1977, I started my first big business, which was my nylon and Velcro surfer wallet business. As I said in a previous chapter, the asset created was bigger than the people who created it. A few years later I created another asset that grew rapidly and again the asset got bigger than the people who created it. Again I lost the asset. It took the third business for me to learn what my rich dad had been guiding me to learn.

My poor dad was shocked at my financial ups and downs. He was a loving father but it pained him to see me on top of the world one minute and in the gutter the next. But my rich dad was actually happy for me. He said after my two big creations and disasters, 'Most millionaires lose three companies before they win big. It took you only two companies. The average person has never lost a business and that is why 10% of the people control 90% of money.'

After my stories about making millions and losing millions, I am often asked an important question, 'Why do rich people go bankrupt?' I offer some of the following possibilities, all from personal experience.

Reason #1: People who have grown up without money have no idea how to handle a lot of money. As stated earlier, too much money is often as big a problem as not enough money. If a person is not trained to handle large sums of money or does not have proper financial advisors, then the chances are very strong that they will either stash the money away in the bank or just lose it. As my rich dad said, 'Money does not make you rich. In fact, money has the power to make you both rich and poor. There are billions of people each day who prove that fact. Most have some money but they spend it only to get poorer or greater in debt. That is why today there are so many bankruptcies being reported in the best economy in history. The problem again stems from people receiving money and then buying liabilities they think are assets. In the next few years, I am certain that many of today's young or instant millionaires will be in financial struggle because of their lack of money management skills.'

Reason #2: When people come into money, the emotional euphoria is like a drug that boosts your spirits. My rich dad said, 'When the "money high" hits, people feel more intelligent, when in fact they are becoming more stupid. They think they own the world and immediately go out and start spending money like King Tut with tombs of gold.'

My tax strategist and CPA, Diane Kennedy, once said to me, 'I have been an advisor to many rich men. Just before they go broke after making a ton of money, they tend to do three things. One, they buy a jet or big boat. Two, they go on safari. And three, they divorce their wife and marry a much younger woman. When I see that happening I begin preparing for the crash.' Again, much like reason number one, they buy liabilities or divorce an asset, which then creates a liability, and then they marry a new liability. They now have two or more liabilities.

Reason #3: When you have money certain friends and relatives tend to become closer. The hardest thing for many people is to say 'no' to people they love when they ask to borrow money. This has not happened to me, but I have seen many families and friendships break up when one person suddenly becomes rich. As rich dad said, 'A very important skill in becoming rich is to develop the ability to say "no" to yourself and the people you love.' The people who come into money and begin buying boats and big houses are not able to say 'no' to themselves, let alone their family members. They end up further in debt, just because they suddenly had a lot of money.

Not only do people want to borrow money from you when you have money, banks want to lend you more money. Which is why people say, 'Banks lend you money when you don't need it.' If things go bad, not only do you have trouble collecting the loans you made to friends and relatives, the banks then have trouble collecting from you.

Reason #4: The person with money suddenly becomes an 'investor' with money, but without education and experience. Again, this goes back to rich dad's statement that when people suddenly have money they think their financial IQ went up also, when in fact it has gone down. When a person has money, they suddenly begin receiving phone calls from stockbrokers, real estate brokers, and investment brokers. Rich dad also had a joke about brokers, 'The reason they are called "brokers" is because they are broker than you.' My apologies to any 'brokers' who are offended, but I think my rich dad's stockbroker is the one who told the joke to him originally.

I had a friend of my family who came into a $350,000 inheritance. In less than six months all that money was lost in the stock market, not to the market but to the broker that 'churned' the suddenly rich person who thought that money made him more intelligent. For those who do not know what churning means, it is when the broker advises the person to buy and sell regularly, so the broker makes the commission on each buy and sell. This practice is frowned upon and severe fines are levied if brokerage houses find their brokers involved in this practice . . . yet it does happen.

As stated at the start of this book just because you meet the qualifications of an Accredited Investor, simply a person with money, does not mean you know anything about investing.

In today's heated stock market, many companies are investing as foolishly as individuals are. With so much money in the market, many companies are running around buying other companies they hope are assets. In the industry it is often called M&As, or mergers and acquisitions. The problem is, many of these new acquisitions can become liabilities. Often the big company that bought a small company ends up in financial trouble.

Reason #5: The fear of losing increases. Many times a person with a poor person's outlook on money has lived a life being terrified of being poor. So when the sudden wealth hits, the fear of being poor does not diminish, in fact it increases. As my friend who is a psychologist for professional day traders says, 'You get what you fear.' That is why so many professional investors have psychologists as part of their team, at least that is why I have one. I have fears like everyone else. As stated earlier, there are many ways to lose money other than through the investment markets.

Reason #6: The person does not know the difference between good expenses and bad expenses. I often receive a phone call from my accountant or tax strategist saying, 'You have to buy another piece of real estate.' In other words, I have the problem of making too much money and I need to invest more money in something like real estate because my retirement plan cannot take any more money. One of the reasons the rich get richer is because they buy more investments by taking advantage of the tax laws. In essence, money that would have been paid in taxes is used to buy additional assets, which provide a deduction against income, reducing the taxes due, legally.

The tetrahedron illustrated earlier is to me one of the most important diagrams for wealth creation as well as keeping and increasing the wealth created. When I show people the diagram, I am often asked why expenses are part of the structure. The reason is because it is through our expenses that we become richer or poorer, regardless of how much money we make. Rich dad often said, 'If you want to know if a person is going to be richer or poorer in the future just look at the expense column of their financial statement.' Expenses were very important to rich dad. He often said, 'There are expenses that make you rich and expenses that make your poor. A smart business owner and investor knows which kind of expenses they want and controls those expenses.'

'The main reason I create assets is because I can increase my good expenses,' rich dad said to me one day. 'The average person has mainly bad expenses.' This difference in good expenses and bad expenses was one of rich dad's most important reasons for creating assets. He did so because his created assets could buy other assets. As he said to me when I was just a kid walking along the beach looking at the very expensive piece of real estate he had just purchased, 'I can't afford this land either. But my business can.'

If you understand the tax laws available to the B quadrant, you soon realize that one of the reasons the rich get richer is because the tax laws allow the B quadrant, more than other quadrants, to spend pre-tax dollars, to build, create, or buy other assets. In fact, the tax laws almost require you to buy more investments with pre-tax dollars, which is why I receive those phone calls telling me to buy more real estate or buy another company. The E quadrant on the other hand, must often use after-tax dollars to build, create, or buy other assets.

## What to Do with Too Much Money

'If you want to be rich, you must have a plan on how to make a lot of money and you must also have a plan on what to do with that money before you make it. If you do not have a plan on what to do with it before you make it, you will often lose it faster than you made it.' One of the reasons he had me study real estate investing was so that I would understand how to invest in real estate before I had a lot of money. Today when my accountant calls and says, 'You have too much money. You need to buy more investments,' I already know where to move my money, the corporate structures to use, and what to buy with that money. I call my broker and buy more real estate. If I buy paper assets, I often call my financial planner and buy an insurance product, which then buys my stocks, bonds, or mutual funds. In other words, the insurance industry produces special insurance products for rich people who are business owners. When a business buys insurance, it is an expense to the company and it often becomes an asset to the owner with many tax advantages. In other words, when my accountant calls, much of the money is already spent according to a predetermined plan. It is spent as expenses that make the person richer and more secure. That is why a financial advisor and an insurance agent for the rich are very important members of the team.

Over the years, I have seen many people start very profitable businesses and still end up broke. Why? Because they did not control their expenses. Instead of spending money to acquire other assets, assets such as real estate or paper assets, they expended it through frivolous business expenses, or bought bigger homes, nice boats, fast cars, and new friends. Instead of getting financially stronger, they became financially weaker with every dollar they made and then spent.

## The Other Side of the Coin

Rich dad often said, 'It is through the expense column that the rich person sees the other side of the coin. Most people only see expenses as bad, events that make you poor. When you can see that expenses can make you richer, the other side of the coin begins to appear to you.' He also said, 'Seeing through the expense column is like going through the looking glass as Alice did in *Alice in Wonderland*. Once Alice went through the looking glass, she saw this bizarre world that in many ways reflected the other side of the looking glass.' Both sides of the coin really did not make much sense to me but rich dad said, 'If you wanted to be rich, you had to know the hopes, the fears, and the illusions on both sides of the coin.'

During one of my meetings with rich dad, he said something that changed my thinking from a poor person to a rich person. Rich dad said to me, 'By having a plan to be rich, understanding the tax laws and corporate laws, I can use my expense column to get rich. The average person uses their expense column to become poor. That is one of the biggest and most important reasons why some people get rich and others become poor. If you want to become rich and stay rich, you must have control of your expenses.' If you understand this statement you will understand why rich dad wanted low income and high expenses. That was his way of getting rich. He said, 'most people eventually lose their money and go broke because they continue to think like a poor person and poor people want high income and low expenses. If you don't make this switch in your head, you will always live in fear of losing money, trying to be cheap, trying to be frugal, rather than being financially intelligent and becoming richer and richer. Once you can understand why a rich person would want high expenses and low income, you will begin to see the other side of the coin.'

## *A Very Important Point*

This last paragraph is one of the most important paragraphs in this book. In fact, this book has been written around this one paragraph. If you do not understand it, I suggest sitting down with a friend who has also read this book and begin a discussion to deepen your understanding of what it says. I do not expect you to necessarily agree with it. It would be good just to begin to understand it. You may begin to understand that there is a world of too much money and you may understand how you can become a part of that world. Rich dad said, 'People who do not change their point of view about money in their head, will see only one side of the coin. They will see the side of the coin that only knows a world of not enough money. They may never see the other side of the coin, the side where the world is a world of too much money, even if they do make a lot of money.'

By understanding that a world of too much money can exist, understanding a little of the tax laws and corporate laws, and why control of your expenses is so important, you can begin to see an entirely different world, a world very few people ever see. And seeing that world begins in your head. If your mental view can change, then you will begin to understand why rich dad always said, 'I use my expenses to get richer and richer and the average person uses their expenses to become poorer and poorer.' If you understand that statement you may understand why I think the teaching of financial literacy is important for our school system. It is also why my educational game *CASHFLOW* can help you see a world of money that few people ever see. The financial state is much like the looking glass in *Alice in Wonderland*. In the game *CASHFLOW*, it is via the mastery of the financial statement that the player moves from the Rat Race of life onto the Fast Track of the investment world, the world that begins with the Accredited Investor.

### How Can Low Income and High Expenses Be Good?

So as rich dad said, 'Money is just an idea.' And these last few paragraphs contain some very important ideas. If you understand fully why low income and high expenses is good then move on. If not, please invest some time in discussing this point with someone who has also read this book. This idea is the pivotal point of this book. It also explains why many rich people go broke. So please do your best to understand this point because it makes not much sense to be creative, build an asset, and make a lot of money – only to lose it all. When I studied the 90/10 rule the one thing I discovered is that the 90% who earn the 10% are people who want high income and low expenses. That is why they stay where they are.

## A *Guide Line*

So the question is, 'How can low income and high expenses make you rich?' And the answer is found in how the sophisticated investor utilizes the tax laws and corporate laws to bring those expenses back to the income column.

For example:

This is a diagram of what a sophisticated investor is working to do.

### This is the Diagram of the 10% who Make 90%

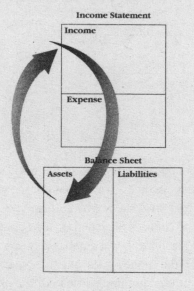

Again the question is, 'How can low income and high expenses make you rich?'

If you can begin to understand how and why this is done, then you will begin to see a world of greater and greater financial abundance.

Compare the previous diagram with the following diagram:

### This is the Diagram of the 90% Who Make 10%

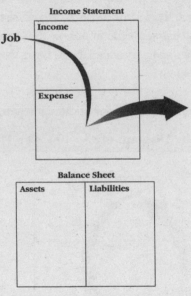

This is the financial diagram of most of the world's population. In other words, the money comes in and goes out the expense column and never comes back in. That is why so many people try to save money, be frugal, and cut back on expenses. This diagram here is also the diagram of the person who will emphatically say, 'My house is an asset.' Even though the money goes out the expense column and does not return – at least not immediately. Or the person who says, 'I'm losing money each month but the government gives me a tax break to lose money.' They say that rather than say, 'I'm making money on my investment and the government gives me a tax break to make money.'

My rich dad said, 'One of the most important controls you can have is found in this question. And the question is, "What percentage of the money going out your expense column winds up back in your income column in the same month?"' Rich dad spent hours and days on this subject with me. By understanding his point of view I saw a completely different world that most people do not see. I could see a world of ever increasing wealth, unlike people who work hard, earn a lot of money and keep their expenses down. So ask yourself the same question. 'What percentage of the money going out your expense column comes back in your income column in the same month?' If you can understand how this is done you should be able to see and create a world of ever increasing wealth. If you are having difficulty understanding this idea, find someone else and discuss how it might be done. If you can begin to understand it, you will begin to understand what a sophisticated investor is doing. I would say it's worth the discussion and why you may want to read and discuss this book often. It really was written to change a person's point of view from the view of not enough money to the view of creating a world of too much money.

## What Is the Value of a Network Marketing Business?

When I speak to network marketing companies, I often say to them, 'You don't know the value of your network marketing business.' I say that because many network marketing businesses only focus on how much money such a business can generate. I often warn them that it's not how much money they make, but much money they can invest with pre-tax dollars that is important. This is what the E quadrant cannot do. To me, that advantage is one of the biggest advantages of a network marketing business. If used properly a network marketing business can make you far richer than merely the residual income the business generates. I have several friends who have made tens of millions of dollars in network marketing and are still broke today. When I speak to the industry, I often remind the leaders of network marketing that a vital part of their job is to not only educate people on how to make a lot of money, it is as important to educate them on how to keep the money they make and it is through their expenses that they will ultimately become rich or poor.

## Why Are More Businesses Better than One?

It is not only network marketing people who fail to realize the true value of their business. I have seen entrepreneurs who are good at building a business yet do not realize the true value of that business. The reason this happens is because there is a popular idea going around today that you only build a business to sell it. That is the idea of a business owner who does not know what a sophisticated investor knows about the tax laws and corporate laws. So instead of building a business to buy assets, they often just build the business, sell it, pay the taxes, put the cash in the bank, and start all over again,

I have had several friends who have built businesses just to sell them. Two friends of mine have sold their companies for cash and then lost all that cash in their next business venture. They lost because the 90/10 rule for business survival is still in effect. These two were individuals from the S quadrant who built B quadrant business. They then sold those businesses to people from the B quadrant. The buyers recognized the often-unseen value of a B quadrant business. So the friends who sold their businesses ultimately went broke, even though they had collected several million dollars. The businesses they sold went on to make the new owners even richer.

A sophisticated business owner and investor would do their best to keep the business as long as possible, have it acquire as many stable assets as possible and then trade the business with as small a tax consequence as possible, while keeping as many of the assets as possible. As my rich dad said, 'The main reason I build a business is for the assets the business buys me.' For many entrepreneurs, the business they build is their only asset because they utilize a single corporation strategy and fail to harness the power of a multi-corporation investment strategy. (Again, to utilize such a strategy requires a team of professional advisors.) This points out that the big advantage the B quadrant has is that the tax laws for that quadrant allow you to spend pre-tax dollars to make you financially richer and in fact, the laws reward you for investing as much money as possible. After all, it is the rich who write the rules.

## *The Power of Expenses*

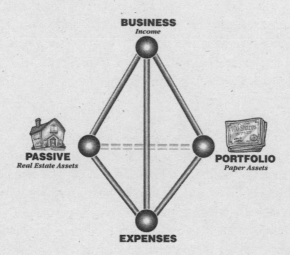

So this is why expenses can be an asset or liability, regardless of how much money you make. One of the reasons 90% of the people only have 10% of the money is because they do not know how to spend the money they make. As rich dad said, 'A rich person can take trash and turn it to cash. The rest of the people take cash and turn it to trash.'

So what is the answer to the question, 'Why do rich people go bankrupt?' 'The same reason poor people remain poor and the middle class struggles financially.' The reason the rich, the poor, and middle class go broke is because they lose control of their expenses. Instead of using their expenses to make them rich, they use their expenses to make them poor.

*Phase Five*

# *Giving It Back*

## Chapter 42

# Are You Prepared to Give Back?

### The Tenth Investor Control: The Control of Giving It Back

Recently a high school classmate of mine, Dan, was passing through town and asked if we could play golf. Dan was always a great golfer and I had not played in months, so I hesitated at first. Realizing that the purpose of the game was to spend time together to renew an old friendship, rather than compete in a round of golf, I agreed to play.

While riding around on the golf cart, being humiliated by Dan's golf game, the conversation turned to what we were doing at this stage of our lives. When I told Dan that I had retired and was building businesses, one to take public and one to be held privately, he became very angry. His anger caused him to accuse me of being greedy, thinking only of myself, and exploiting the poor. After about an hour of trying to keep my cool, I could take no more. Finally I said, 'What causes you to think that the rich are greedy?'

His reply was, 'Because all I see are poor people all day long. I never see rich people doing anything for them.' Dan is a legal aid attorney for people who cannot afford an attorney. 'The gap between the haves and have nots is bigger than ever and it is not improving.

We now have families who have no hope of ever getting out of poverty. They have lost sight of the dream that America was founded on. And guys like you make more and more money. Is that all you can think about? Build businesses and get rich? You've become just as bad as Mike's dad . . . a greedy rich man who only got richer.'

Dan's temper began to calm down as the game continued. Finally at the end of the game we agreed to meet the next day at the hotel's restaurant and I would show him something I was working on.

The next day I showed Dan the game. 'What is the game board for?' asked Dan after we were seated at the table.

Showing him the game, I explained my theory that poverty is caused by lack of education. 'It is a learned condition,' I said. 'It is taught at home. Since school doesn't teach you about money, you learn about it at home.'

'So what does this game teach?' Dan asked.

'It teaches the vocabulary of financial literacy,' I said. 'Words are, in my opinion, the most powerful tools or assets we as humans have, because words affect our brain, and our brains create our reality on the world. The problem many people have is that they leave home and school and never learn or understand the vocabulary associated with money . . . resulting in a lifetime of financial struggle.'

Dan studied the colorful game board while the waitress brought us more coffee. 'So you plan to end poverty with a board game?' he asked sarcastically.

'No,' I chuckled. 'I'm not that naive or optimistic. I created this game primarily for people who want to become business owners and investors. Cash flow management is a basic skill necessary for anyone who wants to be rich.'

'So you created this game for people who want to be rich, not for the poor?' Dan said, his anger rising again.

Again I chuckled at his emotional reaction. 'No, no, no,' I said. 'I did not create this product to exclude the poor. I'll say it again. I created this game for people who want to be rich, regardless of whether you are rich or poor today.'

The look on Dan's face softened, if only a little.

'Exactly,' I said softly. 'My products are designed for people who want to be rich,' I repeated again. 'My products cannot help anyone, regardless of who or what their financial station in life, unless they first want to be rich. My products will not help a rich person or a middle class person unless they too want to become richer.'

Dan sat there shaking his head. His anger was getting higher. Finally he said, 'You mean I've spent all my life trying to help people and you're saying I can't help them?'

'No. I am not saying that,' I said. 'I cannot comment on what you do or how effective you are. Besides that is not for me to judge.'

'So what are you saying?' Dan asked.

'I'm saying you can't help people unless they truly want to help themselves,' I said. 'If a person is not interested in becoming rich, my products are worthless.'

Dan sat there quietly absorbing the distinction I was attempting to make. 'In my world of law and legal aid, I often give advice to people. Many people don't take it,' said Dan. 'I see them again after a year or two and their situation is the same. They're back in jail or they're brought up again on charges for domestic violence or whatever. Is that what you're getting at? Advice alone does no good unless the people truly want to change the situations in their lives?'

'That is what I am saying,' I said. 'That is why the best diet and exercise plan will not work unless the person really and truly wants to lose weight. Or why it is often a waste of time and a disturbance to the rest of the class to have a student in the room that is not interested in learning a subject. It is tough to teach anyone who is not interested in learning. And that includes me. For example, I have no interest in learning to wrestle sharks. So you cannot force me to learn. But my golf game is different. I will study hard, practice for hours, and pay big money for lessons, because I want to learn.'

Dan sat there nodding his head. 'I understand,' he said.

'But I did not show you this game for the getting rich aspect,' I said. 'I want to show you what rich dad taught Mike and me about being generous. About giving money back.'

For the next ten minutes I explained Phase Five of rich dad's plan, pointing out to Dan that it was a big part of rich dad's plan to be generous, to be charitable. I said to Dan as I pointed to the game board, 'Mike's dad taught us five distinct phases of wealth and money. Phase Five was the responsibility of giving money back, after you made it. Mike's dad strongly believed that to make money and hoard it was a misuse of the power of money.'

'So you put Phase Five of Mike's dad's plan on your game board?' Dan asked a little suspiciously. 'Your game board not only teaches people to be rich, but it also teaches people to be generous?'

I nodded my head, 'It was part of the plan. A very important part.'

Having grown up with Mike and me, Dan knew who rich dad was. He had heard about the investment plan rich dad and I had drawn up after I returned from Vietnam. Dan was aware of what I had gone through to learn to be a business owner and an investor. He had lost his temper when I spoke of Phases Three and Four, where I was investing in other business and getting richer. He was now learning about Phase Five.

'As I said, Phase Five is probably the most important phase of rich dad's plan and I purposely built it into this game,' I said.

'So what is Phase Five?' asked Dan. 'Show it to me on the game board.'

I then pointed to the pinkish colored squares on the 'Fast Track' of the board game. The board game consists of two different tracks. One circular track on the inside, known as the 'Rat Race' and the outer more rectangular track known as the 'Fast Track,' which is where the rich invest. 'These pink squares are Phase Five,' I said, pointing to one of the squares.

'A kids' library,' Dan read out loud as he read the corner square where my finger was pointing.

I then pointed at another square.

'A research center for cancer,' Dan read aloud.

'And so is this square,' I said moving my finger and pointing to another square.

'A gift of faith,' Dan said reading the line just below where my finger was pointing.

'You mean you built charitable squares into the Fast Track?' asked Dan. 'The investment track of the very rich.'

Nodding my head I said, 'Yes. There are two kinds of dreams on the Fast Track. Dreams for personal indulgence and dreams for creating a better world with your excessive wealth.'

Dan shook his head slowly, saying, 'You mean Mike's dad taught you and Mike to be charitable as well as rich?'

I nodded my head as I quickly pointed to all the different charitable dreams found on the Fast Track of the game board. 'Rich dad said one of the most important controls an investor had was the control over returning most of the money back to society.'

'He had a reputation as a rich greedy man,' said Dan. 'Many people said terrible things about him, about how greedy he was.'

'That is what most people thought,' I replied. 'Yet Mike and I knew differently. The more money he made, the more money he gave away. But he gave it away quietly.'

'I did not know that,' said Dan. 'So his later years were dedicated to giving all the money he amassed back to society.'

'Well not all of it,' I said. 'He wanted to leave some for his children. The point I want to make is that many people have this belief that the rich are greedy. That belief blinds them to the truth or the reality that not all the rich are greedy. If you open your eyes, you will see that many of the very rich have made tremendous financial contributions to society. Look at what Andrew Carnegie has given back through libraries, Henry Ford through his Ford Foundation and the Rockefellers through the Rockefeller Foundation. My hero, George Soros, the founder of The Quantum Fund, is today dedicating massive amounts of money in the hopes of creating a global society and promoting greater financial understanding amongst nations. But often all we hear about are the nasty things political leaders say about him and his hedge fund.

'John D. Rockefeller not only created his charitable foundation to give away his money, he donated extensively to the University of Chicago, as many rich alumni donate to their schools. Many other ultra rich have founded their own institutions of higher learning just as Stanford founded Stanford University and Duke founded Duke University. The rich have always been very generous to higher education.'

'Vanderbilt University was founded by a very rich entrepreneur,' added Dan.

'I realize that the rich create jobs and provide goods and services to make life a little better. So now you're telling me that they often give the money back to the society,' said Dan.

'That is exactly what I am saying,' I replied. 'And yet many people can only see what they think is the greedy side of the rich. I know that there are greedy rich people, but so are there greedy poor people.'

'So your rich dad gave it back?' Dan repeated.

'Yes,' I replied. 'Phase Five made him the happiest of all the phases. Besides, being charitable increased his expenses, reduced his income, and took him through the looking glass.'

'What?' stammered Dan in confusion. 'What looking glass?'

'Never mind,' I said. 'Just know that being generous made him happy in more ways than one.'

'What did he give to?' asked Dan.

'Since his own father died of cancer, rich dad's foundation gave tremendous amounts of money to cancer research. He also built a cancer ward on a small country hospital, so the country people could be closer to their loved ones when they were hospitalized. Being a very religious man, he also built a classroom building for his church so the church could have a larger Sunday school for kids. And he was a patron of the arts, acquiring artwork from many talented artists as well as donating money to the museums. The best thing is that his foundation is so well directed, that even after his death, it will continue to earn and donate money. Even in death he will still do a lot of good for society. The trusts and foundations he set up will be providing money for many worthy causes for years to come.'

'He planned to have too much money in life and he planned on having too much money in death,' said Dan.

'He definitely had a plan,' I replied.

'So your game *CASHFLOW* really does include everything your rich dad taught you. He taught you how to make the money and how to give the money back,' said Dan.

'I did my best to include the important things rich dad taught me about money in the game. And the importance of giving back was one of the things he taught me,' I replied. 'He taught me to control the acquisition of wealth and he taught me how to control the giving it back.'

'I wish more people did that,' said Dan.

'Oh there will be more people giving more money back,' I said. 'Just look at this baby-boomer generation. Many were hippies in the sixties and they are fast becoming multi-millionaires today. In a few years, the revolution they were a part of will be in full force with cash flow. Many of these one-time hippies and others of that generation are very socially responsible people. What they learned from the sixties, their poor college days, will be brought to fruition in the next few years. Their ideals coupled with their wealth will be a powerful financial, political, and social force in the world. I think that they will do the charitable deeds that our government cannot afford to do today. Many rich boomers will be completing socially responsible deeds they wanted to perform when they were poor . . . but now they're rich.'

'What makes you think they will be generous?' asked Dan.

'Because it is already happening,' I replied. 'Ted Turner pledged a billion dollars to the U.N. and chided people like Bill Gates and others for not being generous enough. In less than three years, after that challenge, Bill Gates alone has pledged $4 billion to various causes . . . and Gates is still a young man. Can you imagine how much he will be donating in his later years?'

'But wasn't that because he was on trial with the federal government?' asked Dan. 'He's just giving money so he can look good?'

'Well, many of the reporters like to point that out in the articles they write about his generosity. But let me ask you this. How many reporters are giving away $4 billion dollars?' I asked quietly. 'The facts are, in 1999 alone, Bill Gates has a full-time staff to give away $325 million. How many reporters are giving away $325 million in 1999? So even if it took an encouraging nudge from Ted Turner, the fact remains that he is giving money away. And the fact remains that this baby-boomer generation of wealthy entrepreneurs will be pressuring each other to be generous. It will be very socially uncool to be rich and not be generous.'

'So Mike's dad was a generous man and he taught you and Mike to be generous.'

I nodded my head. 'And even though many people in town criticized him for being rich, he continued to give quietly. Being generous made financial sense to him as well as giving him pleasure.'

'I really did not know that,' Dan said quietly and almost reverently, having perceived him differently. 'And giving money away made him happy?'

I nodded my head. 'In the later years of his life, I saw a peace come over him that I had never seen before. He had done a lot of good during life and he would continue to do good when his life was over. His life was complete.

'He was very proud of both Mike and me,' I went on. 'He also said he knew I was more like my real dad. He knew I was a teacher and he hoped I would go on to teach others as he had taught me. He wanted me to be both dads . . . a rich man as well as a teacher.'

'And was that it?' asked Dan.

'No,' I replied. 'He couldn't leave it at that. He was always afraid that I would give up along the way. He was afraid that I would not have the persistence to make my investment plan come true, which would mean my financial dreams would not come true. He was always afraid that I would join the quitters of the world, doing what was easy, rather than doing what was necessary.

'Keep going, keep minding your own business, keep being true to your dreams and all your dreams will come true,' I said quietly. 'That was the last advice he gave me.'

Bringing me back to the present, Dan asked, 'So have all your dreams come true?'

'Almost,' I replied. 'I still want to become the ultimate investor and we have just started our Foundation.'

'What Foundation?' he asked.

'When Kim, Sharon and I started CASHFLOW Technologies, Inc., our mission was to "Elevate the financial well-being of humanity."'

'That's a pretty aggressive mission,' Dan said with his eyebrows raised.

'I can see how you would say that but we accomplish our mission every day. We receive calls, letters, e-mails every day from people who have taken action to improve their financial lives. We have been overwhelmed by the response we have from the people using our products. Every time we hear from someone who has improved their financial well-being, we have accomplished our mission.'

'So what about the Foundation?' Dan persisted.

'We created the Foundation for Financial Literacy so we would have a not for profit entity with which to give back. We have been so blessed by our students and customers that we wanted to give back. The Foundation will support other organizations in their efforts to teach financial literacy.

'For example, we have a high school teacher in Indiana teaching *CASHFLOW* 101 and 202 to his students. He has been helping us develop a curriculum that other teachers can use in the classroom. This spring he is going to send his high school students into the elementary schools to teach elementary school students using *CASH-FLOW for Kids*. In fact, we also have the older kids teaching the younger kids in the Boys and Girls Club in Tucson, Arizona. We are so excited by the concept of "kids teaching other kids" that we hope to expand the program worldwide. The Foundation can help make that happen.'

'That sounds great, Robert. It's nice to see you so energized by giving,' Dan said.

'We are still developing the Foundation and its programs. The important thing is to support learning wherever we can. Kim, Sharon and I have been very blessed with success and we want to continue to look for ways to give back through helping others teach financial literacy.'

The Foundation for Financial Literacy was organized and will be operated as a nonprofit corporation for charitable and educational purposes within the meaning of Section 501(c)(3) of the Internal Revenue Code of 1986, as amended, to support needy, educational, charitable, religious, and scientific programs and organizations that support financial education. The Foundation welcomes inquiries at:

The Foundation for Financial Literacy
P.O. Box 5870
Scottsdale, AZ 85261–5870
www.richdad.com

CASHFLOW* Technologies, Inc. supports the Foundation, in part, by donating the time of its staff members and providing office space and services to the Foundation, in addition to financial support.

# *Why It Does Not Take Money to Make Money . . . Anymore*

Recently, while teaching an investment class, I was asked, 'What Internet company would you recommend I invest in?'

I replied, 'Why invest in someone else's Internet company? Why don't you start your own Internet company and ask people to invest in it?'

As stated earlier in the book, there are many investment books written on how to buy assets. This book has been dedicated to learning how to create assets that buy assets. So why not take the time to consider creating an asset, rather than simply buying an asset? I say this because it has never been easier to create your own asset.

### *The World Is 10 Years Old*

On October 11, 1998, Merrill Lynch ran a full-page ad in several of the larger American newspapers, announcing that the world was just 10 years old. Why just 10 years old? Because it had been approximately ten years since the Berlin Wall had come down. Tearing down the Berlin Wall is the event some economic historians use to mark the end of the Industrial Age and the beginning of the Information Age.

Until the Information Age, most people had to be investors from the outside. Now that the world is just over 10 years old, more and more people can invest from the inside, rather than from the outside. When I answered, 'Why invest in someone else's Internet company? Why not start your own Internet company?' I meant, 'It is now the Information Age, so why not become an insider instead of an outsider?'

### *Three Ages*

In the Agrarian Age, the rich were those who owned a castle that overlooked large tracks of fertile agricultural land. These people were known as the monarchs and the nobles. If you were not born into this group, you were an outsider with very little chance of becoming an insider. The 90/10 rule controlled life. Therefore, the 10% who were in power were there because of marriage, birth, or conquest; the other 90% were serfs or peasants who worked the land but owned nothing.

During the Agrarian Age, if you were a good, hard-working person, you were respected; the idea of being diligent was handed down from parent to child. It was also when the idle rich began to be loathed – 90% of the people worked to support the other 10%, who appeared not to be working; that idea was also handed down from parent to child. These ideas continue to be popular and are still handed down from generation to generation.

Then came the Industrial Age and wealth shifted from agricultural land to real estate. Improvements such as buildings, factories, warehouses, mines, and residential homes for the workers were placed on top of the land . . . improvements. Suddenly, rich fertile agricultural land dropped in value because the wealth shifted to the owners of the buildings upon the land. In fact, an interesting thing happened. Suddenly, rich fertile land became less valuable than rocky land, where farming was difficult. Rocky land suddenly became more valuable because it was cheaper than fertile land. It could also hold taller building such as skyscrapers, or factories, and it often contained resources such as oil, iron, and copper that fueled the Industrial Age. When the shift in ages occurred, many farmers' net worth went down; to maintain their standard of living, they had to work harder and farm more land than before.

It was during the Industrial Age that the 'Go to school so you can find a job' idea became popular. In the Agrarian Age, a formal education was not necessary since professions were handed down from parent to child; bakers taught their children to be bakers, and so on. Near the end of this era, the idea of 'a' job, or the idea of one job for life, became popularized. You went to school, got that one job for life, worked your way up the corporate ladder or up the union ladder, and when you retired, the company and the government took care of your needs.

In the Industrial Age, those not of noble birth could become rich and powerful. Rags-to-riches stories spurred on the ambitious. Entrepreneurs started with nothing and became billionaires. When Henry Ford decided to mass-produce the automobile, he found some cheap rocky land that farmers did not want near a small town known as Detroit, and an industry was born. The Ford family became, in essence, the new nobility, and anyone around them who did business with them also became the new, rich nobility. New names became as prestigious as those of kings and queens – names such as Rockefeller, Stanford, and Carnegie. People often respected as well as despised them for their great wealth and power.

In the Industrial Age, as during the Agrarian Age, however, only a few controlled most of the wealth. The 90/10 rule still held true, although this time, the 10% was not determined by birth but by determination itself. The 90/10 rule held true simply because it took great effort and coordination as well as a lot of money, people, land, and power to build and control the wealth. For example, to start an automobile company or an oil or mining company is still capital intensive; it takes massive amounts of money, lots of land, and many smart formally educated people to build that type of company. On top of that, you often must get through years of bureaucratic red tape – such as environmental studies, trade agreements, labor laws, and so on – to get such a business off the ground. In the Industrial Age, the standard of living went up for most people, but the control of real wealth continued to remain in the hands of a few. The rules have changed.

## *The 90/10 Rule Has Changed*

When the Berlin Wall came down and the World Wide Web went up, many of the rules changed. One of the most important rules that changed was the 90/10 rule. Although it's likely that only 10% of the population will always control 90% of the money, the access or the opportunity to join that 10% has changed. The World Wide Web has changed what it costs to join the 10%. Today, it does not take being born into a royal family as it did in the Agrarian Age. It does not require massive sums of money, land, and people to join the 10%. The price of admission today is an idea, and ideas are free.

In the Information Age, all it takes is information or ideas to become very, very, wealthy. It is therefore possible for individuals who are financially obscure one year to be on the list of the richest people in the world the next. Such people often fly past individuals who made their money in the ages gone by. College students who have never had a job become billionaires. High school students will surpass their college student counterparts.

In the early 1990s, I remember reading a newspaper article that said, 'Many Russian citizens complained that under the Communist rule their creativity was stifled. Now that Communist rule is over, many Russians citizens are finding out that they had no creativity.' Personally, I think all of us have a brilliant creative idea that is unique to us, an idea that could be turned into an asset. The problem for the Russians, as it is with many citizens all over the world, is they did not have the advantage of my rich dad's guidance in teaching them to understand the power of the B-I Triangle. I think it is very important that we teach more individuals to be entrepreneurs and how to take their unique ideas and turn them into businesses that create wealth. If we do so, our prosperity will only increase as the Information Age expands around the world.

For the very first time in world history, the 90/10 rule to wealth may no longer apply. No longer does it take money to make money. No longer does it take vast tracts of land or resources to become rich. No longer does it take friends in high places to become rich. No longer does it matter if your relatives came over on the *Mayflower*; it does not matter what university you went to, or what sex, race, or religion you are a part of. Nowadays, all it takes is an idea, and as rich dad has always said, 'Money is an idea.' For some people, however, the hardest thing to change is an old idea. There is an old truth to the saying 'You can't teach an old dog new tricks.' I think a more accurate saying is: 'You can't teach someone who clings to old ideas new tricks, regardless of if they are young or old.'

So when I am asked, 'What Internet company would you invest in?' I still reply, 'Why not invest in your own Internet company?' I am not necessarily suggesting the askers start an Internet company; all I am doing is asking them to consider the idea, the possibility of starting their own company. In fact, many franchise and network marketing opportunities are now available on the Internet. When people simply consider the idea of starting their own B quadrant business, their minds shift from hard work and physical limits to the possibility of unlimited wealth. All it takes is the idea – and we are in the Age of Ideas. I am not suggesting that such people quit their job and leap into starting a company. But I do suggest that they keep their full-time job and consider starting a business part-time.

## The Challenge of Old Ideas

In the stock market today you often hear announcers say, 'Old economy versus new economy.' In many ways, the people being left behind are often people who continue to think in old economy ideas versus new economy ideas.

Rich dad constantly reminded his son and me that money was just an idea. He also warned us to be ever vigilant, to watch our ideas and challenge them when they needed to be challenged. Being young and lacking experience at the time, I never fully realized what he meant. Today, older and wiser, I have tremendous respect for his warning to challenge our old ideas. As rich dad said, 'What is right for you today could be wrong for you tomorrow.'

I have watched Amazon.com, a company without any profits or any real estate, grow faster and become more valuable in the stock market than established retailers such as Wal-Mart, Sears, J.C. Penny, and K-Mart. A new not-profitable Web retailer is perceived more valuable than Industrial Age retailers with solid profits, years of experience, massive real estate holdings, and more assets than any monarch of old. But the new Web retailer is more valuable just because it does not require massive amounts of real estate, money, and people in order to do business. The very things that made Industrial Age retailers valuable in the Industrial Age are making them less valuable in the Information Age. You often hear people say, 'The rules have changed.' I often wonder what the future holds for these older retailers and their investors as more and more Internet companies slice into profit margins, selling the same products for a lower price. In other words, although Amazon.com is not profitable today, it is cutting into the profit margins of companies that are profitable today. What will that mean to job security, pay raises, and benefits for employees and investor loyalty in the future? And what will happen to the value of real estate? Only time will tell.

I believe that many of the new Internet companies will fold and investors will lose literally billions. They will fold because ultimately, profits and positive cash flow are how a business survives. But many Industrial Age companies will also fold because of price competition from these online retailers with no real estate. I recently heard an old-school retailer saying, 'We will make shopping an entertaining experience.' The problem with such thinking is that making shopping an entertaining experience is expensive, and many shoppers will come to enjoy the experience but will still buy on line for a better price.

I have a dear friend who has been my travel agent for years. However, she has to charge me a service fee to write my tickets these days because the airlines have stopped paying her a commission on ticket sales. She has had to release several of her loyal staff and now worries that I will shift to buying my tickets for a lower price on line. During this same period, a person who is not a travel agent and not regulated by the rules of the travel industry started an online company called Priceline.com. Suddenly, with the idea of auctioning off a perishable product known as an empty airline seat, Priceline.com's founder Jay Walker joins the *Forbes* 400 list of the richest people in the world. He does this in just a few years. So he becomes wealthy, and my dear friend lays off staff and counts on her loyal customers to stay with her because she will work harder and provide better service. I am sure she will do OK, but the business she started years ago as her retirement safety net has now become a full-time job with no assurance that it will be of any value whatever when she's ready to retire.

## *Things Have Changed*

Since it does not take money to make money, then why not go out and make a lot of money? Why not find investors to invest in your idea so you can all become rich? The answer is because often, old ideas are in the way.

As Merrill Lynch announced, 'The World Is 10 Years Old.' The good news is that it is not too late to change your thinking and begin to catch up if you already have not started. The bad news is that some-times, the hardest things to change are old ideas. Some of the old ideas that may need to be challenged are the following ideas that have been handed down for generations:

1.  'Good, hard-working person.' The reality today is that the people who physically work the hardest are paid the least and taxed the most. I am not saying not to work hard. All I am saying is that we need to constantly challenge our older thoughts and maybe rethink new ones. Consider working hard in a part-time business for yourself.

    Today, instead of being in just one quadrant, we need to be very familiar with all four quadrants of the CASHFLOW Quadrant. After all, we're in the Information Age, and working hard at one job for life is an old idea.

2.  'The idle rich are lazy.' The reality is that the less you are involved physically in your work, the more your chances are of becoming very rich. Again, I am not saying to not work hard. I am suggesting that today, we all need to learn to make money mentally, not just physically. Those who make the most money work the least physically. They work the least because they work for passive income and portfolio income rather than earned income. And as you know by now, all a true investor does is turn earned income into passive and portfolio income.

    In my mind, today's idle rich are therefore not lazy. It is just that their money is working harder than they are. If you want to join the 90/10 crowd, you must learn to make money mentally more than physically.

3.  'Go to school and get a job.' In the Industrial Age, people retired at age 65 because they were often too worn out to lift tires and put engines into a car on the assembly line. Today,

you are technically obsolete and ready for retirement every eighteen months, which is how fast information and technology are doubling. Many people say a student today is technically obsolete immediately upon graduation from school. Now more than ever, my rich dad's advice of 'School smarts are important but so are street smarts' is even more relevant. We are a self-learning society, not a society that learns from its parents (as in the Agrarian Age) or from its schools (as in the Industrial Age). Kids are teaching their parents how to use computers, and companies are looking for high-tech kids more than college-degreed middle-aged executives.

To stay ahead of the obsolescence curve, continual learning from school as well as the street is vitally important. When I speak to young people, I advise them to think like professional athletes as well as college professors. Professional athletes know their careers will be over as soon as younger athletes can beat them. College professors know that they will become more valuable the older they get if they continue to study. Both points of view are important today.

## *Rich Dad's Advice Is Even More True Today*

For those of you who have read our first two books, you know the difficulty I went through listening to two different dads and their ideas about money, business, and investing. In 1955, my poor dad kept saying, 'Go to school, get good grades, and find a safe and secure job.' On the other hand, my rich dad kept saying, 'Mind your own business.' My poor dad did not think investing was important because he believed 'The business and the government are responsible for your retirement and medical needs. A retirement plan is part of your benefit package, and you are entitled to it.' My rich dad would say, 'Mind your own business.' My poor dad believed in being a good, hard-working man. He would say, 'Find a job and work your way up the ladder. Remember that companies do not like people who move around a lot. Companies reward people for seniority and loyalty.' My rich dad said, 'Mind your own business.'

My rich dad believed that you must constantly challenge your ideas. My poor dad believed strongly that his education was valuable and most important. He believed in the idea of right answers and wrong answers. My rich dad believed that the world was changing and we needed to continually keep learning. Rich dad did not believe in right answers or wrong answers. He believed instead in old answers and new answers. He would say, 'You cannot help but get older physically, but that does not mean you have to get older mentally. If you want to stay younger longer, just adopt younger ideas. People get old or obsolete because they cling to right answers that are old answers.'

Here are some examples of right answers that are old answers:

1.  Can humans fly? The correct answer prior to 1900 was 'No.' Today, it is obvious that humans are flying everywhere, even in space.

2.  Is the earth flat? The correct answer in 1492 was 'Yes.' After Columbus sailed to the New World, the old right answer was obsolete.

3.  Is land the basis of all wealth? The answer before the Industrial Age was 'Yes.' Today, the answer is a resounding 'No.' It takes an idea and knowledge from the B and I side of the Quadrant to make that idea real. Once you prove you know what to do, the world is full of rich investors looking to give their money to you.

4.  Doesn't it take money to make money?' I am most frequently asked this question. The answer is 'No.' In my opinion, it has always been 'No.' My answer has always been 'It does not take money to make money. It takes information to make as well

as to keep money.' The difference is that it has become much more obvious that it does not take money or hard labor to make a lot of money.

I don't know what tomorrow will bring; no one does. That is why rich dad's idea of constantly challenging and updating ideas was one the most important ideas he passed on to me.

Today, I see so many of my friends falling behind professionally as well as financially simply because they fail to challenge their own ideas. Their ideas are often right answers that are very very old answers handed down for generations, from one economic era to another. Some high school kids plan on never having jobs. Their plan is to bypass the whole Industrial Age idea of job security and become financially free billionaires instead. This is why I ask people to think about building their own Internet business – either on their own or through a franchise or network marketing company – instead of just looking for one to invest in. Today's thinking process is very different, and it may challenge some very, very, old right ideas. Those old ideas often make the process of change so difficult.

## *Ideas Do Not Need to Be New, They Just Need to Be Better*

Always remember that once you have mastered the guidelines found in the B-I Triangle, you can virtually take nothing and turn it into an asset. When I am asked what my first successful investment was I simply reply, 'My comic book business.' In other words, I took comic books that were going to be thrown away and created an asset around them, using the principles found in the B-I Triangle. Starbucks did the same thing with a cup of coffee. So ideas do not have to be new and unique, they just have to be better. This has been going on for centuries. In other words, things do not have to be high-tech to be better. In fact, many things that we take for granted today, were very high-tech yesterday.

There are many individuals who spend their lives copying other people's ideas rather than creating their own. I have two acquaintances that make it a practice of taking other people's ideas. Although they may make a lot of money there is a price for taking other people's ideas without their permission or giving credit where credit is due for those ideas. The price these people pay, although they may make a lot of money, is the respect of the people that know they take other people's ideas without permission. There are two people I used to be associated with that I do not associate with today because they make it a practice to take other people's ideas without permission and claim them as their own.

As my rich dad often said, 'There is a fine line between copying and stealing. If you are creative, you have to be careful of thieves who steal ideas. They are just as bad as people who burglarize your home.' Because there are more people stealing than creating, it becomes ever more important to have an intellectual property attorney on your team protecting your creations.

One of the most important technological changes in the history of the Western world took place during the Crusades, when Christian soldiers came across the Hindu-Arab system of numbers. The Hindu-Arabic system of numbers, so named because the Arabs found this numbering system during their invasion of India, replaced what we call Roman numerals. Few people appreciate the difference this new system of numbers has made upon our lives. The Hindu-Arabic system of numbers allowed people to sail further out to sea with greater accuracy; architecture could be more ambitious; time keeping could more accurate; and the human mind sharpened, and people thought more accurately, abstractly, and critically. It was a major technological change that had a tremendous effect on all of our lives.

The Hindu-Arabic numbering system was not a new idea; it was simply a better idea — and on top of that, it was someone else's idea. Many of the most financially successful people are not necessarily people who have creative ideas; many of them often just copy other people's ideas and turn the idea into millions or even billions of dollars. Fashion designers watch young kids to see what new fashions they are wearing, and then they simply mass-produce those fashions. Bill Gates did not invent the operating system that made him the richest man in the world. He simply bought the system from the computer programmers who did invent it and then licensed their product to IBM. The rest is history. Amazon.com simply took Sam Walton's idea for Wal-Mart and put it on the Internet; Jeff Bezos became rich much more quickly than Sam Walton. In other words, who says you need to have creative ideas to be rich? You just need to be better at the B-I Triangle and at taking ideas and turning them into riches.

## *Following in Your Parents' Footsteps*

Tom Peters, author of *In Search of Excellence*, has been saying over and over again, 'Job security is dead.' Yet, many people continue saying to their children, 'Go to school so you can find a secure job.' Many people struggle financially simply because they have their parents' ideas about money. Instead of creating assets that bought assets, most of our parents worked for money and then bought liabilities with that money, innocently thinking they were assets. That is why many people go to school and get good jobs because that is what their parents did or advised them to do. Many struggle financially, or live paycheck to paycheck because that is what their parents did. When I teach my investment classes, a very important exercise is for students to compare what they are doing today to what their parents did or advised them to do. Many times, students realize that they are either following closely in their parents' footsteps or are following their parents' advice. At that point, they have the power to question these old ideas that have been running their lives.

If a person truly wants to change, adopting a better idea is often a good idea. My rich dad always said, 'If you want to get richer faster, simply look for ideas that are better than the ones you are using today.' That is why, to this day, I read biographies of rich entrepreneurs, listen to audiotapes of their lives, and listen to their ideas. As rich dad said, 'Ideas need not be new; they just need to be better – and a rich person is always looking for better ideas. Poor people often defend their old ideas or criticize new ones.'

## Only the Paranoid Survive

Andy Grove, the chairman of Intel, titled his book *Only the Paranoid Survive*. He got that title from Dr Joseph A. Schumpeter, a former Austrian minister of Finance and Harvard Business School professor. Dr Schumpeter expressed this idea of only the paranoid surviving in his book *Capitalism, Socialism, and Democracy*. (Dr Schumpeter was the 'father' of the modern study of growth and change in economics – dynamics – just as Lord Keynes was the 'father' of the study of static economics – statics.) It is Dr Schumpeter's idea that capitalism is creative destruction; a perpetual cycle of destroying the old, less-efficient product or service and replacing it with new, more-efficient ones. Dr Schumpeter believed that governments that allow the existence of capitalism, which tears down weaker and less efficient businesses, will survive and thrive. Governments that put up walls to protect the less efficient will fall behind.

My rich dad agreed with Dr Schumpeter, which is why he was a capitalist. Rich dad challenged Mike and me to constantly challenge our ideas because if we didn't, someone else would. Today, people with old ideas are those who are falling behind the fastest, even though the world is only a little more than ten years old. The world we face today reminds me of the song 'The Times They Are a-Changin'.' A line from that song goes, 'For you'd better start swimming or you'll sink like a stone.' Although that song was written approximately 40 years ago, it will reflect the next 40 years more and more. In other words, just because you're rich or poor today does not mean you will be in the near future.

### *Your Past Success Means Nothing*

In the near future, those who do not risk failing will ultimately fail. My poor dad looked upon failure as a noun, and my rich dad looked upon failure as a verb – and that difference made a big difference over a lifetime. In *Future Edge*, Joel Barker wrote, 'When a paradigm shifts, everyone goes back to zero. Your past success means nothing.' In this fast-changing world, paradigms will be changing faster and faster, and your past successes could mean nothing. In other words, just because you work for a good company today does not ensure that it will be a good company tomorrow. For this reason, Grove chose the title of his book: *Only the Paranoid Survive*.

Even employee benefits are changing. Not only has thc Information Age changed the rules of retirement plans, the change from Defined Benefit Pension Plans to Defined Contribution Pension Plans, the change has also affected some employee benefits. Recently a friend who works for an airline said, 'It used to be easy to get free flights on airlines, which is one of the benefits of being an airline employee. But today, with airlines auctioning off empty seats on line, the planes are flying full and I find it harder to use a benefit I love.'

### *A Tale of Two Texans*

Most of us have heard of Ross Perot and Michael Dell. Both are Texans, and both made their money in the Information Age economy. Yet recently, an article in a financial magazine stated that Perot's wealth has actually gone down substantially while Dell's wealth continues to skyrocket. So what is the difference? It's not the industry, since both are in the information industry. I'll let you come to your own conclusions.

### *The Rules Have Changed*

As this book draws to a close, I will leave you with some ideas about the changes that we all face today, changes that were brought on once the Berlin Wall went down and the World Wide Web went up. In his book, *The Lexus and the Olive Tree*, *New York Times* foreign affairs columnist Thomas L. Friedman describes several changes between the Industrial Age and the Information Age. Some of the changes are:

|   | Cold War | Globalization |
|---|----------|---------------|
| 1. | Einstein's E=mc2 | Moore's Law |

During the Cold War, Einstein's theory of relativity — E=mc2 — ruled. In 1945, when the United States dropped the atomic bomb on Japan, America became the economic power of the world and took military dominance away from England. During the 1980s, everyone thought Japan was about to beat the United States economically, and the Nikkei stock market surged. But Japan's period of economic dominance was short lived because the United States redefined itself. The United States redefined itself because it shifted from E=mc2 to Moore's Law. Moore's Law says that the power of the microchip will double every 18 months. Today, America is the leading world power because it leads in technology as well as weaponry.

If America had remained in the weapons race only, we might be a bankrupt nation like the former Soviet Union. When the Berlin Wall came down in 1989, America's capital markets shifted quickly into the Information Age. That freedom to change quickly is the financial power provided by a free capitalistic society. Japan as well as England cannot change that quickly because both countries have too many ties to the days of the feudal system — otherwise known as the monarchy, an Agrarian Age institution. Unconsciously, those countries are waiting for the monarch to lead them. In other words, innovation is often hampered by traditions. That idea is true for individuals as well as nations. As rich dad said, 'Old ideas get in the way of new ideas.' I am not suggesting getting rid of old traditions, but rather that we are in the Information Age and so we need expanded ideas as well as old ideas.

| Cold War | Globalization |
|---|---|
| 2. Weight of missiles | Speed of modems |

When the Berlin Wall came down, $E=mc2$ changed to Moore's Law. The power in the world shifted from the weight of nuclear warheads to how fast your modem is. The good news is that a fast modem costs a lot less than big missiles; speed matters more than weight.

| Cold War | Globalization |
|---|---|
| 3. Two world powers in charge | No one in charge |

During the Cold War, there were two superpowers: the United States and the Soviet Union. Today, the web makes the idea of a borderless world and a global economy a reality.

Today, the electronic herd, which is the thousands of fund managers who control great sums of money, have the power to affect world politics more than politicians. If the electronic herd does not like the way a country is managing their financial affairs, they will move their money elsewhere at the speed of light. That is what happened in Malaysia, Thailand, Indonesia, and Korea just a few years ago. The same thing could happen to any country. It is not the politicians that have the power today, as they did in the Industrial Age. In the Information Age, it is the power of global electronic money that often dictates a country's affairs.

Bill Gates crossed the border from the United States to Canada. When the customs agent asked him if he had anything of value to declare, he pulled out a stack of floppy disks wrapped in rubber bands. 'This is worth at least $50 billion.' The customs agent shrugged, thinking he was talking to a nut, and let the richest man in the world pass through the border without paying anything in taxes. The point is that the bundle of floppy disks wrapped in rubber bands was worth at least $50 billion. That bundle of floppy disks was the prototype of Microsoft's Windows 95.

Today, super-rich individuals like Gates often have more money and more influence over the world than many large nations. Such power caused the U.S. government, the strongest government in the world, to take Gates to court for monopolistic practices. When that case started, a friend of mine said, 'The frightening thing is that Gates can afford to hire better attorneys than the U.S. government can.' That is because the U.S. government is an Industrial Age institution and Gates is an Information Age individual.

Following in this line of thinking, George Soros wrote in *The Crisis of Global Capitalism* that many corporations had much more money and power than many Western nations. That means there are corporations today that could damage the economy of an entire nation just to benefit a few shareholders. That is how much power many corporations have.

In the next few years, many changes, both good and bad, will occur. I believe that capitalism will be unleashed to its fullest extent. Old and obsolete businesses will be wiped out. Competition as well as the need to be cooperative will increase (e.g., there will be mega-mergers such as the one of AOL with Time Warner). Notice that the younger company buys the older one. These changes are all happening because the genie known as technology has been released from the bottle, and information and technology are now cheap enough for everyone to afford.

## The Good News

The good news is that for the very first time, the 90/10 rule of the rich no longer needs to apply. It is now possible for more and more people to gain access to the great world of infinite wealth, the wealth found in information — and information is infinite, not restricted as land and resources were in ages gone by. The bad news is that the people who cling to old ideas may be brutalized by the changes upon us as well as by the changes yet to come.

If rich dad were alive, he might say, 'This Internet craze is much like the California Gold Rush of the 1850s. The only difference is that you do not need to leave your home to participate in it, so why not participate in it?' He would probably go on to say, 'During any economic bonanza, there are only three kinds of people: those who make things happen, those who watch things happen, and those who say, "What happened?"'

Although I started with Einstein's Theory of Relativity as an obsolete idea from the Cold War, I also think of Einstein as a true visionary. Even then, he recognized an idea that is even truer today — 'Imagination is more important than knowledge.'

The really good news is that for the first time in history, the Internet gives more and more people the ability to see the other side of the coin if they go there with open eyes.

Taking my ideas and creating an asset with those ideas was one of the best challenges I have undertaken. Although not always successful, with each new venture my skills increased and I could see a world of possibilities that few people see. So the good news is that the Internet makes it easier for more people to access a world of abundance that for centuries has been available to just a few. The Internet makes it possible for more people to take their ideas, create assets that buy other assets, and have their financial dreams come true.

### We've Only Just Begun

Karen and Richard Carpenter sung a great song titled 'We've Only Just Begun.' For those of you who think you may be too old to start over again, always remember that Colonel Sanders started all over again at 66. The advantage we have over the Colonel is that we are all now in the Information Age, where how young we are mentally matters, not how old we are physically. After all, Merrill Lynch reported, 'The world is 10 years old.'

## *Your Most Important Investment*

You are making an important investment by reading this book, regardless of if you agree with it or not, regardless of if you understood it or not, and regardless of if you ever use any of the information or not. In today's ever-changing world, the most important investment you can make is an investment in on-going education and searching for new ideas. So keep searching, keep challenging your old ideas.

One of the main points of this book is that you have the power to create a world of not enough money as well as a world of an abundance of money. In order to create a world of an abundance of money it does require a degree of creativity, a high standard of financial and business literacy, seeking opportunities rather than seeking more security, and to be more cooperative instead of competitive. Rich dad guided me in shaping my thoughts by saying, 'You can choose to live in a world of not enough money or too much money. That choice is up to you.'

## *A Final Word*

Rich dad's advice to the average investor at the beginning of the book was, 'Don't be average.' Regardless of whether you invest to be secure, comfortable, or rich, please have a plan for each level. In the Information Age, an age with faster changes, fewer guarantees, and more opportunities, your financial education and investor knowledge is vitally important. And that is why rich dad's advice of 'Don't be average' is vitally important today.

# Robert's Edumercial

### How to Create Your Own Assets and Buy Other Assets From the Inside as Well as the Outside

In the introduction of this book, I stated that the SEC defines the Accredited Investor as a person who earns more than $200,000 a year. I also stated that earning at least $200,000 a year allows you access to some of the best investments in the world as well as some of the worst most risky investments in the world. That is why rich dad did not think that simply earning at least $200,000 a year was enough. He believed that investing in these types of investments required special skills to be able to spot good investments from risky ones.

My educational games, *CASHFLOW*, were created for individuals who wanted to:

1. Take control of their personal finances.
2. Learn how to keep more of the money they make.
3. Learn the basic skills to take their ideas and turn them into assets.
4. Learn the basic skills needed to build businesses that could earn over $200,000 a year. You may recall that the basic skill of the B-I Triangle is cash flow management. One of the reasons why 9 out 10 start up businesses fail in the first 5 years is

because the business owner fails to manage the cash flow to grow the business.

5. Gain some of the financial literacy required to invest in some of the best investments in the world with greater safety.

6. Learn to be an investor who invests with confidence in up markets as well as down markets.

7. Train your thinking to realize that it is possible to live in a world of too much money.

8. Improve your financial literacy and vocabulary.

9. Learn how to solve financial problems by having your money work for you instead of you working hard for money.

10. Have fun while learning and be able to teach the people you love the same skills you are learning.

These are a few of the benefits you can gain from playing *CASH-FLOW*. Included in the games are the basic skills that allowed me to build businesses that made a lot of money, invest in real estate and other businesses safely. It was through the cash flow generated from these investments that my wife and I were able to retire. She was 37 and I was 47. For further details, you can read on about the three different games.

It may be obvious to you after reading this book that investing to be secure and comfortable should be automatic plans designed specifically for you. You may choose to turn your money over to a financial advisor and let the advisor invest your money for you according to your plan. However, investing to get rich often requires a different set of personal skills, skills essential for financial success as well as low-risk and high-investment returns. In other words knowing how to create assets that buy other assets. The problem is that gaining the basic education and experience required is often time consuming, frightening, and expensive, especially when you make mistakes with your own money. That is why I created my patented educational board games trademarked as CASHFLOW.

## Three Different Games

### CASHFLOW, Investing 101:

CASHFLOW 101 teaches you the basics of Fundamental Investing. But it also does much more than that. CASHFLOW 101 teaches you how to take control of your personal finances, build a business through proper cash flow management, and learn how to invest with greater confidence in real estate and other businesses.

This educational product is for you if you want to improve your business and investing skills by learning how to take your ideas and turn them into assets such as your own business. Many small businesses fail because the owner lacks capital, real-life experience, and basic accounting skills. Many investors think investing is risky simply because they cannot read financial statements. CASHFLOW 101 teaches the fundamental skills of financial literacy and investing. This educational product includes the board game, a video, and three audiotapes. It takes approximately two complete times playing the game to understand it. Then, we recommend that you play the game at least six times to begin to master the fundamentals of cash flow management and investing.

**Price: $195.00 (U.S.).** This game is for the person serious about investing in his or her financial future. When people say, 'The game is expensive,' I reply with, 'Yes it is. But so is losing money in business or investments.' The greatest expense for many people is actually the money they are NOT making because of their fear of making a mistake in the market.

After you begin to master the fundamentals of the game, you can teach it to others. We all know that teaching a subject is one of the best ways to learn, because the more you give, the more you receive.

**CASHFLOW, Investing 202:**
The Basics of Technical Investing. After you are comfortable with the fundamentals of *CASHFLOW 101*, the next educational challenge is learning how to manage the ups and downs of the market, often called volatility. *CASHFLOW 202* uses the same game board as *101*, but it comes with a completely different set of cards and score sheets as well as a different video and more advanced audiotapes. *CASHFLOW 202* teaches you to use the investment techniques of qualified investors – techniques such as short selling, call options, put options, and straddles, techniques that can be very expensive to learn in the real market. Most investors are afraid of a market crash. A qualified investor uses the tools taught in *CASHFLOW 202* to make money, while the average investor loses money.

After you have mastered *101*, *CASHFLOW 202* becomes very exciting because you learn to react to the highs and lows of the market, and you make a lot of paper money. Again, it is a lot less expensive to learn these advanced trading techniques on a board game using paper money than trading in the market with real money. While these games cannot guarantee your investment success, they will improve your financial vocabulary and knowledge of these advanced investing techniques.

**Price: $145.00 (U.S.).** Many people say the advanced investor audiotapes alone are worth the price of *CASHFLOW 202*. Note: *202* requires the game board from *101* to be played.

***CASHFLOW, Investing for Kids:*** Could your child be the next Bill Gates, Anita Roddick of the Body Shop, Warren Buffet, or Donald Trump? If so, then *CASHFLOW for Kids* could be the family's educational and fun game that gives your child the same educational headstart my rich dad gave me. Few people know that Warren Buffet's father was a stockbroker and Donald Trump's father was a real estate developer. A parent's influence at an early age can have long-term financial results.

**Price: $79.00 (U.S.) – includes the game, book, and audiotape.**

# Rich Dad, Poor Dad

Robert T. Kiyosaki with Sharon L. Lechter C.P.A.

'The main reason people struggle financially is because they have spent years in school but learned nothing about money. The result is that people learn to work for money . . . but never learn to have money work for them.'

ROBERT T. KIYOSAKI

## Rich Dad, Poor Dad

WILL . . .

Explode the myth that you need to earn a high income to become rich.

Challenge the belief that your house is an asset.

Show parents why they can't rely on the school system to teach their kids about money.

Define once and for all an asset and a liability.

Teach you what to teach your kids about money for their future financial success.

# Rich Dad, Poor Dad 2:
# The Cashflow Quadrant

Robert T. Kiyosaki with Sharon L. Lechter C.P.A.

*The Cashflow Quadrant* will reveal why some people work less, earn more, pay less in taxes and feel more financially secure than others. It is simply a matter of knowing which quadrant to work from and when.

Have you ever wondered . . .

- What the difference is between an employee and a business owner?

- Why some investors make money with little risk while most other investors just break even?

- Why most employees go from job to job while others quit their jobs and go on to build business empires?

- Why, in the Industrial Age, did most parents want their children to become doctors, accountants or lawyers . . . and why, in the Information Age, are these professions under financial attack?

This book will answer these questions and also help you to find your own path to financial freedom in a world of ever-increasing financial change.

**Time Warner Paperback titles available by post:**

| | | |
|---|---|---|
| ☐ Rich Dad, Poor Dad | Robert T. Kiyosaki | £7.99 |
| ☐ Rich Kid, Smart Kid | Robert T. Kiyosaki | £7.99 |
| ☐ Rich Dad's Retire Young, Retire Rich | Robert T. Kiyosaki | £7.99 |
| ☐ Rich Dad, Poor Dad 2: Cash Flow Quadrant | Robert T. Kiyosaki | £7.99 |
| ☐ Rich Dad, Poor Dad (audio tape) | Robert T. Kiyosaki | £14.99 |
| ☐ Rich Dad, Poor Dad (CD) | Robert T. Kiyosaki | £18.99 |
| ☐ Rich Dad's Cashflow Quadrant (CD) | Robert T. Kiyosaki | £14.99 |
| ☐ Rich Dad's Classics (audio tape) | Robert T. Kiyosaki | £35.00 |
| ☐ Rich Dad's Guide to Investing (audio tape) | Robert T. Kiyosaki | £14.99 |
| ☐ Rich Dad's Guide to Investing (CD) | Robert T. Kiyosaki | £18.99 |
| ☐ Rich Dad's Rich Kid, Smart Kid (audio tape) | Robert T. Kiyosaki | £14.99 |
| ☐ Rich Dad's Rich Kid, Smart Kid (CD) | Robert T. Kiyosaki | £18.99 |

*The prices shown above are correct at time of going to press. However, the publishers reserve the right to increase prices on covers from those previously advertised without prior notice.*

**TIME WARNER PAPERBACKS**
P.O. Box 121, Kettering, Northants NN14 4ZQ
Tel: 01832 737525, Fax: 01832 733076
Email: aspenhouse@FSBDial.co.uk

**POST AND PACKING:**
Payments can be made as follows: cheque, postal order (payable to Time Warner Paperbacks) or by credit cards. Do not send cash or currency.

All U.K. Orders          **FREE OF CHARGE**
E.E.C. & Overseas     25% of order value

Name (Block Letters) _____

Address _____

_____

Post/zip code: _____

☐ Please keep me in touch with future Time Warner publications

☐ I enclose my remittance £_____

☐ I wish to pay by Visa/Access/Mastercard/Eurocard

Card Expiry Date

| | | | | | | | | | | | | | | | |
|---|---|---|---|---|---|---|---|---|---|---|---|---|---|---|---|

_____